FORGOTTEN
VOICES
OF THE GREAT WAR

FORGOTTEN
VOICES

OF THE GREAT WAR

A HISTORY OF WORLD WAR I IN THE WORDS OF
THE MEN AND WOMEN WHO WERE THERE

IN ASSOCIATION WITH THE IMPERIAL WAR MUSEUM

MAX ARTHUR

With an Introduction by Sir Martin Gilbert

THE LYONS PRESS
Guilford, Connecticut
An imprint of The Globe Pequot Press

First Lyons Press edition, 2004

Forgotten Voices is a registered trademark

The Lyons Press is an imprint of The Globe Pequot Press.

First published in Great Britain in 2002 by Ebury Press, a division of Random House UK, 20 Vauxhall Bridge Road, London SW1V 2SA

10 9 8 7 6 5 4 3 2 1

Printed in the United States of America.

Text design and typesetting by Textype, Cambridge

ISBN 1-59228-570-8

Library of Congress Cataloging-in-Publication data is available on file.

Contents

Acknowledgments

I wish to thank Christopher Dowling, Director of Public Services at the Imperial War Museum, who offered me this challenging project and gave me wholehearted support. Within the Imperial War Museum I am indebted to Margaret Brooks, the Keeper of the Sound Archive, and her excellent staff, John Stopford–Pickering, Richard McDonogh and Jo Lancaster. I am most grateful to Peter Hart, the Imperial War Museum's eminent oral historian, who gave me much help, not only in choice of particular accounts, but by reading through the manuscript and making some wonderfully robust comments as he did so. Brad King at the Photographic department of the Museum could not have been more helpful with the selection of photographs. At my publishers Ebury Press, I owe an important debt to Jake Lingwood, my editor, who has been a tower of strength throughout. He has been ably supported by his editorial assistant, the most helpful Claire Kingston. I must also pay tribute to the Sales and Marketing force of Ebury Press and in particular thank them for their continued enthusiasm for the book. Steve Cox did a tremendous job in editing the final draft. My agent Barbara Levy, who is also the agent for the Imperial War Museum, helped create the project and has been a hundred per cent behind it throughout and I thank her.

Every transcript of this book was typed by Lorraine Lee with amazing speed and accuracy. In the initial research for the book William Skidelsky discovered interesting material and the good work was carried on in depth and with great diligence by Joshua Levine. He sat alongside me in the Sound Archive for many months and his enthusiasm sustained many long hours. With us for many weeks was my dear friend Ruth Cowen, who brilliantly transcribed many of the tapes. As the book progressed she superbly crafted the major part of the accounts making my task so much easier. I am indebted to her for her professionalism and her passion for the book. Brigadier Sebastian Roberts kindly read through the last draft and made a number of suggestions, which I was happy to incorporate. I am much in his debt.

My brother Adrian, an expert on the British Army, always came up with the right names and regiment and offered sound advice.

Susan Jeffreys was a constant source of encouragement as were Don and Liz McClen who have supported me through all my work over the last twenty years. I would also like to thank Fanny Lewis for her support. She is the widow of the remarkable Cecil Lewis who flew at four thousand feet above the Somme in 1916 and was struck by mud from the devastating explosion at La Boiselle. Cecil was the inspiration for *Forgotten Voices of The Great War*.

I would particularly like to thank Malcolm Brown, the historian, who kindly read through the book and made a number of suggestions.

No oral history of the First World War would be complete without acknowledging the tremendous work of the distinguished historian, Lyn Macdonald. She has, always, been a source of encouragement.

Throughout the writing of this book my good friend Sir Martin Gilbert has devoted endless hours of his time and we have shared many meals going through each year of the book. He has given me wise advice and suggested changes which I have incorporated. I am most grateful to him and in particular for his fine introduction.

Any errors in this book are entirely the responsibility of the author.

Max Arthur
July 2002

Author's Preface

Forgotten Voices of the Great War has been created entirely from the remarkable collection of taped interviews held by the Sound Archive of the Imperial War Museum. It is an archive of extraordinary depth, containing thousands of recordings of men and women who have served or witnessed the wars and campaigns from the First World War to the present.

The First World War archive contains several thousand taped interviews recorded over the last forty years. I have drawn extensively from these interviews listening to hundreds of hours of tapes and reading countless transcripts.

Although the First World War involved many countries, I have concentrated on the Western Front and the Gallipoli Campaign. I have arranged the accounts, as far as possible, in chronological order. Because these are personal accounts, not cold histories, the order in which I have placed them may sometimes seem imperfect. However, wherever possible, I have checked for historical accuracy. The length of these accounts varies, some take many pages, whereas others select the most affecting moments. In some cases, contributors appear several times to tell of different actions in which they were involved. To give all the accounts an historical context, I have included a short history of each year.

What I have sought to do is capture through the words of men and women, what life was like in the First World War. The waiting, the preparation, the battle itself and the consequences of battle. Some of these accounts are raw and horrific, others more matter-of-fact or reflective.

Throughout the book, wherever possible I have sought to use the rank or job description held at the time. Some may register as a Private but later progress to a NCO or a commission, others may change their job. It was not always possible to identify each individual's regiment.

Recalling experiences forty or fifty years after the event can lead to recollections that are understandably not always accurate in every single detail, but what cannot be taken away is the feeling that comes from these interviews and I have tried to capture this intensity. It has been a privilege to listen to the voices of the men and women, many now long dead, and to try to bring to life again their vivid memories. These are their words – I have been but a catalyst.

Max Arthur
July 2002

Introduction by Sir Martin Gilbert

One reads this book with bleeding eyes. It contains, as no other book has before it, the First World War in the raw: its dramas and cruelties, its moments of humour – some of it very black indeed – its drudgery, and its excitement. Max Arthur has chosen a remarkable set of recollections: oral testimony at its most immediate and most revealing.

Each recollection casts light on a different aspect of the conflict; often it is a light that has not been cast before; something that the most diligent of historians may have missed, or the most avid reader of war books not read before.

Every reader will be struck by different entries, and will want to read many of them again and again; among those that most affected me by their power and vividness were:

A man enlisting with a sense of the right: 'In the New Testament neither John the Baptist nor Our Lord ever said anything against a soldier.'

A boy of sixteen lying about his age to enable him to enlist.

The undergraduate convinced – in August 1914 – that the war would be over in time for him to start the new university term on October 7.

In a French café: 'omelettes and café rum for a halfpenny.'

1

Humping sandbags, assembling a Lewis gun, life inside a tank.

Soldiers on leave, in civilian clothes, being taunted by women with the white feather of cowardice.

A French soldier in the pre-khaki days, seeing men 'shot down like rabbits' because their trousers were red.

A soldier reflecting on his charmed life and that of his friend under bombardment 'because nothing struck Johnny, nothing struck me.'

A soldier devastated by the death of his mule under shellfire, sent back to enable him to recover his composure.

Field rations, the moments before an attack, the first rush towards the enemy trenches, the effects of gas.

At Gallipoli, eating a meal on the body of a Turk too heavy to lift out of the trench.

The soldier who dies in a pit of excrement, as his two mates who have taken him to it are themselves too weak to pull him out when he falls in.

The soldier trapped in the bottom of a shell-crater with a dead German: 'Heavens, am I going to spend the night with you!'

Rain, mud, 'rats as big as cats,' lice – 'a real menace' – the stench of horse carcasses.

The death of pals killed at one's sides, the horrifying aspects of death in the trenches.

Tunnelling; and the incredible blast and impact of the mine detonations; 'This was the Day of Judgement.'

Relief at a 'Blighty' wound.

The dead and wounded in no man's land; advancing soldiers unable to stop and help the wounded or comfort the dying; last rites; the death of close companions; sadness.

Scenes at casualty clearing stations: the horrific nature of grave wounds; the much-shelled ground itself 'septic;' the experience of undergoing an amputation.

The trauma of taking part in an execution for desertion.

Armistice: the silence and the sadness as well as the celebration.

The familiar battlefields – among them the Ypres Salient, the Somme and Passchendaele – are here illuminated by those who saw them, fought in them, and lived for the rest of their lives with their memories – memories which in these pages have an extraordinary immediacy and vividness.

The voices in this anthology are real men and women, recalling without restraint that period of their lives when death was a constant companion, fear ever-present, noise and danger the hourly accompaniment; and when the business of the day – the hours between dawn and midday – was the whole compass of life, overshadowed by the vision, and imminent reality, of death.

This anthology is a powerful evocation of the First World War, as seen from the perspective of those who were called upon to serve. It is also a memorial to the hundreds of other soldiers – known and unknown – who appear in it, who did not survive beyond that midday; their story told by others, often by their closest friend, and perpetuated in this book by a master chronicler.

Sir Martin Gilbert
July 2, 2002

1914

Well, a lot of people thought it would be over by Christmas.
I was never one of those.

In the glorious sunshine of June 1914 there was no thought of war, no international crisis and no hint that the crowned heads of Europe were poised to tumble one after the other. The assassination of the heir to the Austro-Hungarian Empire by a Serb-sponsored terrorist on June 28 was neither predictable nor inevitable. Yet within weeks, millions of men were on the march. On August 4 with Austria and Germany already at war with Russia and France, and with German troops marching into Belgium on their way to Paris, Britain declared war on Germany.

Thus it was that the main body of the British Army was shipped to France. Unlike their allies and enemies, recruited by mass conscription, the British had a small professional army of volunteers: even with the recently created (1908) Territorial Force and all the reserves mobilised, the British had fewer than 750,000 men in uniform, of whom 247,432 were regulars with the colours. France, prepared since 1871 for another war with Germany, had 823,000 men in service in 1914; by the end of August they were reinforced by some 2,870,000 reservists reporting for duty. For all the excellence of their pre-war training and vastly higher standards, the six British infantry divisions could make little strategic difference to the 1914 campaign in western Europe. France had 62 divisions; Germany fielded 87; Russia had 114.

The British Expeditionary Force (BEF) disembarked in France in August while the French launched an all-out offensive to recapture th∈

provinces of Alsace and Lorraine, annexed by Germany after the war of 1870. Unwittingly the French were playing into the hands of their opponents: the German strategy, honed over years by the General Staff, was to gamble everything on a knockout blow in the West. The French assaults collapsed in ruin while a colossal outflanking movement took place: the German 1st and 2nd Armies swept in a wide arc through Belgium and into France intent on swinging around to seize Paris and strike the main French armies from the flank and rear.

The first major action involving the British Expeditionary Force took place on August 23 amid the slagheaps and pitheads of the coalfields at Mons. The outnumbered British regulars gave the German conscripts a bloody nose before withdrawing. There was some hard marching ahead, although the epic rearguard action by II Corps at Le Cateau on August 26 gained valuable time. During the last week of August the French succeeded in withdrawing in good order to the river Marne. Their commander, General Joffre, jettisoned pre-war strategy and reorganised his forces for a counter-strike on the approaches to Paris. On September 5 to 7 French attacks from the direction of Paris dislocated the main German thrust, which had outrun its supply depots with grave consequences for its artillery and transport units (all horse-drawn). Joffre raced between his subordinate headquarters in a sports car, coordinating the actions of the French armies. By the end of the year he had sacked two out of five army commanders, nine corps commanders and half his seventy-two divisional commanders. By contrast, General von Moltke, the German Commander-in-Chief, lost control of his army commanders and, ultimately, of himself. He attempted to command by radio from his remote headquarters once the armies had outrun their telephone lines, but the temperamental machinery broke down and the French listening post atop the Eiffel Tower monitored the transmissions.

Eventually, Moltke sent one of his staff officers to drive between the German army commanders and order them to fall back to defensive positions if he deemed it necessary. Germany's grand strategy had failed. The confusingly fluid frontline of August and September congealed all the way to the North Sea, leaving the rival armies confronting each other along 460 miles of hastily dug trenches. The new German Commander-in-Chief, General von Falkenhayn, ordered a last attempt to break through to Dunkirk and Calais at the end of October but the attack was stopped by the British and French at the Belgian town of Ypres. This halted the German advance but left the British in an exposed salient. Indeed, all along the front the Germans were able to pull back to defensive positions and entrench themselves on the high ground.

Although two German corps were diverted from France to the Eastern Front for the struggle against Russia, it was clear that the main theatre of war would remain the Western Front. While Germany was obliged to stiffen its Austro–Hungarian allies with increasing numbers of divisions, the main body of the German army remained in France and Belgium facing the British and French.

Private Reginald Leonard Haine
1st Battalion, Honourable Artillery Company

My first reaction to the outbreak of war was more or less a blank, because I really did not think much about it. I was only just eighteen, and right at the start I didn't think that it would affect me to any extent. I was an articled clerk to a firm of chartered accountants and I was due for a fortnight's holiday. I went on that holiday on August the 4th.

When I came back I went back to the office on the Monday morning and a friend of mine phoned me and said 'What are you doing about the war?' Well, I had thought nothing about it at all. He said, 'Well, I have joined my brother's regiment which is the Honourable Artillery Company. If you like, come along, I can get you in.'

At lunchtime I left the office, in Southampton Row, went along to Armoury House, in the City Road, and there was my friend waiting for me. There was a queue of about a thousand people trying to enlist at the time, all in the HAC – it went right down City Road. But my friend came along the queue and pulled me out of it and said, 'Come along!' So I went right up to the front, where I was met by a sergeant-major at a desk. My friend introduced me to the sergeant, who said, 'Are you willing to join?' I said, 'Yes Sir.' He said, 'Well, how old are you?' I said, 'I am eighteen and one month.' He said, 'Do you mean nineteen and one month?' So I thought a moment and said, 'Yes Sir.' He said, 'Right-ho, well sign here please.' He said, 'You realise you can go overseas?' So that was my introduction to the Army.

Private William Dove
16th Lancers

War had been declared, and the following Sunday I went with a friend of mine to Shepherd's Bush Empire to see the film show. At the end they showed the Fleet sailing the high seas and played 'Britons Never Shall Be Slaves' and 'Hearts of Oak.' And you know one feels that little shiver run up the back and you know you have got to do something. I had just turned seventeen at that time and on the Monday I went up to Whitehall – Old Scotland Yard – and enlisted in the 16th Lancers.

Private Thomas McIndoe
12th Battalion, Middlesex Regiment

It was seeing the picture of Kitchener and his finger pointing at you – any position that you took up the finger was always pointing to you – it was a wonderful poster really.

I was always a tall and fairly fit lad. When I confronted the recruiting officer he said that I was too young, although I had said that I was eighteen years of age. He said, 'Well, I think you are too young, son. Come back in another year or so.' I returned home and never said anything to my parents. I picked up my bowler hat, which my mother had bought me and which was only to wear on Sundays, and I donned that thinking it would make me look older. I presented myself to the recruiting officer again, and this time there was no queries, I was accepted. Birth certificates were not asked for, although I had one, not with me but I had one. My mother was very hurt when I arrived home that night and told her that I had to report to Mill Hill next morning. I was sixteen in the June.

These young recruits are taking the oath.

William Ewen
English student in Germany
One sensed a tremendous expectancy of war in the near future. A favourite bestseller in all the bookshops was *Weltmacht oder Untergang* – World Dominion or Decline. I bought a copy of it and read it myself. Oh! They had the plan for the conquest of the whole of Europe laid out bare. One could feel tremendous resentment in the British attitude towards Germany. We were the band of fellows, we had brought about this *Einkreisung* – this encirclement of poor unfortunate Germany that seemed to worry them all so much. We had a music hall song – 'Tis the Navy, the Fighting Navy, We will keep them in their place, For they know they will have to face, The gallant little lads, in Navy blue.' Oh, they resented that one!

Robert Poustis
French student
When I was a boy, in school and within the family, we often spoke about the lost provinces – Alsace-Lorraine, which had been stolen from France after the war of 1870. We wanted to get them back. In the schools the lost provinces were marked in a special colour on all the maps, as if we were in mourning for them. When I became a student and went to the university, there was always the same ardent feeling. Speaking together we would say maybe war is coming. Sooner or later, we'd say, we don't know when, but we, the young people in those times, we very much wanted to get back the provinces.

In the first days of mobilisation there was of course a lot of enthusiasm. Everybody was shouting and wanted to go to the Front. The cars, the railway wagons loaded with soldiers were full of tricolour flags and inscriptions: 'A Berlin, à Berlin.' We wanted to go to Berlin immediately, with bayonets, swords and lances, running after the Germans. The war, we thought, was to last two months, maybe three months.

Mary Hillyer
Women's National Land Service Corps

When the war broke out I had just left school. My father was a doctor in a small town in Somerset, and my mother was a perfect sweetie but a doormat really. When the war broke out I overheard them saying, 'Of course we shall have Mary with us for the war.' Well, Mary thought otherwise, and when I read in the paper about a course being opened at Sealham College for women who wanted to go on the land I decided that that was what I was going to do. I went off to the post office and removed my life savings of £12.10/- and wrote to Sealham College. I was completely, utterly and absolutely innocent, as we all were on the course. I think we were fourteen of us to begin with and we joined the Women's National Land Service Corps. It wasn't the Land Army proper because women on the land were not recruited until the end of 1915. Well, off I went to Sealham College. I remember looking on the board one morning and for my first job, I saw, 'Will Miss Hillyer please take the sow to the boar.' I overheard one of the other girls say, 'Oh well, she hasn't got far to go.' So I harnessed the sow with a halter and marched her down the road, then popped her into a stable at the Boar Hotel. And I thought I'd done my job rather well, but when I came back, of course, there was an almighty row.

These girls were all from very good homes. None of them knew quite why they wanted to go on the land, but they all realised that they did. We knew we'd earn no money, we just wanted to do it. At the end of the course we had to put our names down on the local labour exchange and I suppose I was unlucky, I got the last job left. The advertisement said: 'Farmer requires a Land Girl. Twelve cows to be milked twice a day. Forty head of cattle to be fed. Two hundred loads of mangels to be drawn in. Calves to be fed, and if any time left over, the milk to be separated.'

This was an isolated farm, 1,700 feet above the river between Dartmouth and Totnes – completely and utterly lonely. I got up at five every morning to milk those cows, never once in daylight. I separated the milk, then went into the farm and put a colossal faggot on the fire. The family then appeared and we had breakfast. I then went out and

A sergeant measures recruits for their uniforms.

fed the cattle and did all the jobs of the day. One just went on doing it, very often until nine at night. I didn't realise what an enormous amount of work I did. I stuck it for six months.

Kitty Eckersley
Mill worker

I worked in the mill, I was a ring-spinner, and we worked six days a week, from six o'clock in the morning until half-past five at night, and I got the large sum of fifteen and six a week. Anyway, I had a nice friend and we used to go out at night – and we met these two young men, and I liked mine very much and he liked me. So eventually we started courting, and I learned that he was only in lodgings, that he had no father and no mother, and that he was a very steady young man, very big and fair, and he was all that a young woman would wish to see. He was a lovely man, really good, and he was a member of St. Cross's Church at Clayton. We eventually made our minds up that we would get married, but we wanted a house, so we saved our money up, and eventually got a house in Clayton for three and sixpence a week which we furnished. He would go to his work and I would go to the mill. We were very happily married. Very, very happy because we were very much in love, he thought the world of me and I thought the world of him. And at times, at nights when he used to be at home, I had lovely hair in those days, and he used to do my hair up for me, in all kinds of styles.

And then it came to be that the war started. Well, we had a friend in Canada who had enlisted over there, and when he came back, he visited one night and asked us, 'Would we go to the Palace?' He had booked seats for the Palace and would we like to go? We didn't know what was on, of course, but it was a great treat for us. So we went. And when we got there everything was lovely. Vesta Tilley was on stage. She was beautifully dressed in a lovely gown of either silver or gold. But what we didn't know until we got there was that also on stage were Army officers with tables all set out for recruiting. She introduced those songs, 'We Don't Want To Lose You, But We Think You Ought To Go' and 'Rule Britannia,' and all those kind of things. Then she came off the stage and walked all round the audience – up and down, either sides, down the middle – and the young men were getting up and following her. When she got to our row she hesitated a bit. I don't quite know what happened but she put her hand on my husband's shoulder – he was on the end seat – and as the men were all following her, he got up and followed her too.

When we got home that night I was terribly upset. I told him I didn't want him to go and be a soldier – I didn't want to lose him. I didn't want him to go at all. But he said, 'We have to go. There has to be men to go.'

Elizabeth Owen
English schoolgirl

I was seven and I was playing in the garden when I was asked to go and speak to my grandmother. She said, 'Now children, I have got something very serious to tell you. The Germans are fighting the British, there is a war on and all sorts of people will be killed by these wicked Germans. And therefore there must be no playing, no singing and no running about.' And then she took from us all our toys that were made in Germany, amongst them a camel of which I was very fond.

Then we heard that the khaki men were coming to take away all the horses from the village. Everything in the village was done by horses. The station was about a mile or a mile and a half away and the train was met by a brake drawn by horses. The milk was delivered by horses and the butter used to be collected from the farms and brought in by horses to the butter market. There was a farmer who had a lovely pair who we called the prancers. He thought he would try and hide these horses but the khaki men found them. They tied them all together on a long rope, I think there was about twenty – all horses we used to know and love and feed. Then they started trotting them out of the village and as they went out of sight we were all terribly sad.

Private Godfrey Buxton
Royal Army Medical Corps
I'd had one year up at Cambridge and then volunteered for the Army. We were quite clear that Germany would be defeated by the 7th of October when we would go back to Cambridge.

Captain Philip Neame
15th Field Company, Royal Engineers
I was stationed at Gibraltar when war was declared, and we officers there were afraid that the war would be over quickly, and that we should miss it because we were not part of the British Expeditionary Force. We were all keen soldiers, and if there was a war in which the British Army was taking part we were all only too anxious to be at the Front.

Private F. B. Vaughan
12th Battalion, Yorks and Lancs
I said to the boss, 'I want to join the Army, I want to be released from my job.' So he said to me, 'Here in the steelworks you are doing just as much for your country, just as much for the nation, as though you were in the Army.' Well, I couldn't see myself catching the 8:40 to Brightside every morning and leaving for home in the afternoon, doing little jobs in the evening, and all the time my pals were suffering – probably dying somewhere – they were serving their country. I couldn't see myself carrying on in that particular way, so I said 'I'm awfully sorry but I have made up my mind, I must go.'

And he saw that I was determined and he said, 'Well then, go to the wages office and they will pay you whatever is due to you. But we shall not save your job for you when you come back and we shall not pay you anything while you are away. I said all right, I accept those conditions. My mind was made up, the die was cast, and when I finally joined the Sheffield Battalion, as 256, Private F. B. Vaughan, Sheffield Battalion York and Lancasters – all at a bob a day – you know I was a very happy man.

Captain Philip Neame, Royal Engineers, pictured here as a Colonel on General Staff.

It was not just a sudden decision that I made to join the Army. My pals were going, chaps I had kicked about with in the street, kicking tin cans or a football, and chaps I knew very well in the city. And then if you looked in the newspapers we saw that Canadians were coming, Australians were coming, South Africans were coming – they were catching the first available boat to England to get there before the war was over.

Then when you went to the pictures you'd be shown crowds of young men drilling in Hyde Park or crowding round the recruiting office, or it might be a band playing 'Tipperary.' The whole thing was exciting, and even in the pulpits – although it started rather shakily at first – they eventually decided to come down on the side of the angels and blessed our little mission.

I don't know whether patriotism entered into it or not, possibly so. We were stirred, I know, by the atrocities, or the alleged atrocities, when the Germans invaded Belgium and France. The other great factor was that the womenfolk, fifty per cent of the population, were very keen on the war. Before long they were wearing regimental badges, regimental buttons, little favours in their hats or coats, and they were offering to do the jobs men had done in civil life, so that men could be released. Some of them would stop us in the street and say, 'Well, why aren't you in khaki?' In other words the whole effect was cumulative, but we were not pressed, we made our own decisions.

Private Godfrey Buxton
Royal Army Medical Corps
During that time one was naturally trying to find out what the Bible said, and it was interesting to find out how many battles in the Old Testament were 'by the word of the Lord.' And in the New Testament neither John the Baptist nor Our Lord ever said anything against a soldier – only told them to do their job within the limits of war. These things in my young mind built up to a confidence that if death was abroad, if wrong was to be resisted, a Christian should be right in amongst it.

Rifleman Norman Demuth
London Rifle Brigade

As well as being given white feathers, there was another method of approach. You would see a girl come towards you with a delightful smile all over her face and you would think to yourself, 'My word this is somebody who knows me.' When she got to about five or six paces from you she would suddenly freeze up and walk past you with a look of utter contempt and scorn as if she could have spat. That was far more hurtful than a white feather – it made you curl up completely and there was no replying because she had walked on.

However, I was given a white feather when I was sixteen, just after I had left school. I was looking in a shop window and I suddenly felt somebody press something into my hand and I found it was a woman giving me a white feather. I was so astonished I did not know what to do about it. But I had been trying to persuade the doctors and recruiting officers that I was nineteen and I thought, well, this must give me some added bounce because I must look the part, and so I went round to the recruiting offices with renewed zeal.

Private Clifford Lane
1st Battalion, Hertfordshire Regiment

I was working as a clerk in the secretary's office of the Post Office in St. Martin Le Grand. I had already enlisted in 1913 in the 1st Battalion, the Hertfordshire Regiment in the Territorial Army, and we were mobilised on August 4th while we were at camp at Shorncliffe.

Private F. B. Vaughan
12th Battalion, Yorks and Lancs

So far we'd been individualists, so far we'd been Mummy's pet or something like that, we had a will of our own and it came rather hard to start to obey commands, but gradually we knew how to form fours, right wheel, left wheel, and all the rest of them. We became in other words a disciplined body of men and then the training consisted largely of route marches. Then we learned how to excavate the ground and make trenches and the country itself of course was well known to us.

A portrait of Private Clifford Lane, 1st Battalion, Hertfordshire Regiment.

Derbyshire hills, Derbyshire dales, we marched about, all over the place.

Fixing bayonets is one of the most wonderful things in the Army. The sergeant-major was telling the troops how to fix arms, how to fix bayonets, and he said, 'When I says fix, you don't fix, but when I says bayonets you whips 'em out and whops 'em on.' And that was the style of some of our sergeants and sergeant-majors who had been old sweats in the Boer War. They were fine chaps, and good soldiers.

Rifleman Henry Williamson
London Rifle Brigade
During our training in Crowborough in Sussex it was a month of great heat, we sweated tremendously. We carried about 60 lb. of ammunition, kit and our rifle. We got blisters, but we did about fifteen or sixteen miles a day, with ten minutes' halt every hour. We lay on our backs gasping, water bottles were drunk dry, people in cottages, women in sun bonnets come up with apples and jugs of water and we passed some of the battalions who had been in front of us whose headquarters were in some of the poorer quarters of London, and I remember so well the dead white faces, many with boils, lying completely exhausted, sun-stricken in the hedges, hundreds of them.

Rifleman Norman Demuth
London Rifle Brigade
When I enlisted in the ranks of the London Rifle Brigade I found that my mother enjoyed a kind of spurious reflected glory. You see, she was in a local sewing group and of course everybody talked about their sons in the war, and my mother said, 'Oh Norman has just enlisted,' and this apparently created a great sensation as I was considered to be much braver for having enlisted in the ranks, and for going about fighting a war with all those coal miners and people I had never met before, than if I had got a commission. But it was rather unfortunate because the boy who lived next door was a 2nd lieutenant, and although my mother enjoyed basking in this reflected glory she did not like it much when we happened to meet this boy and I swung up a good salute. After this had

happened once or twice when I was on leave she said, 'You know it's a pity you haven't got a commission – then he could salute you.' When the mothers were seeing us off at Waterloo you could see an enormous sense of pride on their faces.

Marjorie Llewellyn
Schoolgirl in Sheffield

As a young schoolgirl I remember there was great excitement in Sheffield when the posters went up showing Kitchener saying 'We Want You' and a number of our young men joined up – they were the pick of the city. They were highly educated, most of them, what was called the officer class. And they went to the Town Hall, signed on, and then to their great disappointment were sent home again. This of course was very unexpected. They had expected to be in uniform straight away and rush off to win the war, which of course everyone thought would be over by Christmas. However, they had to go each day to the drill hall and sign on again. Then they were sent down to the Bramall Lane Football Ground and to Norfolk Park where they were drilled and learned to dig trenches, and this went on for quite a long time. They felt they were playing at soldiers, not really doing what they intended. However, soon they were put into a camp a short distance out of the town and there their training began in earnest. They were kept up there pretty well full time, but they did get a bit of leave and come down now and again, and would go to the famous pub, The Three Merry Lads. They were very excited of course because they were quite convinced that now we were in the war, it would soon be over. This went on for some time and then eventually their training was completed and we saw them going through the streets marching off to the war.

Private Tom Adlam
4th Battalion, Hampshire Regiment

Well, a lot of people thought it would be over by Christmas. I was never one of those who thought that at the beginning. But I put it down about a year. I think most of us thought it would last about a year. We thought it couldn't go on longer than that.

Heinrich Beutow
German schoolboy

My memories are those of a child of course. I was in a small German garrison town in 1914 and I remember very well the tremendous enthusiasm. Of course, we schoolboys were all indoctrinated with great patriotism when war broke out. My father was an active infantry officer and I shall never forget the day when they marched out to the trains. All the soldiers were decorated with flowers, there was no gun which did not show a flower. Even the horses I think were decorated. And of course all the people followed them. Bands playing, flags flying, a terrific sort of overwhelming conviction that Germany now would go into war and win it very quickly.

Corporal Stefan Westmann
29th Division, German Army

I was a medical student when I received my call-up papers. They ordered me to report for military duty in a clean state and free of vermin at an infantry regiment in Freiburg, in Baden. We had no idea of any impending war, we had no idea that the danger of war existed. We served in our blue and red uniform, but on the 1st of August mobilisation orders came and we put on our field grey. At 2 o'clock in the morning of the 4th of August we marched out of Freiburg with torches – silent, without any music, without any singing, and with no enthusiasm. We were really weighed down by our kit, which weighed 75 lb. per man. We crossed the Rhine over a very wobbly pontoon bridge into Alsace.

Doris Beaghan
English schoolgirl

We had been on holiday in France for ten days. Although there had been rumours of war, my father didn't believe them. But then war broke out, so we made our way to Le Havre by boat. We went to a hotel, had a clean-up and then went out in the town and then the excitement began. It was absolutely incredible. The British Expeditionary Force was coming in. The soldiers were marching in, all singing. French people, all excited, madly waving, dashing about and rushing up to the soldiers, pulling off their buttons as keepsakes, kissing them and oh! terrific excitement! It was marvellous that here they were. So we stayed there during the day and then we got the boat to Southampton at night. We arrived in the early hours of the morning and went up to London and there the contrast was incredible. From the excitement in France to the gloom of London. Everybody there with long faces and an 'Oh, isn't it terrible' sort of attitude. You could hardly believe it was possible, that there was such a change from the two sides of the Channel.

Private Dolly Shepherd
Women's Emergency Corps
One day I was with my boyfriend, who was in the Yeomanry, and my auntie, and one of her German friends – she had married a German, you see, like Queen Victoria. Anyway this day my auntie said, 'There's talk of war. Do you think we'll have a war?' And this German friend of hers said, 'Oh yes, yes, yes. Oh we shall capture your country. You will all be Germans.' Of course later on, when war did break out, auntie had to register with the police because she was married to a German. When the police said to her, 'Why did you marry a German?' she said, 'Well, why did Queen Victoria marry a German?' And then, of course, directly the war started, I joined the Women's Emergency Corps. I went part-time up to this school in Baker Street. I could only go in the evenings, but we had to give whatever time we could. I was a private, while people who could give all their time became officers. We had to supply our own uniforms – we bought everything.

It must have been with the permission of the War Office or someone, because a Grenadier Guardsman came to give us drill. Form fours, you know, real square-bashing. And he would say, 'And about turn, about.' And he'd wait for a minute or two – and of course us in hobble skirts! And after he said, 'Turn!' he'd say, 'Do you know what you look like? A lot of jelly bags!' It was so funny, really. But he really did put us through it. We had him for about a month, I suppose. He taught us the drill because we had to have discipline. And he was quite right, you can't do anything without discipline. Then we had First Aid, that came next. First Aid and Home Nursing. And then signalling – semaphore and Morse. We had to be proficient in whatever we might be called upon to do. We couldn't say, 'I can't do it,' there was no such a word as can't.

We first of all worked up to a company, then finally we had enough people for a battalion. One day we had a route march to the Mansion House, and of course people were giggling and laughing and saying, 'Women soldiers! Just imagine having women soldiers. Whoever thought of such a thing!' They certainly sneered at us. Well, for one thing they threw a brick through our window. But no, I didn't support them in those days. We thought, 'Oh, those women. Who wants to vote anyway!' I suppose I was too young to think about it. And they were chaining themselves up and that kind of thing. But none of them joined the Emergency Corps, I do know that. I didn't meet any that had been suffragettes.

Sergeant Stefan Westmann
29th Division, German Army
During our advance through Belgium we marched on and on. We never dared take off our boots, because our feet were so swollen that we didn't think it would be possible to put them on again. In one small village the mayor came and asked our company commanders not to allow us to cut off the hands of children. These were atrocity stories which he had heard about the German Army. At first we laughed about it, but when we heard of other propaganda things said against the German Army, we became angry.

Private Frank Dolbau
French Army
At our first battle at Morhange on the 19th of August, unsupported by artillery, against heavily fortified positions, we had attacked. We were shot down like rabbits because you know for them we were a real target,

as we had red trousers on. When we were fired at we were like sitting ducks in the field, you see.

BRUSSELS FALLS, AUGUST 20

Germaine Soltau
Belgian schoolgirl
I was in Brussels, and at an age when all events seem to leave a permanent impression on you. Of course we were not expecting the Germans to invade Belgium, we were hoping they would respect our neutrality, so the invasion came as a very great shock to us all. We had heard in Brussels what was happening at the frontier – the killing, the shooting, the atrocities and of course it was awful, but the fortresses of Liège were holding and that gave us some hope. Brussels then was very silent, and the Grande Place had never been so beautiful, with all the big flags flying on the old historical buildings. But there was much sadness and emotion.

Then on the 18th of August the government in Brussels left the capital to go to Antwerp. Soon Liège fell and the Germans were on their way to Brussels. They were preceded by streams of refugees, telling us more stories of atrocities in the villages and small towns of the Ardennes. We heard about friends from a little village – the young woman who was shot dead in front of her child just after her husband had been taken away to be shot. That happened hundreds and thousands of times, always the same story.

Then on Thursday the 20th of August, a date I will never forget, the Germans entered Brussels. It was a glorious day of sunshine but in my mind I still keep a vision of grey, these grey-clad hordes marching in the streets. It was a sinister, greenish grey, even their helmets were covered in grey. They had with them all their heavy guns, field kitchens and officers on horseback, and it all went in long, long, endless streams of grey. And the dust that was raised by all these thousands of feet and all those weapons of war – one had the feeling that the dust was hiding the sun. And their music, the music that we were going to hear for four years and three months – the sound of drum and fife and always the same tune. It made us cry when we heard that and thought about our soldiers and of the Allies on the front line. And then in the evening, on our beautiful Grande Place, they put up their field kitchen and started making their soup.

Fusilier William Holbrook
4th Battalion, Royal Fusiliers
There was a periodical going at that time called *John Bull*. It was published by a man named Bottomley. Well, when we got to Cowes and were waiting on the beach I saw on the side of a house, covering the whole wall, a placard advertising *John Bull*. The words were 'The Dawn of Britain's Greatest Glory.' That was all it said. I was lying there, and I thought to myself, I wonder whether it will be or not.

The journey across was peaceful. We had no escort, nothing. When we got there we camped for about three or four days then we went and trained at Le Havre, and then it was up to the Front. We went on a cattle-truck type train, eight horses and forty men. We marched from there to the Front – of course we did not know where we were going, and the whole brigade came together. We were the 9th Brigade.

Before we got to Mons we went through a place called Frameries, a mining town about ten miles from Mons. It was wonderful there, the people came out and cheered and shouted and gave us food and a tremendous welcome.

BATTLE OF MONS, AUGUST 23

Gunner Walter Burchmore
Royal Horse Artillery
We had reached a village about three miles from Mons in our advance towards the German armies and we were enjoying the hospitality of the villagers when quite out of the blue came the order 'Prepare for Action. Get mounted.' We obeyed it immediately, rode out of the village about a couple of miles. We came into action on the high ground overlooking

Mons. We immediately engaged the German artillery and that developed into a regular artillery duel in and around Binche, where we were firing in support of our infantry and cavalry who occupied it in the early morning. It was quite obvious that the Germans didn't intend to give us any rest and we quite made up our mind that we wouldn't give them any either. The infantry during the afternoon were driven out of Binche by sheer weight of numbers. Then developed quite a number of charges and counter-charges, which were very exciting and most interesting. We gave them all the support we could with our guns. We dealt very severely with a squadron of German cavalry who'd appeared on our right. We suddenly saw these people coming, didn't realise who they were at first and we said, 'By crikey! It's bloody Germans!' so we started gunfire immediately. We fired on open sights, fuse nought, and they got about two hundred yards from the guns and they wheeled to the left and galloped away to the left and rode right into a squadron of our own cavalry who dealt with them and finished where we'd left off.

Then quite suddenly we got the orders that we were going to try and retake Binche. This was in the early hours of the 24th. We did very well. The battle went on for several hours and I thought that we were going to take the place but I doubt very much whether we could have held it if we had. However, we were very disappointed when we were ordered to break up the battle and retreat. But we were thankful the Germans had withdrawn after this very severe battle because we were feeling thoroughly tired. We were completely exhausted, thoroughly hungry, and I don't think we were capable of any reasonable further movement. There was only one thing that managed to keep us going and that was the knowledge that we were fighting for our very lives.

As we withdrew we had the advantage of the 1st Division guns, and after that we looked after ourselves by fighting about a dozen rearguard actions until we reached Landrecies. There we put our heads down for about ten minutes, replenished the limbers, then fought another rearguard action all the way to Le Cateau. There we supported the 2nd Army Corps with our guns.

Heinrich Beutow
German schoolboy

After the initial enthusiasm and patriotism came a wave of quietness, because then the first death lists were published in the papers. And my mother – she was English – was suddenly surrounded by women of the regiment, the wives of the other officers of course, and most of them – because my father's regiment was one of the first to march over the border into Belgium – were widows. And even as a child, I must say, it gave me a great shock to see that most of the officers were dead and killed during the first weeks. A lot of the younger soldiers were dead and the whole feeling of enthusiasm faded away very quickly, in my opinion. The world became grey after that.

THE MONS RETREAT

Fusilier William Holbrook
4th Battalion, Royal Fusiliers

I could see the Germans coming down in waves. They were not in formation. As far as I could see there was quite a number of them, more men than we had. I only fired a bit because I was behind the company with the officers. I don't think I was nervous when the action started, everything happened so suddenly. But it was all new to me – it was new to all of us. You didn't really think about that. Shells seemed to worry me a bit, the bursting of shells.

When I returned after the first message, I had a bit of a job to find my way back. I had been gone about half an hour I suppose, and when I came back they were still firing. I took up a position and shortly afterwards, I suppose about three in the afternoon, I had to take another message down, and by then I had got an idea that there was something happening. I got down with this message and when I got away I started going back and met some troops coming down. And a fellow said, 'Where are you going?' I didn't know them – they weren't from my battalion – so I told them and he said, 'You'll have a job – you know they're retiring from the river.' And I said, 'Retiring?' He said, 'Yes, I suppose that's the message you've got,' and I said I didn't know. So I had to go a different route to avoid the troops coming down. When I got back to where we were before, they had gone! I did not see anybody. The Germans were just over the bridge. I wondered what the hell had happened. So I cleared off as quick as I could. I picked up some other fellows, some stragglers, and so of course I was behind the troops retiring and before the Germans advancing.

As we went towards Mons I saw a man with a pack mule who showed us how close we were to the line. Then just as he put his head out to one side, he was suddenly shot clean through the head. I thought, God what's happening? And then I saw some of their artillery on the road where I had been. Of course I came back and picked up some other fellows and somehow we got back, but I didn't find my regiment.

Later we were told that we had fallen back to draw them into a position to make a counter-attack on them, to draw them into a trap. Then that they'd surrender – that they'd be captured.

The Germans were not using rapid fire as much as we were. Our gunners were very rapid. The fire from the river bank was more like machine-gun fire. It really was much faster than the German fire. Our fire was terrific. We were firing fifteen rounds a minute. The Germans were suffering a lot of casualties as far as I could see. But they were reinforced – they did not fall back from the river bank. In fact they were doing their best to get across. We were stragglers in between the Germans and the British lines, and as we gradually went along there were other men joined in. When we got to the outside of Mons, an officer came along. He said, 'Get up. Get everyone together, we'll have to stick together and defend ourselves.'

The thing that upset me most was the refugees, thousands of refugees coming from Mons and mingling with the troops. They were pushing all sorts of things. They seemed to be flabbergasted, they didn't seem to think it was possible that they had been driven back. They did not know what to think. Of course, we could not understand their language. They went across fields, the nearest route to get away, while we kept to the roads.

Gunner J. W. Palmer
26th Brigade, Royal Field Artillery

After advancing several days into Belgium and passing these refugees, many of them with their little dogcarts and piled with their pitiful possessions, prams, children, one thing and another, we found ourselves eventually going the same way as the refugees, so we knew very well we were no longer advancing into Belgium. And our road got more congested with refugees and we got mixed up with the infantry, who in turn were getting more and more tired. The infantry were carrying in the region of 100 lb. on their back, which we did not have. And so their feet got worse and worse. A lot of it was due to the fact that a number of them were reservists and had been called up just prior to the outbreak of war. They were fitted out with kit, including 'ammos' (that's the old army word for boots) and they were very heavy. Before the war we were able to break them in, but they didn't get time. They were put straight on a march which lasted for about 150, 160 miles with only a very, very few rests and if they got those boots off they couldn't get them back on again, consequently their feet were bleeding.

Of course, all the time we were retiring the Germans were coming on and having all the food and that imaginable from the houses. We were told then we must live off the land, we must get everything we can from empty houses, otherwise the Germans would have it. Well, I remember seeing the Munsters, they got about five cows in front of them and they tried to drive them along the road in front of them and I think they were going to kill them at night. Those cows knew more than the Munsters. First of all one would go in a field one side, and one would go in a field the other side. I don't know how many they got away with. I don't think the Munsters had beef for supper.

The position over the rations for both men and horses was rather precarious. There were days when we went without rations of any kind or water. The horses were more or less starved of water. On the retreat we went to various streams with our buckets, but no sooner had we got the water halfway back to them, than we moved again. We had strong feelings towards our horses. We went into the fields and beat the corn and oats out of the ears and brought them back, but that didn't save them. As the days went on, the horse's belly got more up into the middle of its back, and the cry was frequently down the line, 'Saddler – a plate and a punch!' This meant that the saddler had to come along and punch some more holes in the horse's leather girth to keep the saddles on.

BATTLE OF LE CATEAU, AUGUST 25

Private Charles Ditcham
2nd Battalion, Argyll and Sutherland Highlanders
On the night of the 25th at one in the morning my battalion went into a factory in the village of Le Cateau. And at 4 o'clock we moved out hurriedly because the German Uhlans were at the other end of the village. So we took up our position to do a rearguard action for the Expeditionary Force. All this meant was that the company was put in a cornfield and we were told to dig ourselves in. So we just made a bit of a hole in the ground with your trenching tool and then took up a position. Then the party started when the Hun came along. It was what made me realise what war was about. We just lined up in the cornfield, one company on the right, one company on the left, Middlesex and other people, all mixed up. And these Germans came in their hordes and were just shot down. But they still kept coming. There were sufficient of them to shove us out of the field eventually. And then, the realisation what war meant – when I saw my company sergeant-major for instance, a fellow called Sim, who was wounded in the mouth. He was going back dripping blood. And there were various people getting killed and wounded.

What I shall never understand is what I was supposed to do with a bugle in the front line during the battle, except to blow if my platoon officer, who incidentally became a prisoner of war, had told me to. But what he would have asked me to blow I wouldn't honestly know. I mean I couldn't blow ceasefire because it didn't mean a thing. And afterwards, according to later accounts, it was an orderly retreat. Well, as one who took part in the orderly retreat, I didn't think it was very orderly. On my way out I met another drummer and on our way back we met the corporal of the drums, a fellow called Balfour. And this chap had been very badly wounded so we took him back to the aid post in a church in the village of Le Cateau.

When we arrived, it gave me the shock of my life to see all the badly wounded people there – there were stretcher cases and walking cases, the church was full of them. So we left this wounded fellow and just followed the tribe, I didn't know where it was going. The only thing that I am very thankful for was seeing an old soldier who had served with my father, who was driving the ammunition wagon in my company. He was taking back two Clydesdale horses – the wagon had been dumped – and he dragged me onto the back of one of these Clydesdales. And I sat on that thing half asleep till I arrived at St. Quentin the following morning. When I fell off it, I could hardly walk.

THE RETREAT CONTINUES

Sergeant Thomas Painting
1st Battalion, King's Royal Rifle Corps
We were not allowed to have white handkerchiefs in case we used them as a white flag. We had to go and buy a red handkerchief. I remember the first bit of French I learnt was 'mouchoir rouge,' handkerchief red. On the morning of the 21st of August we started to march up to Mons, scorching hot. The French roads were cobbles, terrible to march on, and Route Nationale straight as a die. You could see for miles in front of you. The road seemed endless.

After Givry we pushed on a couple of miles north-east in the direction of where the German Army was coming and dug some trenches there. Number 70 Battery RFA was on a ridge just to our left. A couple of German aeroplanes came over, spotted the guns' flashes and opened fire. Then Jerry's artillery started searching the ground, which cut one section of my trench to pieces. The gunners had three of their guns knocked out of action but the gunners were jolly good and crawled from one gun to the other and kept them going. As one gun was knocked out, they got into action again. Jerry played a searchlight on us during the night, and we thought we were going to be for it, but early the next morning our retirement started and we made our way to Bavay, where the Germans shelled us. We moved off, but one of their cavalry regiments stopped the shells which were meant for us. We were very pleased to see that. On the 25th we got as far as Maroilles and anchored down. That was at the same time as the Germans made an attack at Le Cateau. We had a night operation there alongside the Berkshires. Then we had to carry on with the retirement the next morning.

During the day we saw our first French troops. I was surprised to see them and what they were wearing. Their cavalry went into action with their cuirasses on and plumed helmets; the infantry wore red trousers, a long blue overcoat and were wearing their war medals from the African campaign. They were going into action at Guise with no camouflage. But they suffered badly and had to retire.

During that day we joined up with the Guards Brigade again. On the 27th we got to beyond the fortress of La Fère, where we had a break. General French saw us there. He seemed in good spirits, that bucked us up a bit. Then we marched on to Amigny. We had a kind of day's break there. I suppose the action at Le Cateau and at Landrecies and Maroilles caused Jerry to pull himself up a little bit, because he didn't press us.

On we went in this really sweltering weather. On the night of the 31st we reached Coucy-le-Château and the next morning we marched through Soissons, where we had a few hours' halt on the River Aisne. We then had to hold a bridge at St. Bandry until it was blown up by our engineers. Then we were off again at dawn. It was always dawn.

We slept in the fields, just anchored down for an hour or so, and then moved again. Our food was dished up from ration carts which we ate on the march. Bully beef was issued in seven-pound tins. Well you couldn't expect someone to carry that weight so we used to open our tins and share it out. That was our ration, bully beef, biscuits and water: No time for anything else, seven-pound tins!

FIRST BATTLE OF THE MARNE, SEPTEMBER 5–10

Sergeant Thomas Painting
1st Battalion, King's Royal Rifle Corps

We fought a rearguard action at St. Bandry then marched to Haute-vesnes, where we halted. The colonel came along and said, 'Who's in charge here?' I said, 'I am, Sir.' He said, 'Right, down the road a little way, turn left and join in the next attack with C Company, range fifteen hundred yards.' We formed up on the right of C Company and then we made an attack on this German Jäger Battalion, a horse and rifle battalion such as we were. The colonel's fifteen hundred yards was over a cornfield which had been ploughed. It was just stubble, no cover at all. We had only two machine-guns in the battalion. As soon as we started, our machine-gun sergeant was killed at fifteen hundred yards range.

We went forward as we had been trained – one section would advance under covering fire of another section, leapfrogging each other as the others were firing to keep Jerry's heads down. My company was going in with their bayonets when suddenly Jerry put up a white flag. We were really surprised. We took four hundred and fifty prisoners. I said to one of them, 'Why did you pack up when you've got so much ammunition?' He said, 'Well, your fire was so accurate we couldn't put our heads up to shoot at you.' We lost twelve killed and sixty wounded, they had lost about one hundred and eighty men. We had to guard them all night. They slept nicely on straw while we had to guard them and give them half our rations!

The next day it rained in bucketfuls and we were wet through to the skin but we found a farmyard, lit a fire and stood there practically naked while we dried our clothes. We felt an enormous sense of pride after the strafe at Hautevesnes. It was absolutely a field day, fire and movement, fire and movement, one section firing while the other moved, inter-communication with each other, extended order. It really was an absolutely set-piece operation. And what was more satisfying to us was that it was a crack battalion, a Jäger battalion, and we had held them. The Germans were not going to get their way.

In the battle of the Marne where Allied Forces held the German advance, the Middlesex Regiment's transport comes under fire. The man in the centre has been badly wounded in the face.

Lieutenant Edward Louis Spears
Liaison officer with the Headquarters of the French Vth Army on Western Front

I was introduced to General Joffre. I had never even seen a picture of the man and I was astonished to find a big, heavy, bulky individual walking up and down the square with his hands behind his back. He had his kepi tilted well forward to protect his eyes, he had very light eyes, he was an albino in fact. He had pepper-and-salt hair, a pepper-and-salt walrus moustache, and was wearing a black tunic, which fitted extremely badly, sloping outwards from the third or fourth button down. Also ill-fitting red breeches and abominable gaiters, which as a cavalry officer I was very critical of. I watched him very carefully because here was an important man, perhaps the most important man on the whole of the Allied side at that time, who was commanding enormous forces counted in hundreds of thousands of men, perhaps as many as a million or more.

Joffre had an extraordinary habit of arriving at headquarters and getting out of his car in an enormous coat with a cape on it, even in hot weather. The General Commanding, and the Staff, would come up to him expecting to be told something but he'd listen to them. I have known cases where he has walked straight into his car again without uttering a single word. Always listening.

It was a very strange thing to see a single man exercising his will over a mass of about a million men. The fate of his country was in the balance, and he had to satisfy the political requirements of the British government and face a catastrophic situation, while never, never getting rattled. He was always in bed by 10 o'clock. He always ate enormously, took a little walk with one of his favourite ADCs after meals, and that was about all. I actually saw him on the afternoon that he decided on the battle of the Marne. He was sitting astride a hard chair in a dusty little French school courtyard, and he swayed backwards and forwards as he was deciding what he was going to do.

It was an extraordinary thing; very few people can have seen anybody with such a burden placed on his shoulders with nobody to help, just weighing the pros and cons of this movement and that movement, what orders to issue. It lasted quite a long time, perhaps a couple of hours, and then he got up, his decision was made, and the orders went out that night.

BATTLE OF THE AISNE, SEPTEMBER 14–28

Sergeant Thomas Painting
1st Battalion, King's Royal Rifle Corps
At the battle of the Aisne we got over the river and onto the high ground over a mile in front of the Aisne. We knew there was about a brigade of Jerries against us and we were only seven platoons. During the fight we got pushed back about three hundred yards, we had to leave our wounded and dead. The Highland Light Infantry and Worcesters came up. Private Wilson of the HLI and one of our men attacked a machine-gun. Our man got killed but Private Wilson killed the machine-gunner and captured the position and got the Victoria Cross. Our man got a wooden cross. That's the difference, you see. One killed – one a Victoria Cross.

REINFORCEMENTS

Rifleman Henry Williamson
London Rifle Brigade
Then the orders came through, I remember, in the tented lines on Crowborough Heath. They came down early in the morning with the colour sergeant of the company. The fellows rolled over and kicked their legs in the air and cheered and cheered and cheered, tremendously excited. I was not excited, I was apprehensive. I did not believe the war was going to be over by Christmas, I had a feeling from having talked to chaps from Mons in the local hospital that it wasn't altogether going to be a picnic.

Private Ascan Klee Gobert
Uhlans Regiment, German Army
During the first days of the war I joined a Lancers regiment, and because I could ride and shoot I was at the Front within six or seven weeks. This experience for a young boy of twenty who eight or nine weeks ago was at home was very new and adventurous. Further, there were only two or three volunteers in this squadron of experienced soldiers. They were between twenty-two and twenty-seven years old and they all had a profession, while we were students, so the life was very new for us. They were accustomed to everything, while we had never lived with a horse. The horse was the main thing for the next forty or fifty months. I never had a bed until I think November 1915, because we had always to sleep with the horses in granges or elsewhere.

Trooper George Jameson
1st Battalion, Northumberland Hussars
We gradually drifted sideways from Zeebrugge and arrived on the Mole at dusk. By the time we'd got our horses and everything off, the town was in darkness, there wasn't a light anywhere. There wasn't a person in the streets. But as we were riding through the town the clatter of the hoofs brought all the lights on and the doors open, and all the men and wives and girls came rushing out and embracing us. Bottles of wine, loaves of bread and all sorts were thrust upon us. You talk about a triumphal entry. It wasn't in it.

Private Reginald Leonard Haine
1st Battalion, Honourable Artillery Company
After I joined we stayed at headquarters for about a week. We were kitted out in terrible old uniforms, it wasn't modern stuff at all. And within a fortnight we'd been inspected by His Majesty King George V and we went off to Essex, to Aveley, into camp. The rumour was that we were going to train for six months there and then go to Egypt. We were a battalion of about eleven or twelve hundred strong and most of us had had Officer Training Cadet experience, we weren't completely green. I mean we all knew a bit about shooting and parade work and that sort of thing.

We were at this camp for about a week when there was a panic one evening while we were on the ranges. We went back to camp and they said, 'You're leaving tomorrow morning for an unknown destination.' Well, at that time we hadn't got proper rifles, we'd got the long rifle but not the ordinary service rifle. We hadn't got webbing equipment. We'd got this white webbing stuff but that night we were kitted out with the right stuff. But we hadn't a clue how to put this webbing together.

But by 6 o'clock in the morning we were ready and departed by train, without saying goodbye to one's family or anything. I remember that I wrote a postcard when I was in the train and chucked it out of the window at a station hoping that it would be delivered to my people at home, that was all. That was on the 18th of September, and we arrived that evening at Southampton and embarked that evening. And well, that was the start of things. But at the same time I thought the same as everyone else. 'It'll be over by Christmas and you've got to get out soon otherwise you won't see anything.' But I don't know if it was my opinion or everybody was saying it – that was the whole thing about it.

FALL OF ANTWERP, OCTOBER

Sergeant Richard Tobin
Hood Battalion, Royal Naval Division
On a brisk October morning we arrived in the threatened port of Antwerp. The people lined the street, they cheered, they waved, there were flowers and wine. The war was young and so were we. We felt gallant, they felt relieved. Out to the trenches we went. We settled, opened reserve ammunition, fixed our bayonets and said, 'Now let 'em come!'

Night came but not the enemy. We posted sentries and settled down, but not for long. Heavy rifle fire broke out on the left, then on the right. We manned the firing step and peered over. Searchlights from the fort swept the front. We could see nothing. We held our fire and felt neglected.

Morning came but still no enemy. Suddenly high in the sky was a train-like rumble and whistle followed by an explosion. Smoke and flame shot up in the city. An old hand said, 'Them's howitzer shells. The bastards must be a dozen miles away.'

At intervals throughout the day these rumbling shells rolled over, flames shooting up after each explosion. Then the oil tanks by the dockside were alight. The smoke gathered over the port to join the autumn mists and the glow from the fires. It looked like hell. We could only wait. We felt useless.

On the 8th of October an order came, 'Prepare to move.' Just at the back of our trench was a deserted farm. Odd men had gone scrounging in the farm and as we were about to move, an officer shouted to me, 'Sergeant, see the farm's clear.' Coming back through an outhouse, I saw some pails of milk and I did a most unsoldierly action. I emptied my half-full water-bottle and filled it full of milk. We soon got orders to move to the right and onto the road and we thought, 'Ah, they won't come to us. We're going out to them.'

On reaching the road, instead of turning left to the enemy, we turned right to the city and we received the most deadening, soul-racking order a soldier can receive. Retreat. We picked our way through the burning buildings, past the flaming oil tanks to the flaming pontoon bridge the engineers had built for us to cross and then destroy. On each side of the bridge stood hordes of refugees of every kind – children, women, nuns, priests. This was the bridge of sighs. They had been stopped so we could cross. The flare from the burning lit their faces, expressionless and hopeless, and we felt ashamed. An officer called to me, 'Sergeant! Shout "Break Step!"' It should have been 'Break Hearts!'

We were soon across and in open country. After a few miles we arrived at a Belgian village, marched into a cobbled square, and the orders were, 'Rest where you stand. Be ready for any alarm.'

'Sad' is not a soldier's word – browned off, fed up, yes, but the only time a soldier is really and deeply sad is when his line of duty takes him among refugees, those weary, shuffling, hopeless columns, chiefly women, children and the aged, carrying or pushing-pulling pram, wheelbarrow, farm cart, piled high with their world and often perched on top – granny. If his unit is rushing forward, pressing these weary souls aside so that the troops could get ahead and engage the enemy – he is sad, but feels he's giving them hope, but if his army is in retreat and they are in the press at the side of the road, the troops and guns rush past to take up another fighting position, he is sad but ashamed because he knows they think he is running away.

Just by was the church. Straw had been placed all round it and there were dark forms lying on it. My pal and I moved to the straw and were about to settle when we noticed two young women. With a mumbled apology, we were moving away when a voice said in good English, 'Don't go, please.' We squatted down, and I saw that one of the young women was nursing a whimpering baby. For something to say, I said, 'Is your baby all right?' With a sad smile she said, 'It's not my baby. I don't even know its mother. We are tired and hungry.' My pal and I emptied from our haversacks two tins of sardines and army biscuits. She sighed and said, 'The baby needs milk.' 'Milk!' I swung my water-bottle round. I think even the baby was surprised. Quite soon, we fell in and marched away. The British government had lost a water-bottle, but a baby found a meal.

FIRST BATTLE OF YPRES, OCTOBER–NOVEMBER

Captain Reginald Thomas
Royal Artillery
We were terribly short of hand grenades, in fact I don't think they were even invented at that time. But we really needed something to hurl at the enemy. We were so close to them that occasionally we could take pot-shots, but to get something actually into a trench was a very different thing.

And so with Philip Neame's aid – he was a sapper and I was a gunner – we concocted some jam-tin bombs. I helped Neame with this little factory he was running with empty jam tins and made one or two excursions behind our lines to buy ingredients. I was able to find a shop that dealt in explosives and we got some gun-cotton and some blasting detonators. Also I was still in the mounted section, so was able to get our farriers to cut up old horseshoes and other bits of old iron to put in the bombs.

So we made these hand grenades out of jam-tin bombs and just hurled them into the German trenches. They were very successful. The War Office of the government eventually supplied us with bombs that were exactly the same shape as the jam tin – they were rather handy things to hold, you see, and you could throw them twenty or thirty yards. You couldn't have had a nicer missile to hurl. We did rather well with them.

Captain Philip Neame
15th Field Company, Royal Engineers

It was important that we developed hand grenades, because the Germans were well supplied with well-made ones and started using them in trench warfare and we had no proper reply. Although there was an official British hand grenade it had hardly been used at all in peace-time training, and there was a very limited supply of it. Therefore the Royal Engineers in France started devising home-made hand grenades called bombs. These were made out of empty jam tins which were filled with rivets, hobnails, and any small bits of metal, and the explosive was usually two small bits of gun-cotton with a detonator and the necessary bit of fuse projecting from the end of the jam tin. That first winter of 1914 the sappers were kept busy manufacturing as many as were needed. Hand grenades were very useful, because trenches are all designed with traverses between each fire bay, for the purpose of pre-venting the enemy, if they should capture a length of trench, from enfilading the whole thing. You can't shoot the enemy in the next fire bay, and so the only way of getting at him is by lobbing a hand grenade over the traverse. The hand grenade goes off with a terrific explosion and will probably kill or wound all the soldiers in that length of trench. That's why they were so useful in trench warfare.

Trooper George Jameson
1st Battalion, Northumberland Hussars
We pushed on up the Menin Road and got into Gheleveldt. In those days grub was very chancy, we didn't see much food. We were detached from supplies to a large degree, and they were very slow coming forward. So we were always on the hunt for something to eat or drink.

So when we got into the chateau at Gheleveldt I said to my blokes there, 'You get downstairs to the cellars and see if you can find anything to eat.' And all they could find was champagne! So the whole lot of us, we had about four bottles each stuffed into the strapping round our saddles. Jogging about on a horse didn't help it at all, so there were corks popping all over the place – champagne all over the horses' flanks. It didn't last very long.

Private Clifford Lane
1st Battalion, Hertfordshire Regiment
We moved to the Front in thirty or forty London omnibuses. When we boarded these omnibuses everybody wanted to get on the top because it was quite a nice day, fairly bright for November. But we had not been going very long before it started to rain, so we got thoroughly soaked. We must have travelled for quite a few hours, for it was dark when we eventually reached our destination, Vlamertinge.

We were lined up and given a very generous issue of rum. I didn't even drink beer. So in no time we were quite euphoric really. We were quite happy. We did not know where we were going, but the moon broke through the clouds and it was a lovely night. And I can remember, as we marched along, we passed a Roman Catholic priest who removed his hat and murmured his blessings.

We spent a cold night in a field. In the morning we were told to go up a wooded hillside where we found dugouts. We could rest there much more comfortably – in a dugout you could lay down. We stayed that day, but did not go to sleep. When it was light we simply came out to survey our surroundings.

We could see a road running towards Ypres from our hillside, and on it we saw a group of French soldiers. While we were watching there was the sound of heavy gunfire and, after a few seconds, three violent explosions. When the smoke had cleared we saw this group picking up one of their number and immediately start to dig a grave for him, so the shell had killed him. That was the first time we realised what the war was about – what the Germans could do.

Sergeant Stefan Westmann
29th Division, German Army

All of a sudden the enemy fire ceased. Complete silence came over the battlefield. Then one of the chaps in my shell-hole said, 'I wonder what they are up to,' and another answered, 'Perhaps they are getting tea.' A third one said, 'Don't be a fool, do you see what I see?' And we looked over the brim of our shell-hole and there between the brick heaps, out had come a British soldier with a Red Cross flag that he waved at us. And he was followed by stretcher-bearers who came slowly towards us and collected our wounded. We got up, still completely dumb from fear of death, and helped them to bring our wounded into our trenches.

Rifleman Henry Williamson
London Rifle Brigade

It is true to say that we enjoyed our first visit to the trenches. The weather was dry, we went through a wood under Messines Hill. We were brigaded with regulars who wore balaclava helmets. The whole feeling was one of tremendous comradeship, and these old sweats who were survivors of Mons and Aisne, they had no fear at all, and any apprehension we had of going in under fire was soon got rid of in the trenches.

We could also go in estaminets and have omelettes, and café rum for about a halfpenny, it was great fun. We had to go on working parties at night in the woods, and then after four more nights we were in the trenches again, back slithering into the trenches and doing it all over again.

One night in the second week of November there was a tremendous storm blowing, lightning was flashing and flares were still going up. Rain splashed up about nine or ten inches in no man's land, and it went on and on and on. That stopped the first battle of Ypres which was raging up north. Our sector north of Armentières ceased. The condition of the latrines can be imagined and we could not sleep, every minute was like an hour. The dead were lying out in front. The rains kept on, we were in yellow clay, and the water table was 2 ft below. Our trenches were 7 ft deep. We walked about or moved very slowly in marl or pug of yellow watery clay. When the evening came and we could get out of it, it took about an hour to climb out. Some of our chaps slipped in and were drowned. They couldn't even be seen, but were trodden on later.

We were relieved after the fourth night and some of us had to be carried out. I noticed that many of the tough ones were carried out, while the skinny little whippersnappers like myself could somehow manage, we got out somehow as we had not the weight to carry. We marched back – slouched back – and eventually got to our billet at Plug Street (Ploegsteert), a mile and a half away. We fell on the floor and slept, equipment on and everything. Everything was mud-slabbed – overcoats, boots and everything. We were dead beat.

Private Clifford Lane
1st Battalion, Hertfordshire Regiment
When we came out of the line we were marched along a road again, but by this time it was getting frosty. The French roads were all cobbled and they were getting quite slippery. We didn't know where we were going. We knew we were going out of the line. We marched along fairly happily for a time, but it was getting quite hard work. We'd gone two or three weeks without any real sleep, we hadn't had our boots off for three weeks and we'd had no proper food, nothing hot anyway. Anyway, we marched along for a few miles, and as I say, men began falling out.

And the regimental sergeant-major came along with his stick and he gave them a walloping till they got up and started marching again, because you could not possibly leave them there, they would have frozen to death. Anyway, those of us that were still fairly fit, about ninety per cent of us, we marched along, I suppose, for another hour or so, then we saw some fires burning in the distance. And it was a stopping place for us. They'd built up these fires and made huge dixies of tea for us, and rum. That was marvellous. This was about the middle of the night, I suppose. Well, we had this tea and rum and off we went again.

Our morale stayed high too, I must say that. It was amazing really. Even when they'd realised when we were up against it – we were going to have a very rough time, but they did not sort of lose their optimism, not at all.

When we got into Méteren it was a kind of miner's dream of home – the houses were right onto the pavement, it was a very poor place really, and we simply flopped down into the road and just lay there, waiting to find out where we had got to go, where we were to be billeted.

Eventually about ten of us were billeted in a cottage, and when we went in it was simply bare boards, very crude furniture – a very small place really. But there was an old gentleman and his wife and they had two daughters in their twenties, I suppose. And they had one room, quite a small room, where we were to sleep. But it was like going in to Buckingham Palace for us, to get warm. I have never again experienced it. They had one of these long French stoves, right in the middle of their living room, and it was really beautifully warm. It was such a sensation to be warm again, it was wonderful, I've never felt anything like it since.

Nurse Eleanora Pemberton

I had interesting experiences in Boulogne, when I stood with the others on the quay at Boulogne and watched Lord Roberts' little coffin brought down to be put on a ship to go back to England. He had died at the age of eighty-two while visiting the Indian troops at the Front. It was a wonderful sight and a most moving one. A little coffin – a very small one because he was very short, of course. He died right up at the Front, you know, just where he would've wished to die. And he was carried by four Tommies straight from the battle front: covered in mud, puttees stained, muddy boots, hair anyhow – they were carrying their caps – and they carried this little coffin down the quayside onto the boat. And the band played 'The Last Post' and then 'The Dead March in Saul.' It was a most moving occasion. I shall never forget it. I can see it now.

DECEMBER

Private Reginald Leonard Haine
1st Battalion, Honourable Artillery Company

As far as sandbags are concerned, the first time I saw a sandbag in France was when we were paraded one evening at Kemmel, a small town about half a mile behind the lines at Wytschaete. We didn't take these sandbags up empty, as Kemmel had been knocked about, there were lots of broken bricks and that sort of thing. The Pioneers had filled these sandbags and we carried them up one by one to the line. A whole line of us had one sandbag; that's all we could carry because of the conditions of the road.

Of course, going up on a trip like that one was bound to have a few casualties. Sometimes it was a quiet night and you only got one or two fellows wounded, but sometimes you were not so lucky if you'd got a machine-gun on you. They'd got this road taped to an inch and they knew we used it, just as we knew they had to use the road on the other side of the line. But we took these sandbags up to the line and it seemed to me stupid at the time that we had to do a thing like that. Well, of course that attitude only lasted a very short time.

We used to hump these sandbags at night, chiefly, because we couldn't show our noses in the daytime, we were so close to the Germans. And then they did make a tremendous difference. Instead of just living in a ditch one could take rather a pride in building a decent sort of trench, and we got extremely good at improvising these trenches. Of course one problem was that directly Jerry spotted we had got sandbags we were shelled to blazes straight away as he tried to knock the whole thing to bits. But that was the luck of the game.

The shelling was not the big stuff which we had later on in the war, it was chiefly what we called whizz-bangs. They were equivalent to our 18-pounders, they were little chaps. But they were frightening enough, especially when they knocked the sandbags to bits. And then of course, let's face it, we got a lot of casualties with those too.

The finest training for warfare is warfare itself. In a fortnight you learn more than two years of any training can teach you. And so before

Keeping his head down, a soldier of the Honourable Artillery Company peers through a box periscope at enemy trenches.

the end of the year we were a very seasoned battalion and – I say it without bragging – we were as good as any regular battalion in the line. There was nobody behind except people like the Army Service Corps and suppliers. But as far as the fighting troops were concerned we were all very near the front line the whole time. Practically the whole time you had to sleep with your boots on in case things went wrong anywhere. Even if one was in support – not in reserve so much, in reserve you could get your clothes off – but if you were in support you had to sleep in your clothes. The winter of '14 was extremely hard because we had no amenities whatsoever. It was just ditches, the trenches were just waterlogged ditches, and one was often up to one's knees in frozen mud. You could do nothing about it except stick there. The actual fighting was nothing like it was in the later years of the war, the years I know most from a fighting point of view, and of course the casualties and everything then were terrific. But in '14 there were many casualties through sickness and shelling. There was shelling every day but nothing like the intensity of later on.

We had not been trained for any of the tasks we were asked to undertake. It was all improvisation really. The ordinary infanteer, he shot his rifle. And we had a couple of Vickers guns in the battalion, that's all the machine-guns the battalion had in those days. And there were specially trained people who used to have to hump up their ammunition for them, which was a hell of a job. That was because sometimes one had marched two or three miles to get near the firing line, and then we would have to carry not only our own kit with 250 rounds of ammunition, but sometimes they'd ask us to, between two people, carry up 1,000 rounds of machine-gun ammunition as well. And in those conditions in the winter of '14, when everything was as muddy as it could be and there was really no drainage or anything, it was a terrific task. From a physical point of view it was a killing job but we most of us got through it.

Captain Philip Neame
15th Field Company, Royal Engineers

The 8th Division carried out an attack on the 18th of December near Neuve Chapelle, and during the early hours of the 19th – in fact in the middle of the night – I was ordered up to the area of the attack with my Royal Engineers section to help consolidate the captured area. When I got up to the Front, I was told that the Germans were counter-attacking and the CO of the infantry battalion concerned asked me to go up into the line and see what I could do in making our defences strong. I took my sapper section forward, got up into the Front, and heard noise of fighting and bombs exploding – they were called bombs then, they were actually hand grenades. I thought it best to go forward myself. I left my section of sappers – about thirty-six men – under a sergeant in our old front line while I crawled forward up a ditch and got into the German trenches, where our leading infantry were, to see what was happening.

When I got there I saw the infantry officer in command who said the Germans were counter-attacking with bombs, and that his own bombers had all been wounded and that the bombs that were left would not go off. So I went up to talk to one of the remaining bombers whom I found up in the Front and discovered that he could not light our own bombs because there were no fuses left and he didn't know how to light the safety fuse without a fuse. Well, I did know how to because you can do it by holding a match head on the end of the fuse and striking a matchbox across it. So I got up to the Front and started throwing bombs back at the Germans, and that's how the whole affair started. Our infantry were all crowded up into the remaining bit of trench we had captured from the Germans, and the Germans were throwing their bombs at us from two different directions. I had rather a business – being the only one there who knew how to light our bombs – so I quickly shouted for all our available bombs to be sent up to me. I told two or three of the infantry – the West Yorks – to stay in a bit of trench alongside me in case the Germans tried to reach us.

I then started lighting and throwing bombs in the two different directions from which the Germans were throwing bombs at us. I very quickly stopped the Germans bombing from a trench away on the right. Then I had a good deal of bombing coming from straight in front of me, from Germans throwing from about twenty or thirty yards away, and so I quickly threw several bombs as quick as I could. To do this I had to stand up on the fire step and expose myself so that I could see where I was throwing with some accuracy.

Every time I stood up a German machine-gun fired at me, but luckily he was a bit slow and I always managed to pop down again having thrown my bomb before the stream of machine-gun bullets came over more or less where I had been standing. Anyway, after some little time I heard what sounded like shouts and screams from the Germans in the trench where I had been throwing my bombs, so evidently they had been effective. At all events the German bombing eased off, and after about a quarter of an hour or so almost stopped altogether.

And so I was able to hang on to the trench we had captured, having only had to withdraw by one bay, that's to say some eight or ten yards. Then with the West Yorkshire infantrymen I stayed there until the officer in command, Captain Ingpen, came along to see how things were going on. He offered to send more infantry up, and I said, 'No, I don't want any more, these three fellows are quite enough to hold this bit of trench.'

Captain Ingpen told me he had orders to evacuate the German trench and take all his men back to the British line where we'd started the attack from, and so I stayed there for the next half an hour or so holding that bit of line.

And then I got a message to say that all the British troops had got back safely. Mind you, a great many had been killed and wounded by the German bombs and by machine-gun fire before I'd got there. In the bottom of the trench were numbers of our dead soldiers lying there and a certain number of wounded, and we managed to help some of them to get back to our line. And when we finally had a message to say we were to come back I gave a quick two or three bombs as a final goodbye to the Germans – really to keep them quiet while we moved back down the trench.

We then lined the road ditch on our side of the road to stop the Germans attempting to attack. I helped one or two of the wounded get across the road, and in the end I joined up with my sappers and my sergeant. Amongst other things my sergeant and I had to carry a badly wounded infantryman along the road in full view of the Germans because it was quite impossible to move him along the road ditch. The Germans seemed to respect our task because they did not shoot at us, which they could easily have done – we were sitting ducks. We got them into our proper trench where it was much easier to walk along and handed the men over to stretcher-bearers.

I then went back and reported at the battalion, thinking I'd done my day's work, because my task had been to go and prepare the captured German trenches for defence, and as there were no longer any captured German trenches I presumed I could go back to our billets behind the line.

However, the two infantry colonels, of the West Yorks and the Devons, asked me to take my section of sappers back to the front line again and make sure that our original line was in a good state for defence because they were afraid the Germans might now set to and counter-attack. So we patched up breastworks and French defences for the rest of the day.

When I got back that evening the CO of the Devons, Colonel Travers, whom I knew very well from working in the trenches, said, 'I will see that the brigadier knows what you have done today.' I just thanked him and did not think any more about it.

Then when I returned to my field company headquarters that evening and told my OC what happened during the day, he said, 'If you're not careful, Neame, you will be getting the VC.' I thought he was just joking. Six days after the event, our divisional commander, Major-General Davis, came to our billets to wish the people who were not working that morning a happy Christmas. He said to me, 'A happy Christmas to you, Neame, I've recommended you for the Victoria Cross.' So that was the first time I really took it seriously. I just said, 'Well, thank you very much sir,' and his ADC came up to me afterwards and said, 'Well that's a nice Christmas present, Neame, isn't it?'

I had written to my parents about the exciting battle I'd had, but I still did not tell them about being recommended for the VC because I was not convinced that I would get it and didn't want them to be disappointed. However, they heard about it in a roundabout way from an officer in our division whose parents lived near them. This officer had heard all about it and wrote to his parents and it got out that way.

Rifleman Henry Williamson
London Rifle Brigade

On the 19th of December 1914 the Brigade was ordered to make an attack on part of the German trench which enfiladed the Hampshire trench. The attack was to be made in daylight, we were in support of this attack. We were ordered to lie down at the edge of the wood and wait events. There was practically no bombardment because there were very few shells. I think the ration was two a day for our heavy guns – our 6-inch Long Toms they were called, but the shells screamed over us. Two of them burst in our front trench, four burst in no man's land.

Then we heard the hoarse cries and shouts of the East Lancs, who were making an attack, and they were only about five or six yards forward, and the machine-guns opened up and down they went. There were cries and screams, and we, who were in support, lay there for three or four hours. Then the order came, 'The London Rifle Brigade will carry on the attack.' The order was not actually to start, but we were to prepare for it. I noticed my friend Baldwin, on my left, had a white face. I felt drained out and when I tried to get up I couldn't. My knees were wobbling and we lay there another half-hour, then heard with great relief that the attack was not to be repeated.

We went out later and helped the stretcher-bearers to get in the wounded. I remember one man being carried back, and when he was safely inside he sang in a light tenor voice, 'O for the wings, for the wings of a dove, far far away would I rove.' He was said to sing in a church choir before the war. And far away in the woods as we went back rejoicing to have our rum ration, we heard this voice singing as the stars came out. But one poor chap with us, he took a first sip of the rum and gave a shriek and dropped the jar because some fellow back in the rear had stolen the rum and filled the jar with brown Condy's fluid, a powerful disinfectant. This poor fellow had taken a mouthful and it went down into his stomach. We heard he died later.

CHRISTMAS

Private Clifford Lane
1st Battalion, Hertfordshire Regiment
We'd all got these long, thick woollen underpants and vests on and we were soaked right through. When we got back to the trench it was dark, and we tried to get around this little brazier fire, but of course only two or three men could get near anyway so we didn't really get dry. And then they brought us 'Princess Mary's gift box.' And in this box was cigarettes, tobacco and a bar of chocolate, which was very much appreciated. And then we had what the English newspapers called Christmas Dinner. This consisted of cold bully beef and a cold lump of Christmas pudding, that was our Christmas dinner. The English newspapers said the British troops in the front line 'enjoyed' their Christmas dinner.

Private Frank Sumpter
London Rifle Brigade
After the 19th December attack, we were back in the same trenches when Christmas Day came along. It was a terrible winter, everything was covered in snow, everything was white. The devastated landscape looked terrible in its true colours – clay and mud and broken brick – but when it was covered in snow, it was beautiful. Then we heard the Germans singing 'Silent night, Holy night,' and they put up a notice saying 'Merry Christmas,' so we put one up too.

While they were singing our boys said, 'Let's join in,' so we joined in and when we started singing, they stopped. And when we stopped, they started again. So we were easing the way. Then one German took a chance and jumped up on top of the trench and shouted out, 'Happy Christmas, Tommy!' So of course our boys said, 'If he can do it, we can do it,' and we all jumped up. A sergeant-major shouted, 'Get down!' But we said, 'Shut up Sergeant, it's Christmas time!' And we all went forward to the barbed wire.

We could barely reach through the wire, because the barbed wire was not just one fence, it was two or three fences together, with a wire in between. And so we just shook hands and I had the experience of talking to one German who said to me, 'Do you know where the Essex Road in London is?' I replied, 'Yes, my uncles had a shoe repairing shop there.' He said, 'That's funny. There's a barber shop on the other side where I used to work.'

They could all speak very good English because before the war, Britain was invaded by Germans. Every pork butcher was German, every barber's shop was German, and they were all over here getting the low-down on the country. It's ironic when you think about it, that he must have shaved my uncle at times and yet my bullet might have found him and his bullet might have found me.

The officers gave the order 'No fraternisation' and then they turned their backs on us. But they didn't try to stop it because they knew they couldn't. We never said a word about the war to the Germans. We spoke about our families, about how old we were, how long we thought it would last and things like that. I was young and I wasn't that interested, so I stood there for about half an hour then I came back. But most of the boys stayed there the whole day and only came back in the evening. There were no shots fired and some people enjoyed the curiosity of walking about in no man's land. It was good to walk around. As a sign of their friendliness the Germans put up a sign saying 'Gott mit uns' which means 'God is with us' and so we put a sign in English saying 'We got mittens too.' I don't know if they enjoyed that joke.

Sergeant George Ashurst
2nd Battalion, Lancashire Fusiliers
There was still 200 yards between us and the Germans. We did not intermingle until some Jerries came to their wire waving a newspaper. 'What's that lads?' 'Are you going for it?' 'I'm not going for it!' Anyway a corporal in our company went for it. Well, he got halfway and he stopped. I don't know if he'd changed his mind or not, but the lads shouted, 'Go on! Get that paper!' He went right to the wire and the Germans shook hands with him and wished him a merry Christmas and gave him the paper.

He came back with it but we couldn't read a word of it so it had to go to an officer. And there were still fellows walking about on top of our trench at 5 o'clock, at teatime, and not a shot had been fired, although the armistice had officially finished at 1 o'clock. And we could see Jerries knocking about all over the place. It was so pleasant to get out of that trench, from between those two clay walls, and just walk and run about. It was heaven. And to kick this sandbag about, but we did not play with the Germans. Well we didn't, but I believe quite a lot did up and down the place. Eventually, we got orders to come back down into the trench, 'Get back in your trenches, every man!' The order came round by word of mouth down each trench. Some people took no damn notice.

Anyway, the generals behind must have seen it and got a bit suspicious, so they gave orders for a battery of guns behind us to open fire and a machine-gun to open out, and officers to fire their revolvers at the Jerries. That started the war again. We were cursing the generals to hell. You want to get up here in this mud. Never mind you giving orders in your big chateaux and driving about in your big cars. We hated the sight of bloody generals, we always did. We didn't hate them so much before this, but we never liked them after that.

Then we had newspapers coming here from England accusing us of fraternising with the Germans: parsons accusing us of fraternising with the Germans when there had been an armistice on Christmas Day. I wrote back home and told my family off. I said we could do with that parson and the fellows that are writing in the newspapers here, I said. We want them here in front of us instead of Jerry so we could shoot them down for passing remarks like that while nice and safe in England.

Lieutenant John Wedderburn-Maxwell
Royal Field Artillery

There was a party, a couple of hundred yards away, of our troops and the Germans all fraternising. And so I said I was going to go and look at this. And I told the infantry to keep an eye on me, in case anybody tried any rough business, so they'd know what was happening, and I went up and met a small party who said, 'Come along into our trenches and have a look at us.' I said, 'No, I'm quite near enough as it is.' And we laughed at each other, and I gave them some English tobacco, and they gave me some German – I forget what it was – and we walked about for about half an hour in no man's land.

And then we shook hands, wished each other luck and one fellow said, 'Will you send this off to my girlfriend in Manchester?' So I took his letter, and I franked it, and sent it off to the girlfriend when I got back. And then after that I came back, and at midnight we were ordered into action because there was a strong rumour from a German deserter that there was going to be an attack.

Rifleman Henry Williamson
London Rifle Brigade
That evening the Germans sent over a note saying that their Staff was visiting their trenches that night, so the truce must end and they would have to fire their machine-guns. They would fire them high but could we in any case keep under cover in case regrettable accidents occurred. At 11 o'clock precisely they opened up. We saw flashes of the machine-guns going high and it was passed back to Intelligence that the Germans were using Berlin time in the trenches, which is one hour before British time. I suppose that was an important item for Intelligence, and that was the end of our truce. We did not fire, and they did not fire for a day or two, but then the Prussians came in and relieved the Saxons and then we began to lose more men from sniping and we went out after that.

1915

After the gas attack they were reeling around tearing at their throats,
their faces black, while an RAMC sergeant stood by and, well,
I've never seen a man look so dependent. He said, 'Look at
those poor bastards, and we can't do a thing for them.'

France had lost ten per cent of her territory to the German invasion, and a third of her industrial capacity. Nevertheless, French factories poured forth guns and munitions. British plants began tooling-up for production quantities undreamt of before the war. Mistakes were predictable in so hasty a transition to a war economy, optimistic productivity assumptions failed to be achieved, and standards of manufacture were alarmingly variable, particularly with regard to ammunition. A disagreeably high volume of 'dud' shells were passed to the front.

A total of 110 Allied divisions faced 100 German divisions in the West. In the East, 80 German and Austro-Hungarian divisions confronted 83 Russian divisions over a front that stretched from the Baltic Sea to the Carpathian Mountains – more than twice as long as the Western Front. The lower ratio of troops to space, combined with the yawning gulf in professional ability, enabled the Germans to drive the Russians out of Poland (a Russian province since the Napoleonic Wars) and eventually overrun Serbia. Russian pressure on the tottering Austro-Hungarian Army was reduced, but the conquest of a great swathe of Eastern Europe availed Germany nothing. Russia remained in the war and the British and French war economies began to win the 'battle of the factories.'

The Allies did not win on the battlefield, however, despite

bringing to bear increasing numbers of soldiers. The British Expeditionary Force, which had reached a total of ten divisions by the end of 1914, expanded to thirty-seven by the end of 1915 (including two Canadian divisions). The call for volunteers vastly exceeded the ability of the tiny pre-war army to train and equip, let alone command in battle. Veteran officers and NCOs were brought from retirement, but the heavy losses that the pre-war regulars suffered in 1914 were to blunt the efficiency of this brave, enthusiastic but essentially amateur army.

The Battle of Neuve Chapelle indicated that with a well-prepared artillery fireplan the German trenches could be stormed. However, these were small-scale operations, limited both in the numbers of troops employed and the modesty of their objectives: their aim was to advance little more than a mile. The story of 1915 is of progressively larger Allied assaults failing with ever-lengthening casualty lists.

The Germans tried one brief attack in the West that year. On April 22 they made the first effective use of poison gas to attack French and British positions at Ypres. The Allies condemned this as an atrocity but hastened to produce their own chemical weapons. The attack was essentially an experimental raid, in that no follow-up troops were ready to exploit the gap created by the initial success of the gas. This German error was to be repeated by British and French forces later.

The French opened a major offensive in Artois, on a twenty-mile front from Vimy Ridge to Arras, on May 9. Twenty French divisions were involved against just four German, but despite unprecedented artillery bombardments the German defences proved impossible to break. Barbed wire obstructed the attackers' approach; concealed machine guns swept the open approaches, and hidden batteries opened fire suddenly to cut down the French in no man's land. In a series of attacks that lasted into the summer, 100,000 French soldiers were killed.

The French tried again in the autumn on an even greater scale, this time with major British participation. Eighteen French divisions were ordered to assault the German lines in the Champagne sector, supported by 700 guns. Objectives up to fifty miles behind the German trenches were planned to be captured, but the lines barely advanced five miles. At the same time, another thrust at the Artois area involved eleven French and five British divisions: the battle of Loos opened on September 25 and ended on October 8. The German lines remained unbroken, despite the British use of gas and smoke. The slaughter of two British reserve divisions with the loss of 8,000 men, helped end the career of the British Expeditionary Forces commander, Sir John French. He was replaced by the commander of the First Army, General Haig. On the French side, Joffre's reputation suffered, but endured.

The major British and French diversion of 1915 was the attempt to defeat the Ottoman Empire, which had joined Germany and Austro-Hungary in October 1914. An Allied naval attack at the Dardanelles on March 19, 1915 was beaten off. The next decision was to carry out a major assault by ground forces: the Gallipoli landings on April 25, in which Australian troops took part at Anzac Cove, while British and French troops landed at Cape Helles. The Allied forces – including many Indian troops – won a limited beachhead and spent the rest of the year in trench warfare.

HOME FRONT

Private S. C. Lang

I was walking down the Camden High Street when two young ladies approached and said, 'Why aren't you in the Army with the boys?' So I said, 'I'm sorry but I'm only seventeen' and one of them said, 'Oh we've heard that one before. I suppose you're also doing work of national importance.' Then she put her hand in her bag and pulled out a feather. I raised a hand thinking she was going to strike me and this feather was pushed up my nose.

Then a sergeant came out of one of the shops and said to me, 'Did she call you a coward?' I said yes and felt very indignant about it. He said, 'Well, come across the road to the drill hall and we'll soon prove that you aren't a coward.' I got into the drill hall and then the sergeant said to me, 'How old are you?' I told him I was seventeen and he said, 'What did you say, nineteen?' 'No, seventeen.' 'When were you born?' '1898.' '1896?' 'No,' I said, '1898.'

He then said to me, 'Get on the scales.' He weighed me, took my height and said, 'Now we'll go round to the doctor for a medical exam.' The doctor told me to take all my clothes off, which embarrassed me very much. Any rate, I got back to the drill hall, where there were six of us waiting, and the sergeant called out my name. I walked forward and thought, 'Oh that's good, I'm not in,' and he said, 'You're the only so-and-so that's passed out of this six.'

I was astonished because I'd told him I was only seventeen and there I was, almost in the Army. I went to the recruiting office and the officer said something to me about King and country and then he said, 'Well raise your right hand and say I will,' or something like that. Then he said, 'I'm extremely sorry I haven't got your shilling, but we'll let you have that later on,' and to my amazement I found I was being called Private S. C. Lang.

Private William Chapman
Royal Army Medical Corps
Next morning the new draft – fifteen or twenty of us – had to parade with a sergeant-major and a sergeant in command. Their purpose was quite a noble one – to find out what we had been in civil life so that we'd be suitably placed in the Army. So they started:

'And what were you in Civvy Street?'
'Oh, I was a butcher, Sergeant-Major.'
'Sergeant, send him to the quartermaster's stores.'
'What were you in Civvy Street?'
'Well, I was a clerk, Sergeant-Major.'
'Send him to the orderly room.'
Then he came to me. 'And what were you in Civvy Street?'
'I was a theological student, Sergeant-Major.'

Lieutenant William Chapman – Former Private Royal Army
Medical Corps.

'What?'
I said, 'I was a theological student.'
He said, 'What's that?'
I said: 'Well, just I was a theological student.'
'Sergeant,' he said, 'come and ask this fellow what he was.'
So the sergeant came and I was beginning to enjoy it then.
'What were you in Civvy Street?'
I said, 'I was a theological student, sergeant.'

They then walked away and had a little conference. Right, Chapman, Royal Army Medical Corps. They didn't know the difference between theological and biological!

Gunner Frederick Broome
Royal Field Artillery

When the war broke out I was fifteen years of age, but I was already in the Army. I went to France in August 1914 and was there through the retirement from Mons, the battle of the Marne and then the advance to Ypres. It was there that I caught enteric fever and was invalided back to England. I went and visited my father, and he sent in my birth certificate, so I was discharged for having misstated my age on enlistment.

I got a job in Civvy Street and a few months afterwards I was walking across Putney Bridge when I was accosted by four girls who gave me three white feathers. I explained to them that I had been in the Army, and been discharged, and that I was still only sixteen years of age, but they didn't believe me. By now several people had collected around the girls, who were giggling. I felt most uncomfortable and awfully embarrassed and said something about how I had a good mind to chuck them into the Thames and eventually broke off the conversation feeling very humiliated. I finished the walk across the bridge, and there on the other side was the 37th London Territorial Association of the Royal Field Artillery. I walked straight in and rejoined the Army.

Kitty Eckersley
Leather worker

So he went overseas, and I never saw him for about six months. He sent word he was coming home on leave at Christmas, so I was expecting him all Christmas. In the meantime I'd given the work up at the mill, I'd heard there was a better job at a leatherworks – Noblet's Leather works at Ardenshaw it was – so I went for this job and I got it, and it was a lot more money than I was getting.

So I was expected at work when he came home unexpectedly in January. It was a Monday morning and I was almost ready to go. I used to set off at 7 o'clock with a boy who would call round for me – he was only fifteen but he was company for me – and we used to walk there together. And just before he arrived there was a loud knocking on the door and this voice shouted, 'Open the door – the Jerries are here!' and my mother said, 'Oh, it's Percy – I can tell his voice!' And in he came, all mucky and what have you, straight from France. He came in and the boy followed just behind him and said, 'Oh well – she'll not be going to work then!' And I didn't, I stayed at home all the time he had his leave.

But he was very dirty – filthy in fact. Even lousy. And mother said, 'You're not sleeping in one of my beds like that. There's a tub in the back,' she says, 'and you'd better get your things off. Get them shirts and khaki off and whatnot and I'll see what I can do with it.' Eventually we found some old clothes of his that he had worn before, and he had a good rest.

All that day he was tired – he only got six days leave and he'd spent two of them travelling, so he didn't have very long. But the next day he said to me, 'Now Kitty, what would you like for a present? I'm going to buy you a present while I'm home.' I said I didn't know. But I'm afraid I was rather vain in those days, and I was rather an attractive girl, so eventually I said, 'You know, I have seen a beautiful hat down the street, I would like that.' It was in a shop window, and I'd looked at this hat several times. It was a lovely hat and I'd loved it, but it was terrible dear. It was nineteen and elevenpence. Well, we could get a lovely hat then for two and eleven, you see.

Anyway Percy said, 'Well, come on, we'll go and have a look at it.'

And I'll never forget that hat, it was white felt, and it turned up all around, and with me being dark it did look lovely. It had a big mauve feather all round the brim, and it hung over – oh, it was gorgeous. So we got dressed up and I took him to the leatherworks and introduced him to Mr. Noblet himself, and everyone shook hands with him. And how pleased and proud I was to show him off.

Anyway, he went back on the Thursday night. I didn't go with him to the tram but one of my brothers did, with a friend of his. And it seems he told his friend, 'I'm afraid I shall never come back again.' The friend told me this afterwards. Anyway he went, and I went back to work. Afterwards I found out that I was pregnant and wrote and told him.

Mrs. M. Hall
Munitions worker

I'd never been in a factory before, but the crisis made you think. I thought well, my brothers and my friends are in France, so a friend and I thought to ourselves, well, let's do something. So we wrote to London and asked for war work. And we were directed to a munitions factory at Perivale in London. We had to have a health examination because we had to be very physically fit – perfect eyesight and strong. We had to supply four references, and be British-born of British parents.

We worked ten hours a day, that's from eight in the morning till quarter to one – no break, an hour for dinner, back again until half-past six – no break. We single girls found it very difficult to eat as well as work because the shops were closed when we got home. We had to do our work and try to get food, which was difficult. I remember going into a shop after not having milk for seven days and they said, 'If you can produce a baby you can have the milk' – that was it! I went into a butcher's shop to get some meat because we were just beginning to be rationed and I said, 'That looks like cat.' And he said, 'It is.' I couldn't face that.

It was a perfect factory to work in: everybody seemed unaware of the powder around them, unaware of any danger. Once or twice we heard, 'Oh, so and so's gone.' Perhaps she'd made a mistake and her eye was out, but there wasn't any big explosion during the three years I was there. We worked at making these little pellets, very innocent-looking little pellets, but had there been the slightest grit in those pellets, it would have been 'Goodbye.'

We had to do a fortnight on and a fortnight off. It was terribly hard, terribly monotonous, but we had a purpose. There wasn't a drone in that factory and every girl worked and worked and worked. I didn't hear one grumble and hardly ever heard of one that stayed home because she had her man in mind, we all had. I was working with sailors' wives from three ships that were torpedoed and sank *Aboukir*, *Cressy* and *Hogue*, on the 22nd of September 1914. It was pitiful to see them, so we had to cheer them up as best we could, so we sang. It was beautiful to listen to.

After each day when we got home we had a lovely good wash. And believe me the water was blood-red and our skin was perfectly yellow, right down through the body, legs and toenails even, perfectly yellow. In some people it caused a rash and a very nasty rash all round the chin. It was a shame because we were a bevy of beauties, you know, and these girls objected very much to that. Yet amazingly even though they could do nothing about it, they still carried on and some of them with rashes about half an inch thick but didn't seem to do them any inward harm, just the skin. The hair, if it was fair or brown it went a beautiful gold, but if it was any grey, it went grass-green. It was quite a twelve-month after we left the factory that the whole of the yellow came from our bodies. Washing wouldn't do anything – it only made it worse.

Each day we really and truly worked as I've never seen women work like it in my life before or since. It was just magic, we worked and we stood and we sat and we sang. If anyone had come into that factory they would never have believed it could have gone on, because we were such a happy band of women working amongst such treacherous conditions. And there was the cold. I am certain I'd never known brass to be so cold as it was in those factory nights.

But we were just one big happy family. It was amazing and I shall never forget it as long as I live, the way those women worked and talked and chatted about their ordinary everyday experiences, their boys at the Front, but mind you, it was the boys at the Front that we worried about and thought about and that's what made us work like that.

I used to be in Kent quite a lot and I used to see all the troop trains coming – the Red Cross on them, non-stop night and day. I went to Chatham Hospital to see a brother of mine, who was there, from the Front and I saw all the soldiers come in from Hill 60. Never shall I forget the sight as long as I live. They were unhealthy, they were verminous, and they used to say, 'It's Hell.' That was their words, only a few more adjectives with it, but that's their words, 'It was Hell.' But I know that they were glad to see women at home and the nurses who looked after them. There they were, soldiers lying in Chatham Hospital from that battle scene, and how grateful they were for a kindly word from their womenfolk.

AT THE FRONT

Private W. Underwood
1st Canadian Division
I was given seven days Number 1 Field Punishment, which consists of being tied on a wagon wheel. You're spread-eagled with the hub of the wheel in your back, and your legs and wrists handcuffed to the wheel. You'd do two hours up and four hours down for seven days, day and night. And, the cold! It was January 1915, a really cold month, and when they took you down they had to rub you to get the circulation going in your limbs again. And the only reason I was there was because I missed a roll-call.

Private George Hancox
Princess Patricia's Light Infantry, Canadian Army
In the Vierstraat sector in early '15 the German trenches were roughly 200 yards ahead of us on higher ground, which gave them a great advantage. For one thing their trenches drained into ours, and for another they had observation over our positions. Every time our artillery opened up on them at that particular time they would come back tenfold. For every five or six rounds fired by our artillery they would fire fifty to sixty back at us, and it made it rather uncomfortable.

The weather wasn't too good, it was threatening rain and we had a certain amount of drizzle. The trenches themselves were nothing but unconnected ditches, there was no traversing and no revetment, and just a sandbag parapet in front with loopholes. There were a number of flares going up, which gave a very eerie effect, and quite a bit of rifle fire – not too much machine-gun fire. On the whole we found it depressing and disillusioning rather than frightening. We were not so much frightened of being killed and wounded as we were depressed by the conditions, as we had thought we were going to fight a glorious war.

Our main casualties during the first tours were caused by enemy snipers, and it was soon realised that something was going to have to be done about it. So a sniping section was formed in our regiment. These were almost entirely men who'd been big game hunters and were crack shots with rifles. They were used to stalking, and if they had any kind of a target at all, they were sure to hit it. They'd pick out spots where they could get good observation on the enemy lines, and would watch a weak point in the parapet, for example, where it was shallow. As soon as a German went by, they would let him have it. It's very hard to say how many they got, but I think they paid the Germans quite well for any of our men they shot.

Sergeant Stefan Westmann
29th Division, German Army
While the Prince Regent of Bavaria launched an attack on Neuve Chapelle on January the 25th, this was only a feint to get the enemy to concentrate in the wrong area. Our attack was launched against the French and British trenches on the south of the Aire–La Bassée canal.

We got orders to storm the French position. We got in and I saw my comrades start falling to the right and left of me. But then I was confronted by a French corporal with his bayonet to the ready, just as I had mine. I felt the fear of death in that fraction of a second when I realised that he was after my life, exactly as I was after his. But I was quicker than he was, I pushed his rifle away and ran my bayonet through his chest. He fell, putting his hand on the place where I had hit him, and then I thrust again. Blood came out of his mouth and he died.

I nearly vomited. My knees were shaking and they asked me, 'What's the matter with you?' I remembered then that we had been told that a good soldier kills without thinking of his adversary as a human being – the very moment he sees him as fellow man, he's no longer a good soldier. My comrades were absolutely undisturbed by what had happened. One of them boasted that he had killed a *poilu* with the butt of his rifle. Another one had strangled a French captain. A third had hit somebody over the head with his spade. They were ordinary men like me. One was a tram conductor, another a commercial traveller, two were students, the rest farm workers – ordinary people who never would have thought to harm anybody.

But I had the dead French soldier in front of me, and how I would have liked him to have raised his hand! I would have shaken it and we would have been the best of friends because he was nothing but a poor boy – like me. A boy who had to fight with the cruellest weapons against a man who had nothing against him personally, who wore the uniform of another nation and spoke another language, but a man who had a father and mother and a family. So I woke up at night sometimes, drenched in sweat, because I saw the eyes of my fallen adversary. I tried to convince myself of what would've happened to me if I hadn't been quicker than him, if I hadn't thrust my bayonet into his belly first.

Why was it that we soldiers stabbed each other, strangled each other, went for each other like mad dogs? Why was it that we who had nothing against each other personally fought to the very death? We were civilised people after all, but I felt that the thin lacquer of civilisation of which both sides had so much, chipped off immediately. To fire at each other from a distance, to drop bombs, is something impersonal, but to see the whites of a man's eyes and then to run a bayonet into him – that was against my comprehension.

Sergeant George Ashurst
2nd Battalion, Lancashire Fusiliers
At right angles to the British line was a row of cottages in the Le Touquet sector. On the other side of the German line – about ten to twenty yards away – was another row of cottages in German possession.

A lane ran alongside both of them and across the lane was a German barricade.

It was decided that the row of cottages should be occupied, and when we took them over there was no opposition. Jerry was in his houses and he didn't even know till morning that we were in there. The idea was that we stay in the cottages for a while. We didn't know what might happen, you see. He may have risked a counter-attack to take them off us, but then he couldn't shell us because it was too near the German lines – he might have knocked his own houses to blazes.

There were four or five of us in each house. Me and my party stayed in a kitchen in the front row of houses, right next to Jerry. We had a backyard wall but we didn't dare look over it. But it was quiet, there was nothing much happening. Jerry shouted to us and we shouted back. One German shouted, 'I know Manchester better than any of you!' Course then a Manchester fellow started arguing the point. We used to argue like that – it was friendly.

One day we were cooking our stew in a pan on the fire when Jerry decided to have a bit of fun, so he sat down and fired away at the bricks on the top of our chimney, and he knocked one or two down. Our stew went all over the kitchen floor. Jerry just laughed – he knew he'd picked the right time when the stew would be on.

There was no real fighting. From the upstairs bedrooms you could look down and watch Jerry. You could see over the barricade right into a schoolyard lower down, and one of our officers used to snipe away at Jerry in the yard. You could see their heads and he used to try and get them.

One day the officer took a fellow upstairs and showed him the position where he stood, letting him look through the window. But this fellow dozed off in the bedroom and the officer caught him and severely warned him. Then, when the officer caught him sleeping again, he was sent away to be shot. I don't know whether he was or not, but that's what he went away for. A damned good soldier he was too. We felt sorry for the lad – well he wasn't a lad, he was an oldish fellow, about fifty.

Then the Royal Engineers came into our house and started digging a tunnel below us. We were sure that the Germans were also tunnelling this way – I'm certain I heard them quietly working underneath. So we wanted the Engineers to get the thing blown up first.

Anyway, we got word one day that we must retire into our front line. The Engineers had been carting gun-cotton down below, they'd taken enough stuff down to blow all Paris up, so we knew what was going to happen. We cleared out and then the order came, 'Everybody keep well under cover.' Then 'Whoosh!,' the whole barricade went up in blue flames, along with the end house where Jerry was. There were actually chaps hurt in our front line from pieces of stuff coming down and hitting them, and as soon as it was exploded we had to go back to our houses, which were not damaged.

We ran in the backyard and stood on anything we could find, looking over the wall at Jerry's house. We saw a German lying wounded on top of an outhouse when up came another German carrying a ladder, calm as anything despite having five or six of our rifles pointing at him. He put this ladder against the outhouse, walked up it, got the injured man on his shoulder and carried him away while none of us fired a shot. The officer said, 'Don't fire, boys. He deserves a medal, that lad.' So we didn't, we let him walk away with his wounded fellow. He knew we were there, he could see us quite well. Things went a bit quiet after that. And soon afterwards we were relieved.

Trooper George Jameson
1st Battalion, Northumberland Hussars
During one bombardment we had one of our horses killed. The NCO who'd been in charge of the ammunition train that had come up the night before was told, 'Get a party up there with a spare wagon, load that horse on to it, take it away several miles away and have it properly buried.'

Well, this NCO took the horse less than two miles back and thought, 'Oh, these ditches are handy.' So he dumped it in a dyke, covered it over and thought that was that. He couldn't be bothered to cart it five miles back to the wagon line and then find a place to bury it properly when there was a nice ready-made ditch there for it.

Well, in about a week the place absolutely stank to high heaven. A decomposing horse in a ditch that distance away, with the water carrying it all around the network of dykes . . . Well, whew! People said, 'Where's that coming from? Who's responsible for that?' And the officer said, 'I wonder where so-and-so put that horse.' So he sent for him and the NCO had to admit then where he'd put the horse. So he was told, 'Right, you can take the party you had on that lark, and you can go back and dig it up. And you can put it on a GS wagon and cover it with lime and take it right away. And,' he was told, 'when you've got it out you can properly disinfect the whole of that area as well.' And our stock went down a bit after that because we got blamed for it.

We were withdrawn before the Neuve Chapelle battle. The Guards came and took over from us, and they carried out the attack. We were sent out on listening patrols. I had to crawl through a gap in our wire into no man's land and get as near as I could to the German trenches to see if I could hear or detect anything. What they thought I could find out I really don't know because we never could speak German, while the Germans could very often speak English well. So it was a bit of a dead loss.

BATTLE OF NEUVE CHAPELLE

Captain Philip Neame
15th Field Company, Royal Engineers
I was constructing one of the first strong redoubts close to our front line not far from Neuve Chapelle, and this was regarded as rather a showpiece. My CO brought several people up to see this, amongst them Sir Henry Rawlinson, who commanded the corps. He walked all round and was very interested. Actually I'd known him in peacetime – and he'd seen me win a point-to-point race on Salisbury Plain.

Then to my surprise Haig came up – it was Haig who commanded the First Army in which we were – and while I was showing him round the Germans started shelling. They did every morning at about 11 o'clock. Shells went over and some came fairly near – my sappers and a small infantry working party we had were quite used to it. But one of Haig's staff officers – I don't know who it was – got very fussed and nudged me and said, 'Hurry up, hurry up, let's get the Army Commander away.' But Haig took no notice and went on walking round, even slower than before if possible, and asked me questions, and then even talked about camouflage from the air and that sort of thing – it was the very early days of air observation. Anyway he went the whole way round this pretty big redoubt, then slowly walked off down the communication trench quite unmoved.

The chief work before the battle was the preparation of assembly trenches for the infantry to shelter in immediately beforehand. This was because the whole of the infantry of the division had to crowd into the forward area on a narrow front, and so there had to be lines of mostly breastwork or very shallow trenches, owing to the waterlogged nature of the ground. These were laid out and constructed under the supervision of the sappers.

Another preparation was the provision of approach tracks leading up to the Front, but that had to be done with due thought given to concealment. A certain amount of duckboard approaches – that's to say wooden slats fixed to wooden runners – had to be put over ditches and so on, to give a suitable approach to these assembly trenches.

The opening bombardment was the most impressive that I think I heard throughout the war. It was quite brief and had only a limited amount of heavy artillery. It was nearly all field-gun fire, but in the short period that it took place, the guns were fired at such a rapid rate that the noise was absolutely shattering. Where it was accurate against the German breastworks it had a most decisive effect, and our advancing infantry suffered only moderate losses.

On the left part of the brigade on which I was working the artillery bombardment failed. I believe it was because the batteries operating there had only come into their positions at the last moment, and so had not been able to register properly beforehand. That's to say they hadn't had the opportunity of firing shots a day or two beforehand, so they couldn't accurately align their guns onto the proper target.

This meant that the enemy trenches in that bit of the front were barely touched. As our men rose from their trenches, to my horror they were mown down. Throughout the war I was never again to see such dreadful casualties.

Trooper Walter Becklade
5th Cavalry Brigade

I was wounded in the battle and taken to a casualty clearing station. I was beside a fellow who had got his arms bandaged up – I'd simply got my right arm bandaged. He was trying to light his pipe but couldn't get on very well so I offered to fill and light it for him. But when I'd lit it I suddenly realised he had nowhere to put it, as he'd had his lower jaw blown away. So I smoked the pipe and he smelt the tobacco, that was all the poor chap could have.

Corporal Alan Bray

We took up positions near Kemmel Hill. It was foggy and the attack was delayed two hours, which didn't do our spirits much good. Then the time came for us to go over. We had to run forward about fifty yards, up some planks over our own front-line trenches, and then across a meadow where it was almost impossible to run, we could only stagger along. As we were going over these planks about half of us were knocked out – either killed or wounded – and going across the meadow there were a lot more killed.

When we finally stopped and lay down, trying to get what shelter we could from the tremendous rifle fire which was coming over, a sergeant just in front of me jumped up and said, 'Come on men, be British.' So we jumped up again and followed him. He ran about six yards and then he went down too.

Well, then there were about a dozen of us left and we ran on another twenty yards towards the German trenches. Those trenches were literally packed – the men were standing four deep, firing machine-guns and rifles straight at us, and the only shelter we could see was a road which ran up at right angles to the trench with a bank on the left-hand side. We managed to reach this bank but found ourselves looking straight up at the German trenches while they were firing straight down, gradually picking us off. Eventually there was only myself and another chap that weren't hit.

SECOND BATTLE OF YPRES – GAS

Trooper George Jameson
1st Battalion, Northumberland Hussars
When we arrived in the Ypres area we were all tired out. I found an old shed full of junk including an old tin bath. I just pulled all the things out of it and fell into it and went sound asleep.

When we were in that part of the world the Belgians used to hang tobacco in the lofts. We had never seen tobacco like this before and thought, 'Oh, this is good, ready-made smokes.' So we used to take one of these strings of tobacco leaves down and pull the veins out. Then the only thing we could think of doing was to roll them up and tie a piece of thread round them, then try and smoke them. And they were terrible, awful!

Private Alfred Bromfield
2nd Battalion, Lancashire Regiment
The 22nd of April is a day I shall always remember. I was standing in the bottom of the trench cooking my bit of breakfast. It was one of my chief interests in those days and I was very fond of fried bacon and fried cheese. I'd already made a drop of tea in my dixie so I took the lid and put in a couple of slices of bacon that I'd been saving for about three days and fried it up. I used to lay that on a slice of bread, or a biscuit if they had no bread, then chop my cheese up very fine and drop it into the bacon fat with a drop of water so it wouldn't stick. I fried it up till it was bubbling then turned it out, onto the bacon and bread or biscuit, and it was just like a hot cream cheese.

Anyway I was getting on with that when one of our chaps on lookout yelled, 'Cor, look at the lyddite shells busting along Jerry's trench.' Lyddite wasn't used a great deal so we jumped up out of curiosity to see these shells bursting along the trench. We watched about a dozen puffs of yellow smoke coming up from what we thought was lyddite shells until we lost interest and got down into the bottom of the trench again.

About five or six seconds later the lookout yelled, 'Blimey, it's not lyddite, it's gas.' So we all jumped up again and the officer came running out and gave the order, 'Open immediate rapid fire!' He didn't give us any range or anything because being trained soldiers we knew how to judge a range, and so we opened up as fast as we could. It was a real mad minute. Blazing away there into the gas, we didn't know whether we were hitting anybody or whether it was just a blind with the gas coming over.

While we were doing this the rifles were getting hotter and hotter with the continual fire. Fat was pouring out of the woodwork and the muzzles were beginning to extend. Then an Irish medical officer named Captain Tyrrell, realising we needed help, got out the trench and ran along the back with a can of oil in his hand, pouring it on our rifles as he went by. We'd stop firing just long enough for him to splash a drop of oil onto the bolt. All we needed was the bolts to work perfectly, and he managed to get right along the trench.

By that time the gas had reached us and we had no protection at all beyond our own inventiveness – there were no such things as gas-masks or pads in those days. We'd been tipped off that the only way to protect ourselves was by urinating on either our handkerchiefs or soft caps and covering our mouths with them. So we did that for long enough to get a good deep breath, then continued firing. That's how it went on while all the time the gas was still pouring over the top of the trench.

Personally, I wasn't satisfied with those measures, I didn't think it sufficient protection. So I went into one of the trench latrines, which was just a bucket stuck in a hole, and put my head in the bucket. I stopped down long enough until I couldn't hold my breath anymore, then came up, took a good breath of air and went down again.

I came back into the front-line trench because firing had stopped and I realised that the gas had gone right over the trench. We could see it going towards the rear lines. Anyway, we stopped Jerry. He must have been coming over because when we could see out over the open ground again there was quite a number of them laying out there, some of them wriggling about wounded, and quite a number were dead, but I think the greatest havoc was caused by one of our machine-gunners – Jackie Lynn. He was out to the right of our lines in a position where he could enfilade the whole ground in front of the German trenches, and he'd worked his machine-gun the whole time. He was on his own, because his number two and three had already conked out with the gas. So he was firing it on his own and they had to drag him away from that gun – actually pull him away from it. When they got him back he lasted about three days then died of poison gas. But he got the VC for what he did.

Private W. Underwood
1st Canadian Division

It was a beautiful day. I was lying in a field writing a letter to my mother, the sun was shining and I remember a lark singing high up in the sky. Then, suddenly, the bombardment started and we got orders to stand to. We went up the line in two columns, one either side of the road. But as soon as we reached the outskirts of the village of St. Julien the bullets opened up, and when I looked around I counted just thirty-two men left on their feet out of the whole company of 227. The rest of us managed to jump into ditches, and that saved us from being annihilated.

Then we saw coming towards us the French Zouaves. They were in blue coats and red pants and caps and it was a revelation to us, we hadn't seen anything but khaki and drab uniforms. They were rushing toward us, half staggering, and we wondered what was the matter. We were a little perturbed at first, then when they got to us we tried to rally them but they wouldn't stay. They were running away from the Germans. Then we got orders to shoot them down, which we did. We just turned around and shot them as they were running away.

Then, as we looked further away we saw this green cloud come slowly across the terrain. It was the first gas that anybody had seen or heard of, and one of our boys, evidently a chemist, passed the word along that this was chlorine. And he said, 'If you urinate on your handkerchiefs it will save your lungs, anyway.' So most of us did that, and we tied these handkerchiefs, plus pieces of putty or anything else we could find, around our faces, and it did save us from being gassed.

There were masses of Germans behind this gas cloud, we could see their grey uniforms as plain as anything, and there we were, helpless, with these Ross rifles that we couldn't fire because they were always jamming.

Private W. A. Quinton
2nd Battalion, Bedfordshire Fusiliers
The men came tumbling from the front line. I've never seen men so terror-stricken, they were tearing at their throats and their eyes were glaring out. Blood was streaming from those who were wounded and they were tumbling over one another. Those who fell couldn't get up because of the panic of the men following them, and eventually they were piled up two or three high in this trench.

Lieutenant Victor Hawkins
2nd Battalion, Lancashire Fusiliers
The effect of this gas was to form a sort of foamy liquid in one's lungs, which would more or less drown you. A lot of the men died pretty quickly, and others soon came down – they were in fact drowning from this beastly foam. Out of the 250 men we started with at 5 o'clock we were very soon down to about forty or fifty men.

Private W. A. Quinton
2nd Battalion, Bedfordshire Fusiliers
One chap had his hand blown off and his wrist was fumbling around, tearing at his throat. In fact it was the most gruesome sight I'd seen in the war. We manned the firing step, thinking the Germans would be on their way over by this time, but strangely enough they didn't attack us.

When we got relieved we made our way four or five miles back from the line. Going along this country road we were just like a rabble – you know how men are when they're tired and exhausted. Then we passed by an orchard where there must have been two or three hundred men. They were reeling around tearing at their throats, their faces black, while an RAMC sergeant stood by and, well, I've never known a man look so despondent. He said, 'Look at the poor bastards, and we can't do a thing for them.'

Sergeant Cyril Lee
By the 24th of April the scene around Ypres beggared description. I couldn't fathom that war could be like that. I was only a youngster of seventeen, and I'd sought adventure, but when I saw this I thought, 'What have I come to?' With some of the real good old veterans we had with us I wasn't really afraid, but I suppose it was the spirit of adventure that kept me going.

The Cloth Hall in Ypres itself was burning when we went in, and all the little farms around were also alight. There were quite a lot of buildings around the salient, so it made as awful a picture of warfare as anyone could imagine.

We dug in pretty deeply because the shells were coming over in no uncertain fashion. Huge salvos of shells were being pitched into the salient at that time. So much so that it was humorously suggested that the Germans must have had a big field gun for every rifle we had. It certainly appeared like that to us. Every so often we'd hear an 18-pounder of ours fire, but for every 18-pounder that went their way there were dozens of these huge shells coming back, and they straddled our trenches so much that they became almost uninhabitable – we had to get out.

Sergeant Jack Dorgan
7th Battalion, Northumberland Fusiliers
During the attack on St. Julien on the 26th of April a shell dropped right in amongst us, and when I pulled myself together I found myself lying in a shell-hole. There was one other soldier who, like me, was unhurt, but two more were heavily wounded, so we shouted for stretcher-bearers.

Then the other uninjured chap said to me, 'We're not all here, Jack,' so I climbed out of the shell-hole and found two more of our comrades lying just a few yards from the shell-hole.

They had had their legs blown off. All I could see when I got up to them was their thigh bones. I will always remember their white thigh bones, the rest of their legs were gone. Private Jackie Oliver was one of them, and he was unconscious. I shouted back to the fellows behind me, 'Tell Reedy Oliver his brother's been wounded.' So Reedy came along and stood looking at his brother, lying there with no legs, and a few minutes later he watched him die. But the other fellow, Private Bob Young, was conscious right to the last. I lay alongside of him and said, 'Can I do anything for you, Bob?' He said, 'Straighten my legs, Jack,' but he had no legs. I touched the bones and that satisfied him. Then he said, 'Get my wife's photograph out of my breast pocket.' I took the photograph out and put it in his hands. He couldn't move, he couldn't lift a hand, he couldn't lift a finger, but he somehow held his wife's photograph on his chest. And that's how Bob Young died.

But I had to get on. As we moved forward we came across a ditch in a corner of a field where there were some Canadian soldiers. They said, 'You can't go any further than this. The Germans have released gas and we've had to retire to these reserve trenches.' But it was just a ditch to me, so I jumped across it along with the rest of the fellows.

But we'd only gone a hundred yards in front of the Canadians when we encountered the gas. We'd had no training for gas prevention, never heard of the gas business. Our eyes were streaming with water and pain, and all we had was a roll of bandages in the first aid kit we carried in our tunic. So we bandaged each other's eyes, and anyone who could see would lead a line of half a dozen or so men, each with his hand on the shoulder of the one in front. In this way lines and lines of British soldiers moved along, with rolls of bandages around their eyes, back towards Ypres. When we got there, we were directed to a first aid station and lay down in a field. We hadn't even got to the original front line. We'd only got as far as the Canadians' reserve trenches. But we just accepted it. It was war to us.

The day afterwards, the 27th of April 1915, what was left of the Northumberlands were paraded in a field somewhere near Ypres to be addressed by Sir John French, the commanding officer of the British Forces. He praised us for our bravery, but we thought little of him. We just felt, 'Well, he's just come from his office somewhere back in the line and is praising us up now. What did he come here for?' We just accepted it, but we didn't want it rubbed in.

Trooper Stanley Down
North Somerset Yeomanry

On the night of the 12th of May we arrived in our trenches as the first thin streaks of dawn lit the sky, I think it was about 4 o'clock in the morning. The first shell came across and landed not many yards from where I was standing, and the whole earth seemed to tremble at that moment. Sandbags, rifles and equipment went up into the air and a terrific shower of earth came down on top of us. After that the bombardment began in real earnest. Every three minutes – or possibly every minute, one couldn't tell – the shells kept coming and the noise was terrific.

The bombardment went on from dawn until around midday before there was any cessation at all. By that time the trenches were just a quagmire, and the earthworks and barbed wire, such as they were, had been blown to pieces long since. The result was that practically the whole of the front line around the town of Ypres was a series of holes in which men crouched, waiting for the end.

Fusilier Victor Packer
1st Battalion, Royal Irish Fusiliers

I had heard about the previous battles but I couldn't get there fast enough. We had been brought up on the history of the Boer War and patriotism and heroics and everything, and we thought the war was going to be over before we could get there. However, in about half a minute all that had gone. I wondered what the devil I'd got into because it was nothing but mud and filth and all the chaps who were already there, well, they looked like tramps, all plastered with filth and dirt, and unshaven.

We couldn't dig trenches up there, because the ground was so soft

This is a view of the destruction of Ypres.

and wet. We used to fill the sandbags and to get water we used to gouge out a hole at the side of the trench in the bottom of the wall of sand-bags and put everything we could over it, a piece of cardboard or something or other, and in the morning that would be full of water, but it would be teeming with all little black things floating around, but we found that if we boiled it we killed all this stuff and could drink it quite well or brew it up for a drop of tea. Once we attempted to shave in it but it was cold water and it wasn't very clever because we couldn't light fires.

If you smoked you had to be very careful, if Jerry saw any smoke he would send a grenade over because he knew there was someone there, the same thing would give you away, but we got very clever at boiling a billy can, believe it or not, with love letters, letters from home. We would make spills of them and if you kept a constant flame under it you could make the water boil for tea, that was in the daytime. If it was at night, you had to cover it up with your coat or something. Then there were the rats, of course, rats. You would not kill rats because you had no means of getting rid of them, they would putrefy and it would be worse than if you left them alive. I think they lived in corpses, because they were huge, they were as big as cats, I am not exaggerating, some of them were as big as ordinary cats, horrible great things.

In the line, the tours we did were two hours on and four hours off, and during the hours off fatigues used to be carried out, and at night various tasks had to be done such as filling sandbags, repairing damaged trenches and barbed wire and burying dead. The unit came out of the line, crossed the canal and formed up on the Menin Road and marched back to billets where Packer was out on his feet.

Some of those marches back to billets used to be all of twenty kilo-metres, and we used to be very bitter about the officers having horses to ride on but we had to keep on with our old feet just the same. You got so that you still had, in those days, a full pack, 250 rounds of ammuni-tion, water-bottle, haversack, rifle, bayonet, and often you carried a bit of something extra as well. We were daft enough to carry souvenirs in those days like nose-caps of shells and things, or a Uhlan's helmet, whatever we could get like that we prized, but not long afterwards we threw them over a hedge or somewhere. But we were so fatigued, and this takes a lot of believing, the whole battalion would be marching in a column of fours, or what was left of them, they would be half strength or less than that, and periodically you were halted and the order came to fall out on the side of the road. In those days you did literally that: everybody just fell in one solid phalanx all along the side of the road, and then the whistle blew or they had to come shouting to wake you up and get you on your feet again. Those who could not get up to the destination they would send wagons back for the blokes who couldn't make it, and if you wanted to urinate that was so much wasted time from resting.

Trooper Stanley Down
North Somerset Yeomanry
The shelling had started again at Ypres, and by the time we got to the town it looked as though the whole place was on fire. Buildings to the right and left of us were blazing away. We marched in columns of four, and the fires were so intense in the narrow streets that the men on the flanks had to creep in to the middle to avoid the blistering heat. It was particularly bad when the various regiments were halted. During these stoppages one could see the faces of other men by the firelight, and one could see the haggard desolation on their faces as they also surveyed the havoc around them.

I remember seeing an estaminet with the front wall blown out. A little bagatelle table was still standing there with the balls and cues just as the players had left them as they rushed from the scene. Cafés had the remains of mouldering food on the counters, and often one could hear the howling of a starving and homeless dog somewhere in the ruins. Outside the cathedral there was a battered funeral hearse which had probably been abandoned during the funeral service when the shell crashed through the roof. The stench of the horse carcasses being burned in the square was such that it remained in one's nostrils for months afterwards. Altogether it was chaos, with a terrible sense of decay and desolation.

We were relieving men of the 28th Division, and as we passed them coming down they would ask us where we were from. We would say,

Captain Maberly Esler, Royal Army Medical Corps.

'From Somerset,' and the answer would be, 'You'll be jolly glad to get back there when you've had some of this.' One would say, 'What's it like up there?' and invariably the reply was, 'Bloody awful mate.'

Captain Maberly Esler
Royal Army Medical Corps

At first we found wounds were healing very well. In certain cases a wound that was almost healed, next day we looked at it, it was all inflamed again and enlarged, and after a time the sister and I came to the conclusion that they were doing this themselves to prolong their stay in hospital, because they had a real pasting at the beginning of the war and they didn't like it one little bit and they didn't want to go back again. And so we agreed between us not to report this at all; we just said, 'What we'll do is put a blasted dressing over this thing and it'll heal.' They couldn't get at it then, and you found if you did that and kept it on a week the thing was perfectly healed.

The first hut I had was occupied by Sikhs, and they all had wounds through the palms of their hands, and we thought, 'This is very extraordinary, the only part of their body which was exposed to the enemy was their hands,' and we came to the conclusion they must have held their hands up above the trench so that they could be shot through the hand and get invalided home, and that was obviously what had occurred. But never any charge was brought against them, of course. But we formed our own opinion that it must have been that. There were thirty in my ward and they all had hand wounds, all through the palm of the hand. The conclusion was pretty obvious that they had been putting their hands up to be shot at.

For others the mental condition was something varying between depression and relief at being out of the thing altogether. They were frightened, they were timid, they didn't want to go back again any more to the war and very thankful to be in these sort of surroundings. In fact, when I said to one of them, 'I want to get out to the Front to have the experience,' he said, 'You want to get out to the Front? – you must be bloody mad,' and that gave me an inkling that things weren't very pleasant out there.

Rifleman Henry Williamson
London Rifle Brigade
While I was at Armentières I was detailed to form part of a firing squad at the execution of a deserter. He was tied to a post against a wall in his civilian clothes, and we were told to fire at a piece of white cloth pinned over his heart. We didn't know what the rifles were loaded with – some were loaded with ball, others with blank. Then we had the order to fire and pulled the triggers – we knew by the recoil if it was loaded with ball or not. Then the deserter's name was read out on three successive parades, as a warning.

Corporal Alan Bray
One evening while we were in the trenches at St. Éloi I was warned that six of us had to go on a firing party to shoot four men of another battalion who had been accused of desertion. I was very worried about it because I didn't think it was right, in the first place, that Englishmen should be shooting other Englishmen. I thought we were in France to fight the Germans. Another reason was because I thought I knew why these men had deserted, if they had deserted. It was the fact that they had probably been in the trenches for two or three months without a break, which could absolutely break your nerve. So I really didn't feel like shooting them.

Anyway later in the evening an old soldier in another battery told me that it was the one thing in the Army that you could refuse to do. So I straightaway went back to the sergeant and said, 'I'm sorry, I'm not doing this,' and I heard no more about it.

I think one reason why I felt so strongly about it was the fact that the week before a boy in our own battalion had been shot for desertion. I knew that boy, and I knew that he absolutely lost his nerve, he couldn't have gone back into the line. Anyway he was shot, and the tragedy of it was that a few weeks later, in our local paper, I saw that his father had joined up to avenge his son's death on the Germans.

Lieutenant Richard Talbot Kelly
Royal Artillery

I think you are chiefly afraid, you know, of how you will behave when you really meet the worst things that war can produce, and I became afraid of seeing my first dead man. I'd never seen a dead man and was very afraid of seeing anybody killed in front of my eyes. Well, now this bit of line had been fought over a few weeks previously in the battle of Festubert, and some of the old German trenches that we had captured were left lying in a derelict mess. Between our trenches we had dug new ones beyond them and I knew that there was an old stretch of German trench between our first and second line where there were a lot of German and Canadian corpses. One afternoon when things were slack – we were only allowed to fire three rounds per gun per day – I thought I would go and have a look at these corpses and see what I felt. I went along the communication trench and slipped over the side into this German trench. It was very impressive. To begin with, the Germans had run short of sandbags when they had built their trenches in this part of the world, and they had looted the cottages round about and made sandbags out of curtains, counterpanes and tablecloths and any other material they could lay their hands on. So these trenches were the most varied and coloured affairs you could imagine, and faded wonderfully into the wild flowers and cabbages and everything else of the landscape – in fact they produced a camouflage excellence that we never achieved again in the war.

I wandered along this old German trench for a bit and was very interested in the way it was made. I found the odd German cowhide pack, a round cap and bashed pickelhaube. Then suddenly round the bend in the trench I came to a great bay which was full of dead Germans, but they weren't a bit horrible. They had been dead for about six weeks and weather and rats and maggots and everything else had done their stuff. Now they were just shiny skeletons in their uniforms held together by the dry sinews, that wound round their bones. They were still wearing their uniforms and still in the attitude in which they had died, possibly from a great shell burst. It was a most weird and extraordinary picture and I was absolutely fascinated. A skull, you know, grins at you in a silly way, it laughs at you and more or less says: 'Fancy coming here all terrified of dead men, look how silly we look.'

Sergeant Jack Dorgan
7th Battalion, Northumberland Fusiliers

In the first week of June, only about six or seven weeks after we'd arrived in the trenches, the colonel sent for me. He said, 'Sergeant, this morning I've just received information from the war office that leave can be started now. I've chosen you to be one of the first to go home to England for four days.' I came out of his dugout, took off my hat (steel helmets weren't invented then) put it on the bankside and put a bullet through it. I did it so that when I went home wearing a hat with a bullet hole through it, I could say, 'That was a near one.' And that's what I did.

Private Harold Carter

I came home on leave from Ypres for four days. I got home, knocked at the door, and as they opened it I walked in and Mother rushed up as soon as she heard my voice. She was so pleased to see me she threw her arms round my neck and kissed me. Then she said, 'What's all this crawling about all over you?' I said, 'Well, mother, they're lice. Don't worry,' I said, but she was horrified. Of course, she never dreamt that conditions were such out there. I told her I'd have a wash down and dig out my civvy suit. Later on they asked me questions about what it was like over the other side but I didn't tell them too much. I didn't like to pile the agony on them at home. They knew that I'd had a rough time by looking at me – they didn't want telling twice.

On the Saturday I went to a music hall in civilian clothes and as I lined up outside a lady came along and put a white feather into my hand. I looked at it and felt disgusted, but there wasn't much I could do about it. I felt small enough over the white feather incident outside, but as I went into the gallery a chap came out in naval uniform – he might have been a petty officer – and said that no girl should be sitting with a chap unless he was in uniform.

No man should be out of uniform, he went on – if he was out of uniform he was nothing more than a worm and a skunk. He made me feel about as big as a worm. I just sat there, on my own, while people looked at me and I looked at them. I should like to have jumped up and told them I'd just come out of the trenches at Ypres, but I couldn't. I had to take it, and I came out disgusted and went home.

Private Ernest Todd

The day would start about half an hour before daybreak. We would stand right up to the parapet looking over, waiting for Jerry to come if he was going to come, then when it was light enough we'd stand down. The sentries detailed would stand at their posts while the rest of us would get down to sandbags or trench work, whatever work there was to be done. The sentries would be relieved about every two hours.

On a nice summer's day you could think there wasn't a war on really. Looking through the periscope out to no man's land you would see the sandbags of the Germans' front line; you would see the grass and the flowers out front; the birds might start singing if the sun was up on a nice day.

Early in the morning you would have the first planes coming over and a general air of balminess and ease. Breakfast would come up, if there was going to be any, and you would settle down to a day of laziness in the sun, if you could.

The lads would sit on this fire step and talk and sing. Towards the evening they would get sentimental talking about their homes. We had one chap who was a very good singer, and he used to indulge in his singing and lead us in the chorus. But he was always inclined to get a bit sentimental, so we had to shut him up for obvious reasons – we couldn't stand too much of that.

Then there was the man we used to call Cornet Joe over in the German front line. He used to blow his cornet and play British songs to us. When he played we would shout out, 'Damn good, Jerry!' and, 'Give us another one, Joe!' As the lines weren't too far away he would ask us what we wanted to hear and we would say, 'Give us the old Bull and Bush.' So he would play that and we would sing it, and sometimes that session would last half an hour. We would have mouth organs, of course, and well, there was nothing else to do but talk, reminisce and sing.

Yes, during those summer months of 1915 you could forget that there was a war on, you really could. It did happen sometimes – people would forget and get careless, and before you knew where you were they had got a bullet through their head while sitting on the latrine or something.

Corporal Charles Quinnell
9th Battalion, Royal Fusiliers

The one thing we used to look forward to every night was our issue of rum. That was very, very acceptable. It used to come up with the rations in a 2-gallon stone jar, and that was given to the company sergeant-major, who used to issue out four lots, four mess tins, to each platoon sergeant – there were four platoons in the company – and the platoon sergeant would come along the trench of a night-time with a big tablespoon and this mess tin full of rum. The cry was 'Open up' and you'd open your mouth up and he'd pour this tablespoon full of rum down your throat.

Sergeant Alfred West
Monmouthshire Regiment

One of my boys was about the ugliest man I've ever seen. He was short, stumpy, and most uninteresting to look at. Well, one time I was down for a rest with my machine-gun team when we realised old Sam was missing. We watched out for him, then suddenly we saw him walk up to a cottage on top of a hill. We found out he had a little agreement with a lady – and that when she started to hang clothes on the line, that meant her old man had gone out. When the signal came you couldn't hold Sam back – he was up the field.

Out of the line, the boys were all wanting women. And the women, knowing this, used to put a sign in the window saying, 'Washing done here for soldiers.' I've seen up to twenty men waiting in one room, and there were probably others upstairs. Afterwards these women used to sit on the end of the bed, open their legs and flick this brownish stuff around their privates, ready for the next man.

We used to have a week's leave in Paris and some of the boys would return full of pox. On the train back, they used to have braziers to keep you warm, and one particular boy who'd been to Paris a few times said he had sat too near a brazier with his legs open, that he had gone to sleep, and when he woke found his trousers nearly alight and his privates burned. That's what he said had gone wrong, but it wasn't that. He'd come back with pox, and his penis was nearly falling away, it was so rotten.

There was another nice chap who had it too, and although he was in the Red Cross he couldn't do anything about it. The unfortunate part was that his parents were coming from England, at their own expense, to see him, and he'd gone and got this syphilis. Poor fellow, he was shattered. The doctors used to have parades to tell fellows what to do to prevent it. They had a tank of water and showed you how to put this tube into your penis and turn the tap on. The weight of the water would fill up your bladder and you'd pass it all out again along with any infection. I went in there one night and the old doctor who had been giving the lecture that afternoon came in and washed himself, then did what he'd told everyone else to do.

Sergeant George Ashurst
2nd Battalion, Lancashire Fusiliers
Armentières was like a busy little village with a few streets, not a great big place. It was still fully occupied by civilians. We got into the estaminets and we were drinking vin blanc of course. The place was full. This estaminet I was in, this particular night, it was absolutely crowded and there were five women in there and it was five francs a time if you went with them, up the stairs and in the bedrooms. And fellows were going in, coming out, going in, coming out. One night the padre walked in the estaminet and the stairs leading up to the bedrooms were full. There was a man on every step waiting his turn to go in with a woman. The padre came over to us. We were sat there, me and Tom and a couple more at a little table. You can imagine how he dressed us down. 'Have none of you any mothers? Have none of you any sisters?' and all that sort of thing. He said, 'I shall report this to the colonel.' He reduced our time in the town.

I didn't fancy the women at all. They were so common. Tom said: 'Are you going up there?' I said, 'No. Not with them things.' They were all sorts of ages, the women. The first thing she does is grab your five-franc note. Then she unfastens your flies and has a feel and squeezes it, sees if there's anything wrong with it. Then she just throws this cloak off and she's on the bed, you know, ready for you. That's what happened. Then, when you've finished, she has the kettle boiling there with some herbs in to give you a bit of a swill with it, for safety's sake, for disease, you know. But, no I didn't go up there, not with that lot. Most of the troops did, because I tell you the stairs were lined with them.

Private Thomas McIndoe
12th Battalion, Middlesex Regiment
When we arrived in France a memo was issued by Lord Kitchener, which said that in recent months quite a number of the Expeditionary Force had rendered theirselfs unfit for duty through negligence in contracting venereal disease. This must stop forthwith as the War Office take a very poor view of the number that's been rendered unfit for duty.

When we got to Number One Rest Camp on the hill at Le Havre, I saw a number, all different units, engaged in digging pits and sweating profusely. And in conversation to one of the inmates I found out that they were undergoing a course of treatment, a German treatment named 606 which necessitated an injection of mercury into the system. This mercury apparently took effect quicker if the victim overheated his body in working and so rid himself of this complaint.

Then we got a memo on the notice board. 'The victim's parents or his wife or his relatives would be notified in the future if any man rendered himself unfit through contracting venereal disease.'

Private Clifford Lane
1st Battalion, Hertfordshire Regiment
Fleas, yes. Every man in the front line was in a state of – every man in the front line had fleas after about two or three weeks. Fleas used to get into the seam of your underclothes, and the only way to get rid of them

Private Thomas McIndoe, 12th Battalion, Middlesex Regiment.

was to get a candle and go along the seams with the candle and you could hear the eggs crackling. And the extraordinary thing is these lice were so bad in places, I've seen men taking their shirts off with the skin of their backs absolutely raw where they'd been scratching. And there was no way of getting rid of them at all. We used to have sent out a chemical called Harrison's pomade. We used to use that but it wasn't very effective. Lice were a curse, were a real menace to us. For one thing, you had very few chances of getting a good sleep anyway, and when you had the lice with you there to irritate you, drive you into a sort of frenzy almost – the whole thing was that the lice were in the dugouts.

Private Thomas McIndoe
12th Battalion, Middlesex Regiment
Rats! Oh crikey! If they were put in a harness they could have done a milk round, they were that big, yes, honest. Nearly every morning, a bloody great thing would come up and stand up on its back legs and gnaw at something. I used to line the sights up and give them one round of ball. Bang! And blow them to nothing.

HOOGE, JUNE 16

Private George Clayton
175 Tunnelling Company, Royal Engineers
The Germans had started tunnelling and blowing our trenches up, and we were urgently required to get there and give them some of their own back. We were taken to the front line of trenches in Sanctuary Wood, as near to the Germans as we could go, and then the officer said, 'Well, I think we'll sink the shaft here.'

We told him none of us had ever done any sinking, and he said, 'You call yourselves miners and you've never done any sinking?' Where we were from, there were special teams who went from one colliery to another to do the sinking. But this officer was from Australia and he'd been used to prospecting for gold. Eventually he said, 'Well, we'll have to make the best we can of you,' and so we started to make an inset of about four foot square in the side of the trench nearest the Germans.

We then made a vertical shaft about twenty-five feet deep, using a rope ladder like the ones you see on ships. There'd be two of us working in the shaft at any one time, one digging and one filling sandbags. It was a twenty-four-hour job, and you'd be relieved after a couple of hours. We used entrenching tools, picks and shovels, and the full sandbags were wound up, two or three at a time, with a windlass. Then some Gurkhas carried them off to an area of low-lying ground. The Gurkhas would never go down the shaft – 'No going down there, Johnny.' At twenty-five feet we got to water and had to use a lift and force pump worked with a handle. The Gurkhas would work the pump.

When we finally got to the bottom we made a straight tunnel towards the German trenches. We had a surveyor called John Warnock, who took the bearings, and we worked under his instructions. The tunnel was framed by wood on all sides like a box, so there was no danger of it falling in on you. It was lit by candles – you'd make a candlestick out of clay and stick it onto the side. For ventilation we had a blacksmith's bellows on the surface and an open hosepipe into the tunnel. It gave us sufficient air, and you knew that if the candle went wonky it was an indication that there wasn't enough oxygen.

We were digging through a grey clay in the Ypres Salient that was easy enough to work, so you could get ten yards done on a shift, and thirty yards in a day – ten days of that made three hundred yards. We were heading towards the Hooge Chateau, where the cellar had become the headquarters of the German officers. When we got there we laid it with explosives, then stemmed it with sandbags and tree trunks to stop the force of the explosion blowing back towards us. Then we ran the wire back up to the support line. When the Hooge Chateau was finally blown up I was about 250 yards away watching from my trench, and I saw the earth come up and shake the ground. It made a dull thud like an earthquake and left a hole like a quarry.

Lieutenant Gordon Carey
8th Battalion, Rifle Brigade

At 11 p.m. we marched into the line in dead silence – it was extraordinarily quiet. This was in the Hooge section. Initially I thought, 'What a bit of luck, no shelling, no nothing.' The only noise, in fact, was made by my troops and the 7th Battalion squeezing past each other in the trenches. There were the sounds of their weapons clashing and that sort of thing, and at one point I thought, 'Well, the Germans will know all about this,' but we were just new to the line, and by 2 a.m. on the 30th of July the relief was complete and the exhausted 7th Battalion had cleared off. And so there we were – we just waited for the dawn and for the men to be able to see for the first time this horrid bit of landscape that they were supposed to cling on to.

I didn't like it as the time went on, I had a sense that there was definitely something wrong – that something was brewing. I was determined that everyone should be up and alert and should have their bayonet fixed because I hated the feeling that something wasn't right. I was at the farthest point away from the crater when the thing happened, so dramatically and so suddenly that at first I was quite incapable of any comprehensive thought at all. The first idea that flitted through my mind was that the end of the world had come, and this was the Day of Judgement, because the whole dawn had turned a ghastly crimson-red. And then, as I began to come to my senses, I saw four or five jets of flame passing across the trench that I had been in just one minute before. There was a horrible hissing sound and a nasty oily black smoke at the edge of the flame. They were using flamethrowers – we'd never seen or heard of them.

When I did manage to think with a little sense, I clambered out behind the trench to see what was happening. And it was then that I realised the Germans were coming over into my bit of trench. The light was very dim but I could see the enemy jumping in, and I had no doubt whatsoever that they must have been jumping right on top of my men. The men couldn't possibly have been doing anything other than lying in the bottom of the trench until the flames stopped. So the Germans must have jumped in on top of them with bayonets.

Captain Maberly Esler
Royal Army Medical Corps
In our front-line dugout we had first aid dressing and morphia and that was all. We'd never attempt any major surgery or anything like that in the trenches – one couldn't do it. The only thing you could do was to cover a wound to keep it from getting infected, or stop a haemorrhage by compression on the main vessel if they were bleeding to death.

If a limb had been virtually shot off and they were bleeding profusely you could stop the whole thing by putting a tourniquet on, but you couldn't keep it on longer than an hour without them losing the leg altogether. So it was necessary to get the field ambulance as soon as possible so they could ligature the vessels, and the quicker that was done the better. But even so, several people got tetanus afterwards from an infection in the ground which was carried in shelled areas – very much like it was carried in farmland in the Fens. The ground had been shelled for such a long time it was in a rather septic sort of condition.

But it was all first-aid work. The only value of a medical officer being in a first-line trench was to help the morale of the men. I remember going in the first night we ever went to the trenches, and one fellow who thought I couldn't hear said to another chap, 'Good God, the MO's come up with us – that makes you feel better, chum, doesn't it?' Then I realised that I was doing some good by being there. Medically I felt I was doing no good at all.

BATTLE OF LOOS, September 25–October 10

Corporal Edward Glendinning
12th Battalion, Notts and Derby Regiment (Sherwood Foresters)
During the night of the 24th of September we moved up into reserve trenches almost opposite Hohenzollern Redoubt. As we came up we had passed through many squadrons of British cavalry who were assembling ready to exploit any breakthrough we infantrymen could make the next day. We didn't get any sleep all night, because even before we got there our artillery barrage was blazing away and we sat there huddling in this reserve communication trench. It was a long, dreary,

miserable night. Some chaps were crying, some praying, but most of us were optimistic: we all hoped that we would come through.

As soon as it was light, we were issued with a big ration of rum. You could drink as much as you wanted. We were then told to be prepared to receive orders to advance at any moment. Any moment was a long while coming, which was very trying. It was two hours before we got the actual order to advance. Just before the order we were issued with two additional bandoliers of ammunition, which meant we were carrying a pretty heavy weight of ammunition.

We clambered out of the trench. Some of us had ladders and some got out as best they could. We very soon found ourselves picking our way over the bodies of men who had fallen in the earlier attack and wounded men who were trying to crawl into shell-holes to get protection. We kept on in extended order. For the first two or three hundred yards, there wasn't a great deal of firing. But all of a sudden they opened on us with terrific machine-gun fire, a lot of which came from a tall slag-heap on our right. I sensed we were getting fewer and fewer as we went on. From that time we received no further orders. We somehow took the second line of their trenches, which had been devastated by our artillery. We dug in and got ourselves into shallow trenches. Then the Germans began to realise where we were because they started sweeping us with machine-gun fire. Then they sent over shrapnel shells, but most of that burst behind us. Then they opened up with whiz-bangs. We lost our platoon sergeant and corporal through direct hits. The hours wore on, it became dusk and we were relieved when a detachment of the Guards managed to take our places. They relieved us in much greater strength than we'd been all day. Whereas we'd been one man to ten yards of trench, they had a man every couple of feet. Word was passed along for the Sherwood Foresters to assemble in groups and to withdraw.

Coming back over the ground that had been captured that day, the sight that met our eyes was quite unbelievable. If you can imagine a flock of sheep lying down sleeping in a field, the bodies were as thick as that. Some of them were still alive, and they were crying out, begging for water and plucking at our legs as we went by. One hefty chap grabbed me around both knees and held me. 'Water, water,' he cried. I was just going to take the cork out of my water-bottle – I had a little left – but I was immediately hustled on by the man behind me. 'Get on, get on, we are going to get lost in no man's land, come on.' So it was a case where compassion had to give way to discipline and I had to break away from this man to run up to catch up with the men in front.

Bombadier J. W. Palmer
26th Brigade, Royal Field Artillery
Our lads weren't moved for some days – the dead weren't moved, the wounded were – and for days after when I was laying the wire out I had to pass over those bodies, whose faces were turning more and more blue and green. As a matter of fact it was a terrible sight and we had one or two frosts those evenings which made matters worse. Well, on the left of us, there was the Hohenzollern Redoubt, one of the strongest points of the war at that time, I know our Guards had two or three attempts to do it without any luck at all. I was told to lay a wire up to the Hulluch Crossroads. Well, I went over the first and second line of trenches and I got right up to where some German trenches had been captured when an officer came down and he said, 'Where are you going?' I said, 'I've got to lay a wire to the Hulluch crossroads.' He said, 'You'd better bugger off. We haven't captured it yet.'

Sergeant Charles Lippett
1/8th Battalion, Queen's Royal West Surrey Regiment
We arrived at Béthune, where we stayed the night. We went off on the line of march headed by our band, moving up to attack Hill 70. We hadn't the faintest idea where we were going, but we sang the usual sol-diers' songs – 'Tipperary,' and all those sort of things – we were thor-oughly enjoying ourselves. We had the usual stops, which were supposed to be ten minutes every hour, but actually we halted far more than that because of the chaos on the roads – traffic going up and down, ammuni-tion limbers and walking wounded.

Our first shock was when we met the walking wounded. They said when we were laughing and talking, with an eager to get at 'em sort of attitude, they said, 'You'll laugh on the other side of your ruddy faces when you get up there.' Of course, that didn't mean very much to us at that time, we were members of the Queen's you know, and as Kitchener had said, we were going to do as well as those who had gone before, so we didn't bother very much about that.

Our baptism of fire was our attack on Hill 70 in the Béthune area. We advanced in short sharp rushes and everywhere men falling. I began to get really anxious as I moved forward because I could see men disappearing and didn't know quite what was happening to them because you couldn't see the bullets. My biggest shock, in advancing up that hill, was to come across my own platoon officer, Lieutenant Cressy, who was either dead or very badly wounded. I remember shaking him and telling him to come on, but of course he was dead, so he couldn't.

Then I realised that we had to get on and do something, but there was no one to give us orders – they had all been killed or wounded. The thing that worried me most was the fact that on my back was about 60 lb. of weight and I just couldn't carry it very much further. So I got the man next to me to get out his jack-knife and cut it off, and I did the same for the remainder of the fellows who were there.

In the meantime we were still firing, and as we approached this wire I could see the bodies of men hanging on it, obviously dead or badly wounded, and there were no gaps in it at all. Our artillery had not cut the wire, even firing 18-pounder shells at it. The shell could land in a certain spot and instead of cutting a neat swathe through the wire to allow the troops through, it just lifted great lumps of it up and made the confusion worse. So there was no way of getting through the wire at all. I couldn't even see where the enemy trench was, the barbed wire was so thick and so deep.

Well, we laid down, and how many men there were at the time I don't know, but it was very few indeed. We lay there wondering what on earth to do until some bright spark said, 'We've got the order to retire.' Now I didn't fancy going down that hill again with my back to them, it was bad enough coming up in front. But I knew there was a sunken trench to the right of us, so I got the few men that were around me back into this trench, and temporarily at least we were out of fire.

Well, how long we laid there I don't know, but I realised that we had made a mess of the thing, or at least, someone had, and we were all cut up. I was never going to forget Hill 70.

Corporal Edward Glendinning
12th Battalion, Notts and Derby Regiment (Sherwood Foresters)
In the autumn of 1915 we were doing the routine duty, four in and four out with plenty of work. Then we had orders to clean up as we were going to be inspected by someone high up. We didn't know who it was.

We made ourselves fairly presentable and the next morning set off and marched away. We did about fifteen miles then came to a little valley with a road running along the bottom of it, where we found a lot of other units already assembled. We took our allotted places and waited for three or four hours before anything happened. Then along came a contingent of staff cars. These high-ups got out of their cars and proceeded to mount their charges. I believe there was an orderly flying a miniature royal standard behind the King.

The King rode along the first three or four ranks, then crossed the road to the other three or four ranks on the other side, speaking to an officer here and there. Our instructions had been that at the conclusion of the parade we were to put our caps on the points of our fixed bayonets and wave and cheer. So that's what we did – 'Hip, hip, hooray.' Well, the King's horse reared and he fell off. He just seemed to slide off and so of course the second 'Hip, hip' fizzled out. It was quite a fiasco and you should have seen the confusion as these other high-ranking officers rushed to dismount and go to the King's assistance. They got him up and the last we saw of him was being hurriedly driven away!

Lieutenant George Craike
12th Battalion, Highland Light Infantry
Massive reinforcements crossed the Channel in late September and early October, and I was one of these reinforcements, proceeding to the Loos area where very heavy losses had been sustained by the British Army. My division was the 15th Division and my battalion the 12th HLI. To a young officer and to young soldiers proceeding there after the

tragedy of Loos, life was very troublesome and we had to overcome many difficulties. The chief of these difficulties was frustration in the great defeat which the British Army had suffered.

When we arrived at Loos the trenches were in not too bad a state, considerably damaged, but we were able to take over in due course from the English regiments, which had suffered very badly. The problems for the British battalion commanders were numerous, the principal being organising defence, organising supplies and preparing for impending, so we thought then, German attacks. The other problems were supply and the disposal of the numerous dead lying all about. This naturally could only be done under cover of darkness. To venture out in no man's land in daylight was seeking instant death. The evening burial parties were a feature which went on for several months before the battlefields were finally cleared up. Under cover of darkness each battalion and unit had its share of this very unpleasant task.

One frosty evening practically the whole of our company, including the captain himself, were on a special burial party to dispose of a large number of the 7th East Surreys who had been killed between the 25th and 27th of September. We crawled out of the trenches with caution in small parties, and dealt with the dead by simply pulling them into depressions in the earth, or into shell holes. This was not a pleasant task and occasionally the arms disengaged from the bodies. However, the bodies were placed as far as possible in these holes and covered over with a light layer of earth, this earth being brushed or dug in by the entrenching tools. All the work had to be done on all fours, for to stand erect was courting disaster. In addition the very frequent Very lights of the Germans necessitated instant stillness while these lights illuminated in the sky. The work was slow, laborious and difficult. Before the bodies were actually covered over the main task was to retrieve the identity discs. These discs were found round their necks and were cut off, collected and in due course sent back to headquarters.

Lieutenant Ulrich Burke
2nd Battalion, Devonshire Regiment

When we did read the newspapers it made us angry, especially if you had done a big raid on a battalion scale which would be two hundred yards wide and you had penetrated the enemy to a depth of, we'll say, quarter or half a mile, brought back prisoners. Then you'd read in the paper 'No action on the Western Front.' It didn't seem to warrant, where you'd lost probably fifty men killed and an equal number wounded, a mention. It wasn't big enough, even though the war hadn't been on two years. It used to annoy everybody terribly, 'Very little action on the Western Front.'

Private R. Richards
Royal Engineers

When we finally got to France we went straight up to Dickebusch, and of course it being the latter part of November, it was pretty filthy weather. The Germans were only about fifty yards away and they had highly specialised snipers, which made life pretty unbearable. We could never retaliate properly because this sort of warfare had taken us completely by surprise – we had nothing to lob back at them.

But then all of a sudden there was a violent explosion, and I was blown back about twelve yards. When I finally got up all I could see was smoke, and I could hear the cries and screams of the survivors. As I crawled towards them I could see what remained of the section that had been making these bombs. Some had been cut in two, some in three parts, legs and arms were strewn all over the place and there was that acrid smell of explosion. Well, all my romantic ideals of war completely vanished with that episode. The following day when I was given the job of going round with sandbags, collecting the pieces, we had to rescue some bits from telegraph wires where they'd been blown at great velocity, and we buried them in the common grave.

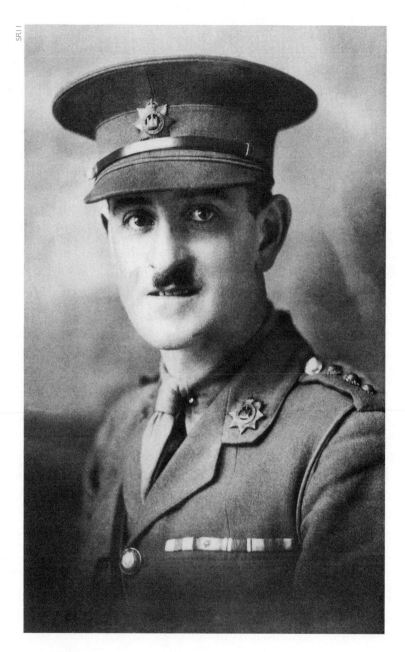

Lieutenant Ulrich Burke, 2nd Battalion, Devonshire Regiment.

Private Clifford Lane
1st Battalion, Hertfordshire Regiment
I can remember that one of my comrades got wounded and this induced in me a sense of desolation which would normally only come if you lost a very close family – a member of your family really, that sort of feeling, for quite a time, you felt absolutely, completely desolate. There is that feeling of comradeship which can't be understood by anybody unless they were actually in the front line in the War. It was the sort of trust between men that rarely occurs.

Sergeant Charles Lippett
1/8th Battalion, Queen's Royal West Surrey Regiment
The men in the line tended to despise conscientious objectors, but it was not until I was appointed regimental policeman that I came in contact with them.

There were, of course, different varieties of conscientious objectors – there were the political ones, the religious ones, and those who just didn't want to bother. But it was not until I had actual contact with them that I could see that there was something at the back of this thing, that neither I or anyone else around me had realised.

One morning it was my job to go into the cell where these people were put prior to their appearance before the commanding officer, and this fellow had scrawled across his cell wall, which was whitewashed, a slogan which I now know well. 'Workers of the world unite, you have nothing to lose but your chains.'

I wondered what it meant and I asked the fellow all about it. He proceeded to explain, and I think that was the start of my political education. But the thing I must emphasise is the treatment we were forced to mete out to these poor blighters because they thought as they did. I remember one man in particular, who absolutely refused to have anything to do with the Army at all, and refused to put on khaki.

Well, we were instructed to take measures to remedy this state of affairs, which included taking him to the baths, stripping him and forcing a suit of khaki on him. We took him to the open compound, and as it was very cold at night we thought he would be forced to wear this khaki to keep himself warm, but he had other ideas. During the night he stripped himself of this khaki and shredded the whole of the suit up and hung it around the barbed wire, and that man walked about all night long without a shred of clothing on him. That was the type of treatment we had to mete out, and I am bitterly ashamed that I was forced to take part in it.

Another fellow I well remember, a great big strapping fellow with a black beard, and we had the lousy job of taking this beard off this man, and I shall never forget now his eyes as he looked at us, to think that we fellow men were doing this to him. We had to do it, I suppose that was our excuse. But ever since then I've admired these men intensely. I would take off my hat to them any time, because I realise that what they did in defying the British military might – and they defied it in every way possible – they had far more guts than we did who were doing these things to them.

Kitty Eckersley

When I found out I was pregnant I went to see them at the leather-works and they said they would find me some light work. So I had a very nice job and worked there until I was seven months pregnant.

And then I'd just given up work on the Friday night when I received the letter on the Monday morning. I had gone to bed on the Friday as usual – I didn't go out very much because I had a very bad time during my pregnancy – the only thing that I could keep in my stomach was carrots. They were very cheap so I had two pounds of carrots every day, it was the only thing I could eat. I was very thin at the time.

Anyway my mother in the meantime had got a little job picking strawberries at a jam factory, and so there was only me in the house. Well, mother had gone to the jam factory and she'd left me in bed. But I heard the postman come and I knew that it would be a letter for me. So I ran down in my nightdress and opened the door, snatched the letter off him and ran in and shut the door again. And I opened the letter and I saw it was from his sergeant. It just said, 'Dear Mrs. Morton, I'm very sorry to tell you of the death of your husband.' Well, that was as far as I could read. I don't really know what happened over the next few minutes, but I must have run out of the house as I was, in my bare feet, and banged on the next door.

The next-door neighbours were a Mr. and Mrs. Hurst, and they let me in. She said, 'Whatever's to do?' and I said, 'Would you read this letter, Mrs. Hurst?' So she did, then said, 'Oh you poor child.' Then they brought some blankets and wrapped me up in them and sent word to my mother, so she came home and they treated me for shock. But his letter was only from his sergeant, so I thought perhaps it was an error. So later on I wrote back to the sergeant, but I had another letter to say that he had also been killed. Then later on, I got the official news.

Private George Jameson
6th Northumberland Hussars

I can't really remember anything after Loos. I can't remember any outstanding event beyond the humdrum business of a war. We just felt, 'Will this never end?' There was a hopeless sort of outlook, a belief that we were there for keeps. That it would never change.

GALLIPOLI

Private Walter Stagles
3rd Australian Battalion, 1st Australian Division

It was pitch dark then all of a sudden the coast, a dim outline of the coast, loomed up. As we got closer, we were all beginning to get tensed up, nervous, wondering what was going to happen as everything was so quiet. Then a single shot rang out and a yellowish light flared up in the sky, and from then on the Turks let loose, machine-gun and rifle fire at the boats. The pinnaces cast us off, the muffled oarsmen took up the row. As soon as the boats grounded it was every man for himself, it was out, do the best you could.

As we scrambled ashore, those that were lucky enough to get there, we found what cover under the cliff we could. As we lay there for a few moments gathering our wind, we slipped off our pack, fixed our bayonets and someone in the crowd – there was no officer – shouted 'Right lads, after the bastards.'

Fusilier W. Flynn
1st Royal Munster Fusiliers

When we woke up on the *River Clyde* in the morning and looked out of the portholes and saw land, they told us it was the Dardanelles and we had to make a landing there. It was Cape Helles. We couldn't see anybody. All we could see was this piece of land shaped like a saucer which gradually went up to a little hill, which was called 141. That dominated the whole beach.

Our cue was when the Dublins came off the warship in cutters. We then had to run down the gangway across the two boats and a steam hopper, and then we only had perhaps 10 or 20 feet to go to the shore.

But the boat had been carried away towards a strip of rock, and the steam hopper and one of the lighters had been cut away and drifted out to sea. The one that was tied to the bow of the ship was all right, but as we ran down the gangway, instead of having two separate gangways either side of the ship, they had connected them. Unfortunately, the first batch had to run across into the lighter, and what with us running down and them running across, and all the bodies piling up, it was like a barricade. They simply fell into the lighters. Some were dead, some were wounded, some weren't hit but got smothered in the pile-up.

Captain Geddes and I managed to get on the first lighter, where the dead were. Captain Geddes, said, 'It's no good Flynn, come on.' But I was weighed down by a big periscope I was carrying for him. We had double ammunition, double rations, double everything. He had the sense to tell everybody to throw their coats off before we made land. All the Dublins never had a chance to drop their coats, they went down, they sank – just disappeared.

I followed Captain Geddes down the gangway and along the gunwale of the lighter, and we laid down in the bow with just enough cover to hide us. He looked back and called for the remainder of the company to come but they couldn't. So he said, 'Well, over we go, we're going to fall into the sea.' I managed to come up once or twice for fresh air, then gradually drifted to my right until I came up by this strip of rock which was piled high with dead. Anyway, I managed just to crawl on the rock, exhausted.

We got along the side to the end of the boat without any mishap, there was about twelve feet of water to go through. The boat was facing ashore. So I dived into the water and crawled along the bottom and eventually came up behind the boat. It just hid us. Although when the waves wobbled a bit it turned the boat's stern into the shore and the enemy could just see us. We didn't realise this until I heard something go by and I said to Captain Geddes, 'My, that was close,' and he said, 'It was, wasn't it.'

It was then that his ear was shot off and I don't know how it missed me, but it did. He said, 'We'd better get ashore, but how can we?' I said, 'We'll have to go underneath, if there's enough room. Wait till the waves lift the boat and shove your rifle in front of you.' Anyway, we managed to scramble on the shore with eight or nine feet to go, and we got behind a bank about five feet high, where we were safe for the time being.

Private Frank Brent
2nd Australian Brigade, 1st Australian Division

There was no co-ordinated effort about it. Just a crowd of Diggers working with each other. Trust each other blind. After we'd been digging a little while, the *Queen Elizabeth* let go two or three of her shells and the sound of those shells was a real tonic. One bloke shouted out 'Share that amongst you, you bastards,' and the bloke next to me was Robbie Robinson, a corporal in my battalion. I can see him now, grinning all over his face and the next thing his head fell on my shoulder. A sniper had got him through the jugular vein. I really think that was my baptism because Robbie's blood spent all over my tunic. After he was laying dead I thought 'Well, I'd better let his people know about it,' and I took his paybook out and wrote his mother's address on a bit of paper. It was somewhere in Fitzroy that she lived but I never wrote to her but I do remember looking at that bit of paper afterwards.

Well, having dug in, there was only one thing to do, was to stop where we'd dug in. If he'd come at us and been successful, he could have got us back into the sea. All during the night, there was plenty of shrapnel and machine guns and snipers as busy as they could be but we lived through. At 9 o'clock the next day, we could see he was bringing up plenty of stuff to have a go, and I think he'd made up his mind to dump us. Half an hour later we could hear him shouting 'Allah' and blowing trumpets. There was quite a lot of heavy firing and plenty from us. They brought up some Indian mountain batteries. Well, they could only dig in about twenty yards behind where we were, because any farther down they'd have been shooting into the hillside. They joined in the general shelling and bombardment and they were firing what they call 'grapeshot.' Well, this was shrapnel that burst the moment it left the gun muzzle and, blimey, we had to scatter each time those batteries went.

Then on the 28th, Royal Naval Division came and we were evacuated from the line into these little humpies just in the sand hills and it was then for the first time since the landing that we'd been able to look round for our cobbers. On the first day, we were just mixed up and running about like a lot of rabbits – nobody could see who was who or what was what. And it was then for the first time we realised what the taking of Anzac Ridge had cost, because hardly any of our mates were left.

Private Frank Brent
2nd Australian Brigade, 1st Australian Division
There were dead and wounded of the 3rd brigade all round and we scampered as hard as we could to a little bit of shelter, dumped our packs and dumped the shovels and the picks – we'd had enough of those – and then somebody said, 'Well, up you go' and away we went up the slope. It wasn't too bad but just half way up somebody shouted out to me 'Alan Cordoner's stopped one.' Well, Alan was one of my best pals and that made me feel a bit better because if they'd got him, I felt 'I'm gonna get them.'

Sergeant Frank Kennedy
3rd Australian Battalion
When we disembarked from our boats on the beach the conditions were indescribable. There were the wounded, dead and dying, rifles left all over the place and the packs the chaps had chucked off when they had advanced in the first assault.

A dressing station had to be arranged and the first order I had was to try and get the bodies carried under cover. But carrying the stretchers down those slopes was about the most difficult thing a stretcher-bearer could do. We were constantly stepping down, stepping down – perhaps stumbling over some bushes – while all the time trying to ease the pain of the chap on the stretcher.

But we carried on, right until the evening, doing our best to get all those that were wounded. You might be coming down from the front line and suddenly you'd hear a mournful cry from a bush perhaps twenty yards away, 'Stretcher-bearers, Stretcher-bearers,' and all you could do was to ease your stretcher down on the ground for a moment, go over and see to the case, give him an injection if necessary or some tablets to ease the pain, and tell him you'd come back for him.

Private Walter Stagles
3rd Australian Battalion, 1st Australian Division
On the morning when the attack came, they came over in two great waves from their trenches, in great hulking mass. They were rather big men, the Turks, fine body of men. As they came over, they were shouting 'Allah!' and blowing their trumpets and whistling and shouting, like schoolboys. As they got closer, within nice rifle range, we had the order to fire and we opened up with rapid fire and brought them down in hundreds, hundreds of them fell, and in front of our trenches. I should think when the attack was over there would be anything from two to three thousand dead or dying in front of our brigade.

Marine Joe Clement
Deal Battalion, Royal Marine Light Infantry
Eventually we made the rocky ground of the first ridge. I fixed up my

Maxim machine-gun behind sandbags at the end of a gully, then sat and waited. It was still dark when we heard trumpets blowing as the Turks came at us in droves from the other end of the gully from where we were positioned. I didn't have to take aim, I just fired and mowed them down. You couldn't miss, there were so many of them. It was like firing into a mass of bodies gelled together.

Eventually they withdrew. But they came again seven times that night and each time we drove them back. Come the dawn, they had gone, only the bodies were left.

Fusilier W. Flynn
1st Royal Munster Fusiliers
We made another big advance on the 29th and got right to the bottom of the whole trouble – that was Achi Baba, which dominated the whole peninsula right out to sea. It was a tidy-sized hill, and it ran right across the narrow part of the peninsula, because the peninsula at its widest part was only three miles from the Narrows to the Aegean Sea.

But anyway, we had lost a lot of men in the trench fighting and then we had the order to retire, what was left of us. There was just one man here, perhaps two another twenty yards away, and so forth, so we had to retire right down to the narrowest part. General Ian Hamilton promised reinforcements if we got ashore within a fortnight, but it was more than six weeks before we got any. We could have walked away with the place.

BATTLE OF KRITHIA – MAY 6

Ordinary Seaman Joe Murray
Hood Battalion, Royal Naval Division
I remember, Yates was a little ahead of Don Townsend and myself. We crawled up more or less abreast, but the bullets were hitting the sand, spraying us, hitting our packs. So we decided, 'How about another dash?' So off we went, near enough fifteen yards. Then we got down again. Then we decided to go a little bit further. We'd got to keep bearing to our right slightly, because we were dodging the line of fire. We

Australian soldiers who took the brunt of casualties in Gallipoli, attend a wounded friend. None have steel helmets, which were not issued until 1916.

decided to go a little bit further and all four of us got up together.

Yates was in front and all of a sudden he bent over. He'd been shot in the stomach, or maybe the testicles, and he danced around like a cat on hot bricks until he fell down on the ground. We decided to ease up a bit. But as soon as we got near him he got up and rushed like hell at the Turks and Bang! He went down altogether, out for the count.

Horton and I were more or less together. Townsend was on the other side and there was a gap where Yates had been. Young Horton was the first to get to Yates and he had just pushed him to see what was wrong when a bullet struck him dead centre of the brow – it went right through his head and took out a bit of my knuckle. Poor Horton, he kept crying for his mother. I can see him now. Hear him at this very moment. He said he was eighteen but I don't think he was sixteen, never mind eighteen. He was such a frail young laddie. He was a steward on the Fyffe banana boats in peacetime. Yates was dead. Horton was dead. Only Don and I were left.

Private Frank Brent
2nd Australian Brigade, 1st Australian Division
It just went on all day. The older battleships in the bay were letting go as hard as they could, and the harder they fired the more confident you felt. So whilst it was about the most precarious position a bloke could find himself in, you sort of made up your mind that, 'Well, we're here, and the only way the enemy can get us off is by carrying us off feet first.'

The dust and the noise – it was so loud you couldn't hear each other speak – went on for a quarter of an hour, then suddenly everything was as silent as the grave. And that was when we had to hop it. The barrage had been so heavy that in the quiet we thought, 'Well this is going to be a cakewalk, there's nothing to stop us.' But the mistake we made was that after we got out of our 'hop-out' trenches our own artillery began to put down a barrage just in front of us and some of it was firing short. You could see your mates falling, going down right and left, and you were face to face with the stark realisation that this was the end.

And that was the thought that was with you the whole time because despite the fact that you couldn't see the Turk, he was pelting us with everything he had got from all sides – the marvel to me was how the Dickens he was able to do it after the barrage that had fallen on him. And sure enough we got within a mile of Krithia village when I copped my packet – as I laid there I said, 'Thank Christ for that.'

Marine Joe Clement
Deal Battalion, Royal Marine Light Infantry
Later I had my machine-gun trained on Krithia which was probably just over a thousand yards away where there was a road used by mule trains. We would fire and make the mules jump about a bit. At night we were sometimes told not to fire in certain directions because we had patrols out. One night the Gurkhas were out there, so we were keeping a close watch. Out of the dark came this voice to warn us not to shoot, 'All right, Tommy, all right.' Then I saw this smiling face coming in and it wasn't till he'd got in the trench that I realised he was carrying the head of a Turk! He had used his kukri.

Private Harold Boughton
2/1st Battalion, London Regiment
One of the biggest curses was flies. Millions and millions of flies. The whole of the side of the trench used to be one black swarming mass. Anything you opened, like a tin of bully, would be swarming with flies. If you were lucky enough to have a tin of jam and opened that, swarms of flies went straight into it. They were all around your mouth and on any cuts or sores that you'd got, which then turned septic. Immediately you bared any part of your body you were smothered. It was a curse, it really was.

Fusilier Harold Pilling
1/6th Lancashire Fusiliers
If you'd looked in the latrines you'd have been sickened. You'd think people had parted with their stomachs or their insides. It was awful. You had to cover it and dig another. It hadn't to be so high or else you could fall down. There were no supports or anything, it was just an open trench, but it was fairly deep.

Ordinary Seaman Joe Murray
Hood Battalion, Royal Naval Division

Dysentery was a truly awful disease that could rob a man of the last ves-tiges of human dignity before it killed him. A couple of weeks before getting it my old pal was as smart and upright as a guardsman. Yet after about ten days it was dreadful to see him crawling about, his trousers round his feet, his backside hanging out, his shirt all soiled – everything was soiled. He couldn't even walk.

So I took him by one arm and another pal got hold of him by the other, and we dragged him to the latrine. It was degrading, when you remember how he was just a little while ago. Neither my other pal nor I were very good – but we weren't like that. Anyway, we lowered him down next to the latrine. We tried to keep the flies off him and to turn him round – put his backside towards the trench. But he simply rolled into this foot-wide trench, half-sideways, head first in the slime. We couldn't pull him out, we didn't have enough strength, and he couldn't help himself at all. We did eventually get him out but he was dead, he'd drowned in his own excrement.

Private Henry Barnes
4th Australian Brigade

We were so close to the Turkish front line that we were constantly on good terms with them, even though we were officially fighting them. We regularly exchanged bully beef and biscuits for strings of figs and oranges. You see instead of throwing a bomb, you could throw a tin of bully beef over, and when they discovered that, you got a string of figs back.

One day I sat on the parapet and after a while walked over and offered bully beef to one Turk, and he smiled and seemed very pleased and passed me two whole strings of dates.

Jack – as we called this Turkish soldier – was very highly regarded by me and all the men on our side. I never heard him decried, he was always a clean fighter and one of the most courageous men in the world. There was no beating about, they faced up to the heaviest rifle fire, and nothing would stop them, they were almost fanatical. We came to our conclusion that he was a very good bloke indeed, we had a lot of time for him.

The Turks were firing bombs as well as rifle fire and it was very difficult to avoid the occasional one that came over. There was one man fell right in front of me – he came over bawling some Muslim phrase and me and the fellow next to me shot him at the same time. We were rather bunched around the entry to the trench and he came through practically on top of my bayonet. He was a very big man and came down right on top of me and none of us could lift him out, he was too heavy. So I literally sat on that Turk for two days – we ate our lunch of bully beef and biscuits sitting on him.

ATTACK ON TURKISH LINES, JUNE 4

Ordinary Seaman Joe Murray
Hood Battalion, Royal Naval Division

We stood there, packed like sardines unable to stand up in comfort, and we still had another hour to go before we went over the top. It was a long hour. Some men were fast asleep on their feet, others just stood staring at the sky. The laddie next to me checked his rifle and ammunition again and again, still not satisfied. Others just stood and stared, silent as the grave. Maybe they were looking forward to it, who knows?

At 11:30 our guns ceased fire just as promptly as they had started. Many lives had depended upon that half-hour bombardment – and we knew it. Had it destroyed the Turkish machine-gun posts? Had the riflemen been killed or driven to cover? We didn't know, we only hoped. I'd never dreamt that even borrowed time could go so slowly.

Of course I'd advanced before – many times. I wasn't afraid of advance. I didn't like it, but I wasn't afraid of Johnny Turk. I'd met him before and beaten him and I could beat him again. But I was afraid – I was afraid of myself. I wondered if I would live long enough to get out of the trench, and if I did, if I would have enough puff left in me to cover that four hundred yards or so across in one mad rush. And if not, and I

Many of the King's Own Scottish Borderers go over the top in the battle of Krithia on June 4.

had to bury my head in that burning scrub, would I have enough courage left to rise again and face that rain of lead?

Those were my thoughts as I stood beside Lieutenant Commander Parsons, my Company Commander, waiting for him to blow his whistle. Then, just before we went over the top, he turned round with the most confident smile and said, 'Five minutes to go men – four minutes – three minutes – two minutes – one minute to go, men. Are you ready? Come on boys, off we go!'

As I was getting out of the trench I could see the Collingwood Battalion leave their trench in perfect formation – it was like they were on a parade ground, three lines of them. Well, this heartened me, because they were to go through us and capture the enemy's third line. But as we lay there we saw them being cut down in a matter of a few minutes, by enfilade fire from a ridge on the right, just in front of the French. Only in ones and twos did the survivors reach the line, and none reached us in the second.

I asked God to help me as I scrambled over the top into that withering fire. Many, many men were killed as soon as they showed their heads, and fell back into the trench. Poor old Lieutenant Commander Parsons only got a few yards. Very few of us reached the Turkish front line and even fewer got through to the second.

The trench was much too deep for us to occupy and as we were getting into position along the parapet I felt a sudden bang in the chest. Then I found myself crawling about on the bottom of the trench trying to find my rifle – my face was stiff and I could only see out of one eye. I eventually got to my rifle and realised that all my equipment had been torn to shreds – my tunic was smouldering, my body was criss-crossed with rips and all the ammunition had gone. Apparently, a machine-gun sweep had caught me and blown the lot off, and down I went. After some distance, I managed to get to my feet. I remember crawling quite a long way.

Private S. T. Sherwood
We landed on Suvla beach and all that first day we were lying there with no orders to attack. Throughout the day the Turks were reinforcing their positions.

I kept in touch with my Colonel – I had to be close to him because I was one of the chief runners who took down messages, but by the time we had reached Point 100, which was our objective, our casualties had mounted terrifically. The Colonel turned to me and said, 'You must go down and find the Brigadier.' It was a verbal message, there was no time for writing it down or anything. The message was, 'Have reached Point 100. Casualties very heavy, am being enfiladed.'

I shot off downhill with this message. On the way I was hit on the top of the head with a nose-cap from a shell, which crushed my helmet and slightly wounded me on the side. I think there was more blood than damage but I didn't look a very good sight by the time I reached the Brigadier General. I explained the position to him and he looked at me as much as to say, 'We haven't been in action two or three hours yet, it was impossible.' But a few minutes later a Lincolnshire runner came up and he had the same tale, their casualties were about seventy-five per cent. I remember the General looking at the Brigade Major and said, 'My God, this must be true.'

Ordinary Seaman Jack Gearing
Benbow Battalion, Royal Naval Division

We knew that the four hundred men of the East Yorks were mostly fresh from training and few had seen action, so every sailor was given two soldiers to look after. We gave them our hammocks, made sure they ate well and gave them our rum. You see, we knew that where they were going would be like Hell on earth, so we gave them all the love we could, because they were going to need it. There was all those feelings, all that silence. That's why I admire the British, they take it and they're quiet.

As we approached Suvla Bay on the night of 6–7 August, it was the darkness before the dawn. I stood on the gangway which had been fitted over the stern to allow the troops to walk down into the motor lighters. As the soldiers followed each other down with their rifles one got hit by a sniper and screamed out. I told him to shut up and put up with the pain or he would frighten the rest – that was my first scream of war.

Allied troops advance on a Turkish trench.

Each day when there was a lull we'd go in and collect the wounded. Some of them were terribly badly wounded, and all so young. Suvla Bay was reasonably flat and the soldiers had made homes for themselves or taken over where other battalions had been before they moved forward. I did my best to cheer them up and encourage them. But most of the time, I was quiet because there wasn't much you could say in the face of all that horror. It was important that they had their own thoughts, they had to come to terms with it in their own way.

Every Sunday we used to try and have a service on board and we sang hymns which were heard by the soldiers on shore. They told us how much it meant to them so whenever we scrubbed the decks we sang out as loud as we could all the old hymns to inspire them: 'Onward, Christian Soldiers,' 'Fight the Good Fight,' anything that was rousing. It cheered us up, too.

I saw quite a lot of the Turkish prisoners on shore. They were badly dressed and always wanted our boots, they were so poor; but they were wonderful fighting men. They didn't give way. We could see them fighting from the ship; they were good. We didn't feel any anger towards them, we had a respect for them!

Fusilier W. Flynn
1st Royal Munster Fusiliers
When we advanced the Turks stood up on their trenches and waved us on. It was hopeless, hopeless. They set fire to all the gorse bushes and it was called Chocolate Hill. They called it Burnt Hill afterwards, so many of the wounded got burnt.

We did get black towards the end. We weren't succeeding at all, all we were doing was losing a lot of men and ships. Every day we were bringing in different men, different faces, all tired, all beaten. And it was so hot that summer, so hot. Then, as autumn came on, we knew things were getting worse on land, even with the reinforcements. We were watching a picture of failure fought out by brave men.

When we withdrew on the 20th of December it was dark. The soldiers were all packed so tight and quiet in the barges making their way to the big ships. We never lost a man, which was remarkable. As we were steaming quietly away I thought of what 'Pincher' Martin, who had done twenty years in the Navy, had said to me a few days after we'd arrived at Suvla Bay: 'We're not going to be flying the Union Jack here.' He was right. We were never going to make it ours.

Marine Joe Clement
Royal Marine Light Infantry

There was continuous rain which filled up the trenches, so we had to sleep on the parapets. The Turks did the same. We had an unspoken truce and didn't shoot at sleeping men. But it was so cold and we were always wet. On Christmas Day we were in the firing line and were served one slice of pudding and seven dates. Two days later we went down into our dug-out to change our clothes only to find our packs with our clean washing under three feet of water. Then, for another treat, they put us into the firing line for New Year's Day.

The first we knew of the evacuation was when the French moved out on the 1st January. We spread out into their trenches to extend the line. We didn't know that Anzac and Suvla beaches had already been evacuated. On the 8th of January we began to destroy food and rifles that were not needed. We then tied empty sandbags around our feet, secured our water bottles so that they wouldn't clank around, and at midnight we moved off. I carried my machine-gun for over five miles in the dark until we reached the beach. As we were walking 'Asiatic Annie' fired several shells. We had come to hate her throughout our time at Gallipoli. The Turks didn't know we were going. Firing from the Asiatic side, Annie had always been a law unto herself.

Ordinary Seaman Joe Murray
Hood Battalion, Royal Naval Division

I thought to myself, 'I don't like sneaking away like this after all this bloody trouble.' I was really distressed in my own mind. I thought to myself, 'We're stealing away. We stole away from Blandford, stole away from Egypt and now we're stealing away from Gallipoli.' I remember when I came towards Backhouse Post, I thought to myself, 'Oh dear me! Poor old Yates and Parsons, all killed and buried here.' When we first went to Backhouse Post I remember how happy and anxious we were to get stuck into the Turks. And now here we were, only a handful left.

As we got further from the line near Backhouse Post, I remembered the advance we had on May the 6th, when more of my pals died, such as Petty Officer Warren and young Yates. I could still hear young Horton crying for his mother as he died. And I remembered Colonel Quilter, a great big chap, a 'straight as a poker' ex-Guards Officer. I remembered him leading the advance and going to his death armed with a huge walking stick. He told us when we were on the boat, just before we landed, that the eyes of the world would be upon us. Well, the eyes of the Turks certainly were, and so were their rifles, but the rest of the world seemed to have forgotten us.

The tears were streaming down my cheeks, I just couldn't restrain them. My eyes were smarting so much I think I walked the rest of the way with my eyes closed. I knew it so well though, I couldn't go wrong.

We were packed up like sardines in this blinking lighter. We were so packed we couldn't move our hands up at all. And it was dark, of course. Apart from being dark outside, it was dark inside – there were no lights and no portholes.

A couple of fellows behind me were pushing and shoving, and all of a sudden the damned thing started to rock, there must have been a shell dropped pretty close. There were hundreds of us in this blinking lighter and then all of a sudden it hit the pier. Those that were asleep were half awake and those that were sick were still being sick and, oh dear me, it was stifling hot!

And then another shell came along and I thought to myself, 'Why the hell don't we get out of here? It may only have been a little while but it seemed hours and then eventually we felt the slow rocking and I thought to myself, 'Well here we are; we're at sea now anyhow.' We'd been dumped into this lighter like a lot of cattle and just pushed out to sea, and nobody gave a tinker's cuss whether we lived or died.

1916

Then the British Army went over the top . . . our machine-gunners crawled out of their bunkers, red-eyed and dirty, covered in the blood of their fallen comrades, and opened up a terrific fire.

In February 1916 the Germans launched a major offensive. General Falkenhayn's strategy was to deliver the heaviest blow he could against France, perhaps calculating that after the hideous losses of 1914–15 the French might conceivably crack. His objective was Verdun, which lay close to Metz, which had been occupied by Germany since 1871, and had served as a major depot for their armies since then. For an attack in this sector the German railway network could ferry hundreds of heavy guns right up to the front-line, together with vast quantities of ammunition.

More than a thousand guns and mortars fired two million rounds at the French front line to open the battle, but despite this, the first infantry attacks that went in near last light on February 21 met heroic resistance from scattered groups of survivors. Additional bombardments were called for and the Germans slowly ground their way forward. However, their rate of advance was little more than a kilometre a day during the first week, and came to a virtual halt in March.

As the battle of Verdun proceeded the French urged the British to advance the date of the Allied offensive to relieve the pressure on their forces. The Somme offensive which resulted became a predominantly British battle. The Germans had fortified their positions on the Somme with professional thoroughness. Three successive lines of defences followed the high ground across gently undulating farm-land. Thickets of barbed wire presented an attacker with the most fearsome obstacles. Machine-guns in concrete strongpoints were deployed with interlocking zones of fire, most sited to fire into the flank of attacking infantry. The chalky soil was excellent for tun-nelling, and German engineers burrowed deep to create almost indestructible shelters for the soldiers manning the front line. German artillery positions lay well back, camouflaged from the air but ready to deluge no man's land with high explosive, their fire directed from the Front by observation positions with telephone lines buried far beneath the shell-torn ground.

The British plan was not unlike General Falkenhayn's at Verdun: to pulverise the enemy trenches with such a weight of fire that the trenches would collapse, the barbed wire would be cut and resistance – at least in the immediate front line – brushed aside. Again like the Germans at Verdun, they anticipated that the greatest danger would be from enemy counter-attacks catching the assault troops disorgan-ised after their initial success. Consequently, the leading waves carried picks, shovels and sandbags with which to fortify their posi-tions once they had captured them. No British artilleryman had ever had so much firepower at his disposal.

The bombardment lasted a week, beginning on June 24. Five days' intensive shelling was planned, with pauses to trick the Germans into manning their front line trenches and unmasking their hidden batteries. It was extended by two days as the attack, planned for June 29, was delayed until July 1 because of bad weather. Zero hour was fixed after first light at the request of the French, who wanted good observation for their artillery; many British officers had wanted to go over the top while it was still dark. The whistles blew at 7:30 a.m. and tens of thousands of men clambered up the assault ladders and into no man's land. They advanced at a steady pace so as not to become disorganised.

The bombardment had failed to crush the enemy defences. In many areas the barbed wire was uncut; field guns firing shrapnel formed a high proportion of the artillery on the Somme, and their ammunition was not effective enough in this role. Nor were the German machine-guns destroyed or even suppressed. The machine-gunners occupied their strongpoints, and across the twenty-mile front British hopes were dashed to the steady stutter of the Maxim guns. The German artillery counter-barrage opened with murderous effect, deluging no man's land with high explosive and in some sectors wrecking the British front-line trenches. On July 1, 1916 the British Army sustained 57,470 casualties, of which 19,240 were killed or died of wounds.

The battle of the Somme continued until November 19. Small-scale attacks by the British took place every week, but there were several concerted efforts across the front. The first and most successful took place on July 14, when General Rawlinson was granted his wish to make a night attack. This took most of its objectives and even led to a brief cavalry attack on the late afternoon of the following day. However, another major push on July 23 failed with heavy loss.

The casualty lists published in Britain staggered the nation, especially as the territorial gains were so negligible. Yet the battle was an equally grim experience for the Germans. The unbending Prussian tradition of 'Halten, was zu halten ist' ('Hold on to whatever can be held') was applied with no regard for the lives of the soldiers. On almost any given day of the Somme battle the Germans launched some sort of counter-attack, in the teeth of massive British fire superiority. If the British gunners failed to wipe out the German infantry in the pre-battle bombardment, they made up for it with deadly accurate fire that smashed many a German counter-blow even as it assembled on its start line. The Royal Artillery fired seven million rounds on the Somme between July 2 and September 15, and by the end of the battle 138 German divisions had been rotated in and out of the front line there, compared with seventy-five at Verdun. On September 15 the British attacked on a ten-mile front between Combles and the Ancre valley beyond Thiepval. Twelve divisions took part, their attack supported by thirty-six armoured fighting vehicles, cover-name 'tanks.'

Mabel Lethbridge
Munitions worker

I was put into a shell-filling shed where I was taught to fill 18-pounder shells. We girls never went into a shed unless there were some of the older workers there to help us, but the older workers were always moaning. They were upset and miserable because there had been so many explosions, and I think they were justified, as we heard that machines we were going to be asked to work had been condemned.

We were continually searched for cigarettes, matches and anything you might have of metal. This went on hour after hour, you were continually pulled out for a search. There was a great feeling of tension all the time, although it was not exactly fear because we were very merry and always singing and very gay. The only difficulty I found when I was put on to one of these machines was that it was very tiring work. The shells were very heavy, and we had to kneel down in front of the machine. When you stood up you just felt you hadn't got any knees, and you hadn't got any back, except one aching mass. That was from all the carrying, the long hours and the weight.

Corporal Charles Quinnell
9th Battalion, Royal Fusiliers

My home town of Woolwich was a very busy place with all the munitions workers, and the place just hummed with activity. There was plenty of money about, some of them were getting four, five and six pounds a week. All my old friends had joined up, so I was very lonely.

One thing I really noticed was that after being with the young fellows in the Army, we were a race apart from these civilians. You couldn't talk to the civilians about the war, you'd be wasting your time. They hadn't got the slightest conception of what the conditions were like and so forth. So after a time you didn't talk about it.

You went home on leave to forget. I know that one of the most pleasurable things at home was mother's cooking, and after army cooking it was very nice indeed. Father was a good scrounger and I lived like a fighting cock for seven days.

It was a life apart from anything that you'd done in civilian life.

You'd become a gypsy, you'd learned to look after yourself, you'd learned how to cook for yourself, to make do, to darn your own socks, sew on your own buttons and things like that.

Sub Lieutenant William Benham
Hawke Battalion, Royal Naval Division

I was working in Barclays Bank in Longton, and wrote to the general manager in Birmingham and said I'd like permission to join the Army after my eighteenth birthday in April 1916. That was unless the bank wanted to star my services, but as I was only the office boy I didn't think they would. They replied very courteously that in view of my limited bank experience they didn't think that they would make an application to the tribunal for me to be retained in the bank. They wished me the best of luck and said they would keep my job for me until I came back.

I enlisted and they were highly delighted to see me. They pushed me in as quick as lightning. I tried to join the Bankers' Battalion, but I found that it had just gone overseas. In point of fact it was cut to pieces at the battle of the Somme in July 1916. Anyway I went to the 31st Royal Fusiliers, which was stationed in an old amusement park outside Edinburgh.

As I was under nineteen, I couldn't be sent to France under an undertaking the War Office had given to parents. Therefore, after I had done my basic training of about fourteen weeks, they had to find jobs for me. I became a regimental policeman, I did a stint as a sergeants' mess waiter, and I was put on sewerage and latrines. I think I did just about every job there was of a non-combatant nature. In August I was transferred to the Duke of York Schools at Dover, where I was put in the officers' cookhouse until October, when suddenly, to my great joy, I was put on a draft to go to France, although I was only eighteen and a half.

I had my draft leave, said goodbye to my mother, came back, drew my identity discs and had my inoculations. I was ready to go overseas. I fell in on parade, very early in the morning, but when the adjutant arrived, he walked down the lines and obviously could see that several of us weren't nineteen years old. So he went back and gave an order that every man under the age of nineteen should take two paces forward or two paces back. Nobody moved. So then he went down the lines again and picked out people he thought were under-age and called for their papers. When it came to my turn he said, 'You're only eighteen. Fall out.' To my horror and sorrow, I was put back from going.

Lieutenant Charles Carrington
1/5th Battalion, Warwickshire Regiment
When they came to us they were weedy, sallow, skinny, frightened children – the refuse of our industrial system – and they were in very poor condition because of wartime food shortages. But after six months of good food, fresh air and physical exercise they changed so much their mothers wouldn't have recognised them. We weighed and measured them and they put on an average of one stone in weight and one inch in height. But far more than that, at the end of six months they were handsome, ruddy, upstanding, square-shouldered young men who were afraid of nobody – not even the sergeant-major. When we'd pushed them through this crash programme of military training, out they went to France in batches.

Gunner Leonard Ounsworth
124 Heavy Battery, Royal Garrison Artillery
We went down to the river and by dinnertime we were out in the Channel. Through an open porthole I saw one of those Scandinavian full-rigged ships heeling over, and in the sun it was one of the most wonderful sights I'd ever seen. She was really moving, too.

So the ship was rolling gently and they started bringing the usual stew up for the chaps. There were seven men on either side of this table and one man at the head serving. As the plates were passed down each side, from my position I could still see the Scandinavian ship, which seemed to be rolling more and more as we got further out into the Channel.

Then I suddenly saw a wave just a few inches below the porthole, and I was about to shout 'Whoa!' when the next one came clean through it – a solid jet of water – and dropped, plonk, onto the table.

The plates immediately upended and deposited the stew in the lap of each man.

Lieutenant Montague Cleeve
Royal Garrison Artillery

I was asked to dinner at the brigade headquarters of the infantry brigadier. There was a terrible din from the machine-guns and shells bursting all around us, but he insisted on having an old-fashioned mess dinner at 7 o'clock promptly. And we sat at a large table in this dugout, and the wine was brought round in decanters.

This was a bit of a contrast to trench life, where we often had to cook our own meals and I used a little bivvy tin that I had. It was a tiny wee saucepan with a lid, and inside the saucepan was a methylated spirits lamp. And what I found to be absolutely marvellous at an observation post was a tin of bully beef, which we had quite often, and I'd fry it on this little stove. It was most delicious.

Gunner Leonard Ounsworth
124 Heavy Battery, Royal Garrison Artillery

Mostly the cooks got frozen meat, cut it up and made a stew, and you went along with your dixie and got so much stew ladled out. Breakfast was two slices of bread with bacon between them, and if you were lucky the cook would dip it in the grease for you. For tea you might get corned beef or sardines, but it was mostly bread and jam for tea. There wasn't any supper unless you'd managed to save any of your own rations. Of course, we used to get stuff sent out from home as well. We didn't do so well when a battle was on. The rations came up pretty regularly, but the signaller was at a disadvantage because you were out on your own and couldn't get back to the battery for any rations.

Lieutenant Montague Cleeve
Royal Garrison Artillery

There were delousing centres behind the lines where men got into a sort of canister of hot water and had a bath. Then they got into another sort of tub that was surrounded by canvas screens. They were deloused and

SR312

Lieutenant Montague Cleeve, a member of the
Royal Garrison Artillery.

given a new set of clothing. I can't remember that happening to our battery, but it happened a great deal to the infantry, poor things, who couldn't avoid lice in the front line.

Corporal Sidney Amatt
7th Battalion, Essex Regiment
When it was daylight you were set to cleaning up the trenches of all things. That's one thing about the British Army – they never allowed you any time to yourself if they could find a job for you to do. We used to have to go along the trench and pick up cigarette ends, matchsticks, cigarette packets and anything else that had been lying about. We'd get it all nicely tidied for when the officer came and had a look round – they used to come at about 9 o'clock in the morning if it was fairly quiet. We made sure everything was all shipshape, and while it wasn't really necessary I suppose it kept our minds off the terrible times we were having.

Our overcoats used to come about halfway down between our knees and our ankles. And when it was muddy – and it was nearly always muddy – the bottom part of our overcoats got absolutely sodden and it would delay our progress and drag us down. But the French, who were nearly all fine, big-bearded men, had uniforms made so that the front part of the overcoat used to fold back and button up at the rear. That way they were almost free from the waist down, and only their trousers and boots got muddy, and it didn't lag them down. That's one thing I noticed about the French uniform.

Sergeant W. Daniels
Royal Artillery
My first experience in the trenches concerned the padre, who we called the chaplain then. He arrived from brigade headquarters, and I was pleased to see a man of that description risking his life to come into the front-line trenches. He asked me how I felt in regard to God, and was I frightened? I said I was frightened, more than once. He asked me my age and I said I was sixteen, which was much too young to be out there. 'Would you like me to pray, or would you like to pray with me?' he then

Men of the East Yorkshire Regiment move to the Front.

asked. I said I'd very much like to, and we knelt on the fire step – which was the step we stood on to fire at the Germans – and prayed there while the others in the traverse looked on. I was leg-pulled after that, but I told them exactly what I'd said to God, that I hoped he'd save me from death. And I really think without a doubt that praying to God did save my life.

Reverend John Duffield
Chaplain, Lancashire Battalion, Bantam Brigade
One night I was in the line – I was helping the medical officer in his job and doing my own at the same time – when two men came in. The first was one of our men and the other was a German, and they were both wounded. Our man said to the doctor, 'Here's a job I made for you doctor, and he made this one for me.' What could you do with men like that? They were grand.

Lieutenant Godfrey Buxton
6th Battalion, Duke of Wellington's Regiment
We didn't have dentists in any great number until 1916. Then when the dentists came over and the men got their teeth put right, and the dead ones pulled out and so on, it certainly got them into another era of health, because their food could then be properly digested. It seems a small thing, but it was of tremendous value when these dentists came and improved teeth.

Until then I don't think the public were as conscious of the value of teeth. And I believe it began a tremendous change in the attitude of the working classes after the war – quite new to what had happened before it.

Lieutenant Montague Cleeve
Royal Garrison Artillery
Before the wireless was invented we had to do the whole thing by telephone lines. We put them in the trenches for protection, but you can just imagine the confusion. In some trenches there may have been up to twenty lines all mixed up. Occasionally I think they may have been

coloured, red, blue and yellow, or something like that, but not always. And whenever a shell burst in a trench, as thousands did, they bust all the lines and there'd be complete confusion, with mud and lines and debris everywhere.

The signallers, who were marvellous in our battery, had a terrible job to find all the bits and pieces and to join them together again. It was absolutely hopeless in those seven days before the bombardment of the Somme, because the Germans knew exactly what was going to happen and shelled the place to blazes, so nobody had any communications after that. So the telephone system was a complete failure.

Major Jock McDavid
6th Battalion, Royal Scots Fusiliers

Out of the first car came this well-known figure dressed in a long, fine-textured waterproof. He was wearing a *poilu* helmet and a Sam Browne belt holster with a revolver stuck well into it. He was followed by his staff, and I could hardly believe my eyes when I saw the second car, which was piled high with luggage of every description. To my horrified amazement, on the very top of all this clutter was a full-length tin bath. What the hell he was going to do with all this I couldn't think. This very well-known figure came forward, gave a warm handshake, and introduced himself as Lieutenant Colonel Winston Churchill.

After his arrival all sorts of military and civilian VIPs came to visit us. The military types came along mostly, I think, to see if there was anything they could criticise about his duties as a battalion commander, but they didn't find much. I do remember one voice being raised. The brigadier came up late one afternoon and spotted a gap in the parapet that had been made that day. It had only been repaired the night before, and the little brigadier turned to the CO and said, 'Look here, Colonel Churchill. This is a very dangerous thing, to leave this gap unprotected.' And the colonel, turning and fixing him with his piercing eyes, said, 'But you know, sir, this is a very dangerous war.'

Lieutenant Graham Greenwell
4th Battalion, Oxford and Buckinghamshire Light Infantry

An older officer in my regiment, Alan Gibson, said, 'Let's go over and have a drink with the Second Coldstream.' Off we went and they were playing a cricket match behind the line. While we were there watching the cricket, chatting away and having a drink, up came a young chap on a bicycle who looked about fourteen. This was the Prince of Wales. The poor chap was always trying to sneak up to the front line but was never allowed to. He had been taken onto the staff at General Headquarters, where he made great friends with some of those flying blokes, particularly a chap called Barker who got a VC later. He got into terrible trouble for taking the Prince up on several occasions over the enemy lines and was nearly court-martialled for that. The Prince, to do him justice, wanted to get in on the act and serve as a regimental officer in the Grenadiers. He went and bearded Kitchener – who everyone was terrified of – at the beginning of the war and said, 'What does it matter if I do get killed? I've got four brothers.' And Kitchener said, 'I'm not in the slightest worried about you being killed, Sir; what we can't afford is to have you taken prisoner.' All that was part of the thing that irked the Prince of Wales.

Corporal Reginald Leonard Haine
1st Battalion, Honourable Artillery Company

There was a drill to apron wiring. You had angle irons and small pickets and rolls of wire and each man knew his exact job. First of all you put up a fence of pickets at such-and-such a distance apart. And then you put these little angle irons down and you made a fence of about four strands of barbed wire, right along the thing. And about ten or twelve feet in front of you and also behind you, you zigzagged the wire through these angle irons right down to ground level.

Then you ran strands of wire along those bits that you'd angled from the fence down to the angle irons. And then if you'd got a lot of wire left you didn't want to say you hadn't used it, so you bunged it all inside and hoped for the best. But it was a job one took an enormous pride in. You had to site your wire properly of course. You didn't site it straight across in front of you, you sited it at an angle to the trench, the reason being that it was difficult for anybody to get through the wire. It took an awful lot of getting through. And the tendency was for anybody who ran up against the wire to try and get nearer their objective – and they would automatically come down the wire if it was angled to your trench.

You had to leave gaps in the wire, but you had to leave them so they couldn't be seen as gaps from the German trenches. So they were staggered, but you knew where the gaps were. If there was to be a major assault, the wire would be cut. And of course one prayed that the German wire would be cut, which it never was of course. The finest artillery in the world couldn't destroy the wire, especially the enormous wire they had on the Somme.

Lieutenant Stefan Westmann
German Medical Officer

At the battle for Verdun I was a medical officer with an artillery formation. We had taken Fort Douaumont and had observation posts set up looking far into the enemy countryside. One day, I got a telephone message that a man up on an observation post had complained of heavy pains in his stomach and vomited. Apparently this was an abdominal emergency and I had to go up.

There were two communication trenches, one going up and one coming down, and the French artillery knew exactly where they were and fired on them without pause. So before I went, somebody told me to take a gas-mask with me. I'd never seen a gas-mask before, but we knew that the French artillery now fired gas shells onto the German positions. So up I went with this gas mask, which consisted of a piece of surgical gauze with a bit of cotton wool soaked in a certain fluid.

We actually had two observation posts – very strong bunkers – and there was my man with an acute appendicitis. We carried him down to an underground area protected by reinforced concrete where the French had established a little operating theatre. There were two German surgeons constantly on duty, and by chance one of them was from Berlin, my native town.

We operated on this man, but then the tricky question arose as to how to bring this man back into the German line, together with the other casualties which were up there. It was decided to do it at night.

One day I wandered through the casements and found one that had been bricked up. Somebody had written on it, 'Here lie 1,052 German soldiers.' I asked what that meant and they told me a whole battalion was in that casement. It had been used to store barrels of fuel for the flame-throwers and somebody must have been very careless as the whole thing blew up. Nobody was left – they couldn't even get at them, so they just bricked it up.

Lieutenant Tom Adlam
7th Battalion, Beds and Herts Regiment
At times life on the Western Front was bloody awful. When we were training behind the lines, we'd march with only our groundsheets round us to keep out the rain, then we'd have to dry out at night. We'd strip down to our pants then hang our trousers round the fire on sticks and things to dry them out. And there were men who were worse off than us – at least we had inside billets. And we had our baggage so we could get changed. But the men were remarkably cheerful. In fact the wetter it was the more cheerful they seemed to get. I had a great admiration for the British soldier in those days. The soldiers in France took the rough with the smooth remarkably well.

Private Michael Bawden
3rd Canadian Army
One afternoon in late spring, a few of us were resting about twenty-five feet behind the front trench, just talking quietly, when one fellow suddenly leapt to his feet and yelled, 'Stewart's been killed.' Within a minute, a man came from the front trench and told us that Stewart had indeed been killed, by a nose-cap that ripped his spine. During the next two weeks, this fellow had the same feeling about others, and was kidded to such an extent about it that finally he was nicknamed 'Hoodoo Bill.' After that he refused to mention any of these things that he felt and became a nervous wreck, almost ready to be sent back.

Here stands a rather bemused Royal Fusilier (right with rifle) with captured Germans.

Corporal William Skipp

We had a sniper's post, which was just a sheet of metal two inches high and a foot wide – just a hole big enough to put the end of a rifle through. Well, we had two boys who were orphans, they'd been brought up together, joined up together and been all the way through together. They were standing in the trenches and one said, 'What's this, George, have a look through here,' and he had no sooner approached it than down he went with a bullet through his forehead. Now his friend was so flabbergasted he too had a look, and less than two minutes later he was down the trench with his friend.

Lieutenant Montague Cleeve
Royal Garrison Artillery

We officers were living in a marvellous chateau filled with fine furniture, and I remember my delight at finding a newish violin, which I was able to play. That was a great joy to me because I hadn't touched a violin for so long. In this chateau we were absolutely in the lap of luxury – and this was only a few hundred yards from the gun position.

But the digging we had to do to get into that gun position was simply gigantic. It was about ten feet deep and forty long, and we had an awful job manoeuvring the guns into it because the caterpillars were useless. They could get them into the right neighbourhood, but then we had to manhandle these enormous monsters, which weighed several tons. We had to push them into their positions, we couldn't pull them.

But when we got them there, they were very well concealed. We camouflaged them by putting wire netting over them threaded with real grass. In fact it was so well concealed that one day a French farmer with his cow walked straight into the net and both fell in. We had an appalling job getting this beastly cow out of the gun position. The man came out all right, but the cow! In the end the general, who happened to be nearby, joined in and it was one of those delightful moments when you all burst out laughing, it was so comical. It turned out to be enormous fun. There were lots of comical episodes like that, which were a great relief, really, from the tension we were all suffering from.

Lieutenant Charles Carrington
1/5th Battalion, Warwickshire Regiment

When you came out of the line you were mentally and physically tired and hoped you were going to get a rest. But you didn't get much of a physical rest because almost every night you had to go on working parties up to the front line. The worst part was that for the last mile or two everything had to be carried by hand – somehow or other you had to get up all the food, drinking water and necessary equipment.

This included rifle ammunition, machine-gun ammunition and trench-mortar ammunition, which was very clumsy, awkward stuff to handle. Then you had to carry enormous bundles of sandbags, balks of timber, planks, ready made-up duckboards and, worst of all, coils of barbed wire. Barbed wire is the most damnable stuff to handle. It was made up in coils that weighed half a hundredweight that we carried on a stick over two men's shoulders. You were very likely to cut your hands to ribbons before you got it there.

Although people talk about communication trenches and duckboard tracks they generally weren't there, and if they were, there was every probability that the enemy were going to shell them. The nicer-looking they were the more dangerous they were, because the enemy spotted them. So going along a trench meant stumbling along a dark wet ditch with an irregular floor and a right-angled turn every few yards so that you can't see where you're going. To manoeuvre these cursed things round a corner was something so fatiguing it can hardly be described.

One has to remember too that the men who did it were physically tired out when they started. But it had to be done. The ammunition had to get there, the barbed wire had to reach the Front to protect the soldiers who were fighting, and if you were going to get any comfort at all you had to have the planks and trench boards. So you'd go cursing and stumbling along in the dark, slipping into holes and tripping over wires. And you knew that if you made the least noise the enemy would open fire. Worst of all was the traffic problem, because there would be several parties of this kind going through the labyrinth of trenches, and you could have a jam as bad as a London traffic jam.

Then somebody would have to get out on top, and if it was you you'd stand there, exposed, with the feeling that the whole German Army was looking at you. Then you'd struggle down again and perhaps get your stuff to the front line and hand it over without disaster. But then it was two or three miles back again, stumbling through the trenches, then perhaps five or six miles back to your billet, where you'd finally arrive at dawn.

Captain Graham Greenwell
4th Battalion, Oxford and Buckinghamshire Light Infantry
I was made a company commander just before the Somme battle. I was twenty. I remember my commanding officer saying he had to wait eight years before he was a captain. It was a great responsibility but that, of course, never worried me. After all, boys at this time were leaving Osborne and instead of being sent to Dartmouth, being sent straight through and posted to battleships and finding themselves, instead of dogsbodies, having to land burly troops under fire on the beaches of Gallipoli. I think it was Mrs. Sidney Webb said, 'There are people in England who are born to give orders and there are people who are born to take them.' It's true, isn't it? A boy of eighteen, public school, he's had two years as a fag and another two years going up. Then he either was or wasn't selected to be first a house prefect then a school prefect. He rightly or wrongly was given responsibility at a very early age.

For the first time, you were really in command of a couple of hundred men – four platoons – perhaps four or five officers under you, in my case sometimes they were older. You ran your own show. You were in command not merely of the fighting side, but the domestic side of it, the economic side, the human side and everything else. To have that responsibility at twenty is a tremendous spur and achievement.

Sergeant Ernest Bryan
17th Battalion, King's Liverpool Regiment
I asked the brigadier if it was possible for his brigade major to put our equipment on, and he said certainly. So I got two privates, Lewis gunners, to put everything on him – bombs in the pockets, sandbags, spade, kit, rations, extra ammunition round the neck – all of it. Then I said,

'How did you feel, Sir?' and the brigade major said, 'It's a hell of a weight.' So I said, 'You haven't started yet! You forgot the rifle, you've got to put that up, and how are you going to carry it, slung over your shoulders? You can't, because you've got to have it in your hand ready, but you can't take it in your left hand because in that you've got a pannier which weighs 46 lb . . . There's a farm field at the back of here that's just being ploughed – try walking 100 yards and see how you feel, and that's a playground to what we'll all have to go over on the Somme.' He said, 'You feel very strongly about this,' and I said, 'Wouldn't you, Sir? Wouldn't anybody?'

Lance Sergeant Charles Quinnell
9th Battalion, Royal Fusiliers

Sixty men and two senior NCOs out of each battalion had to be labourers for the RE mining parties. We were billeted in French barracks in Béthune, and the idea was that three parties of thirty men would attend to each mine. There were three mines at Givenchy, known as Ducksbill 1, Ducksbill 2 and Ducksbill 3.

As you walked along the trench all you saw of the mine was a wooden-framed doorway about four feet high and two wide. Behind it was a staircase that went thirty feet underground and opened up into a room about eight feet by eight. In the centre of that room was a four-feet-square shaft, and over the top of that was a wooden windlass and a rope. The shaft went down another twenty feet or so. At the bottom of the shaft was another doorway facing the German lines, and that was the entrance to the tunnel. The tunnels were a continuation of this wooden framework that went straight ahead under the German lines.

Now these lads were miners, they were sent from mining districts such as Staffordshire, Leicester, Yorkshire and Northumberland, and they were really masters with their tools. Their principal tool was a bayonet, and they would stick that into the face then with a twist of the wrist bring out a big cheese of clay, which was put in the sandbags and passed along the tunnel to the bottom of the windlass. That was then wound up and an endless chain of men took them up the staircase and threw them over the top.

Every now and again we'd have to stop work, and we'd always leave one man down there at the face, who'd sit on a sandbag with a stethoscope pressed up against the wall, so he could hear the Germans working. If he could hear the Germans working you knew you were quite safe, it was when he didn't hear a noise you knew the Germans were going to blow. One day I crept up to the chap who was listening, and whispered, could I have a listen? He handed the stethoscope to me and I could distinctly hear the Germans talking.

It was clay there, and while these timber frames were very good every joint leaked, and as you were bending down all the time and they were only four feet high your back got absolutely sodden because it was drip, drip, drip on you all the time. We pumped the mine for days on end but couldn't make any impression on the water. The bottom tunnel was absolutely filled and it started coming up the shaft. This puzzled the RE officer, who went out one night and found a crater immediately above the tunnel. The Germans had been pumping water out of their mine out into this crater, so of course we were getting the full benefit of it. So he cut the German hoses and that had an immediate difference and we got our mine clear of water.

They were a rough lot, but by God these miners were brave men. They used to mooch into the trench, they had a rifle but they didn't know how to fire it. They weren't supposed to, they were just miners. You could always tell a miner, he never bothered to clean his buttons. He was a miner, he wasn't one of these posh soldiers.

We had a sergeant who came to us when the Dardanelles were evacuated, a very regimental type of man. His first day in the trenches two of these miners slummocked along into the front line – they used to walk along with their heads down and took no notice of us and we took no notice of them. Anyway, this sergeant didn't know who they were and he yelled out 'Halt!' Then when they didn't attempt to halt, he gave the order again, but when they didn't obey he brought up his rifle and bang, he shot the first man through the head. Then he did exactly the same with the other man, so a bullet went through both of their heads. He killed them stone dead. He was later court-martialled and reduced to corporal.

These Northumberland Fusiliers are in jubilant mood after capturing German gas masks and helmets at St. Eloi.

Corporal Clifford Lane
1st Battalion, Hertfordshire Regiment
They'd get down to where they thought was near enough under the German line, then they'd have a gallery either side. The idea was not only to blow up the German mine but prevent them blowing you up. And we used to have to go down there when the mine was finished, with a candle and a rifle, and sit there for two hours, and listen to see whether the Germans were mining round about. And in fact they used to break into our mine sometimes. When they did that they'd pour gas into it, that would kill anybody. The Germans always had gas and they used it. I think that was one of the worst experiences, the claustrophobic effect of sitting down there for two hours. If our people were shelling you could hear the 'bomp' going over there, and there you were listening, tensed up, to hear whether they were going to break through. Two hours of that was quite a strain.

Gunner Leonard Ounsworth
124 Heavy Battery, Royal Garrison Artillery
I remember a most unusual thing when we were out in the open before the Somme battle. There was a bank, about two feet high, with just a bit of shelter from the morning breeze, and there was very heavy dew in the morning. This was evening, the sun was going down, and suddenly there was a swarm of huge beetles, each about an inch long, coming from the enemy side just above ground level. Where they'd come from or where they were going I don't know, but they never deviated. In the end we moved a few yards either side of this stream of huge beetles. They marched along for half an hour or more.

Lieutenant W. E. Walters-Symons
Royal Garrison Artillery
The initial softening bombardment, for the battle of July the 1st, extended over a period of seven days. In a howitzer battery we were given daily programmes for the destruction of earthworks, and portions of trenches which had to be carefully ranged on, and subsequently annihilated. The enemy trench system was usually in the form of a very

strong front line, according to the configuration of the ground, and support line anything between 200 and 400 yards in the rear. The two were connected by communication trenches, and behind the support line there was a reserve line somewhere between 300 and 500 yards away. All this had to be dealt with, trench junctions demolished and a general annihilation of the area in which the enemy was living.

The task was carried out each day and meanwhile, while the heavier guns were annihilating earthworks, the field artillery were busy cutting the dense wire protecting the German front line, endeavouring to cut paths for our assaulting infantry at zero hour. We fired about 800 to 1,000 rounds per day, the equivalent of many tons. It took twelve men to man an 8-inch howitzer, the shell of which weighed 200 lb., and the preservation of manpower necessitated careful reliefs which took place every four hours.

At 5:30 the barrage came down. It consisted of light artillery on the front line coupled with light howitzers. Three hundred yards beyond that came down the heavier natures. The 6-inch, the 60-pounder, the 8-inch, the 9.2s, and the 12-inch and the 15-inch howitzers were allotted special targets and strong points such as fortified villages. Within a few moments the air vibrated with the concussion.

Lieutenant Stefan Westmann
German Medical Officer

For a full week we were under incessant bombardment. Day and night, the shells came upon us. Our dugouts crumbled. They would fall on top of us and we'd have to dig ourselves and our comrades out. Sometimes we'd find them suffocated or smashed to pulp. Soldiers in the bunkers became hysterical – they wanted to run out, and fights developed to keep them in the comparative safety of our deep bunkers. Even the rats became hysterical and came into our flimsy shelters to seek refuge from this terrific artillery fire.

For seven days and seven nights we had nothing to eat and nothing to drink while shell after shell burst upon us.

Lieutenant Colonel Alfred Irwin
8th Battalion, East Surrey Regiment

We had a lot of warning that the battle of the Somme was coming. It was such a big show, and the first of its kind. I'm quite certain the Boche knew as much about it as we did. He knew when we were coming, and if he hadn't the barrage would have told him, as for the two or three days before the Somme it was intensive, in order to break up the wire in front of the front line.

We were all very young and optimistic, and for myself, I didn't think much about the future. I took it for granted that the wire would be cut, that we'd massacre the Boche in their front line, get to our objective and then be sent to do something else next day.

I was battalion commander on the first day and it was difficult to know exactly what to do. One's instinct was to get on with the chaps, and to see what was going on. On the other hand, we'd been warned over and over again that officers' lives must not be thrown away in doing something they oughtn't – in fact that commanding officers should lead from behind, and only go forward when the attack had lost its impetus. And that's what I tried to do.

Captain Nevill was commanding B Company, and a few days before the battle he came to me with a suggestion. He said that as he and his men were all equally ignorant of what their conduct would be when they got into action, he thought it might be helpful – as he had 400 yards to go and he knew it would be covered by machine-gun fire – if he could furnish each platoon with a football and allow them to kick it forward and follow it.

I sanctioned the idea on condition that he and his officers really kept command of their units and didn't allow it to develop into a rush after the ball. If a man came across the football, he could kick it forward but he mustn't chase after it. I think myself, it did help them enormously, it took their minds off it.

The 1st Lancashire Fusiliers fix bayonets before the attack on Beaumont-Hamel in July.

Captain Charles Carrington
1/5th Battalion, Warwickshire Regiment

I got up at dawn, I was acting-adjutant of my battalion on the morning of the 1st of July. I went up to take to my command post in the trenches, from where we could see over the country between Gommecourt and Serre. Messages were coming in from the front companies to say that they were all in order and that everything was right. We tested our lines back to the artillery. I can only say that I have never been so excited in my life. This was like a boy going to play for the first time in his life. That's how I felt. The noise rose to a crescendo such as I'd never heard before. A noise which made all bombardments that we'd heard in the previous day seem like nothing at all. And the effect of the bombardment created a sort of hysterical feeling.

Fusilier Victor Packer
1st Battalion, Royal Irish Fusiliers

We had been in and out of the line at Beaumont-Hamel and we'd watched the sappers and miners at work. They had sapped out under the German lines and used trolleys to bring back the spoil, which had to be disposed of away from the view of German planes. They packed 200 tons of high explosive as a charge. At about 7 a.m. La Boisselle went up.

The whole village actually lifted up out of the earth. First of all there was a tremendous shake, the earth moved about a yard backwards and forwards, and there were lots of receding vibrations until it became still again. By that time we were all lying flat on the ground, but we got up in time to see the whole of this place lifting up, and I suppose because it was such a big thing it seemed to be incredibly slow. It went up as slowly as anything and whole houses starting splitting and falling apart in the air. Great elm trees were going up, their roots turning upside down, they must have gone up a tremendous height in the sky. When they reached the top they disintegrated into bits and pieces and dust and clouds, and although we were so far away as it fell, we got pieces of brick and masonry falling into the trench around us.

Lieutenant Cecil Lewis
Royal Flying Corps

During the build-up period we were taking photographs of the lines to see what new digging had been done, what the effect of the bombardment was and so on. Meanwhile the batteries were being piled in, night after night, as soon as it fell dark. One had a tremendous feeling of war and what it meant when everything was in position and they began to build up towards the main bombardment. I did many evening patrols when the whole of the ground beneath the darkening evening was just like a veil of flashing sequins, but each one was a gun.

Two days before the attack opened we had to get some photographs that were badly needed. We were down to about a thousand feet in murky weather, with a cloud bank overhead and this grey swathe on one side, and when one saw these continuous flashes one had the feeling they were firing at us – this was ridiculous, of course, but quite terrifying at the time. Then having finished the photos and got out of the buffeting one thought – well, heavens alive, I've come through. Because many of my friends were hit by these barrages, you know, destroyed by a direct hit from a passing shell.

It was a fantastic sight when the hurricane bombardment started because every gun we had – and there were thousands of them – had all been let loose at once. You could hear the guns above the roar of the aircraft like rain on a windowpane. And then at 8 o'clock there was the blast on the Boisselle salient, and suddenly the whole earth heaved and up from the ground came what looked like two enormous cypress trees. Great, dark, cone-shaped silhouettes which lifted the earth three, four, five thousand feet up. We watched this happening and a moment later, of course, we struck the repercussion wave of the blast and it flung us backwards.

Captain Charles Carrington
1/5th Battalion, Warwickshire Regiment

At zero I sent back a message to brigade headquarters to say we were ready and we were going to deliver our smoke cloud. Then the moment we could see the outburst of smoke and gas from our front line, driving and blowing in the right direction towards the Germans, somebody shouted, 'There they go!' I looked over to the left and here were the London Scottish who were on our left, running forward across the three or four hundred yards of green grass towards Gommecourt Wood. Then they vanished into the smoke. And then there was nothing left but noise. And after this we saw nothing and we knew nothing. And we lived in a world of noise, simply noise.

Trooper R. J. Mason
10th Hussars

We crouched in the shallow narrow trench almost shoulder to shoulder. I was next to an officer and had to get him something out of his own haversack because he couldn't turn round. Shortly after he told us we had only five minutes to go.

When the whistle went everyone climbed up the scaling ladders and through the holes in the front of the trench. Once outside, we formed up in line with our rifles in front of us and started the move forward. It was two or three hundred yards to the enemy line. We moved forward slowly, we didn't run, and for the first short distance there seemed to be no casualties, but soon it became apparent that men were going down rather thicker than one realised.

Then we came to a sunken road that had to be crossed at an angle. It was, unfortunately, a spot marked by German artillery and machine-gunners, so we very soon afterwards found that only a few of us were still going forward. My officer called across to me and said, 'You stick to me, and I'll stick to you.' I said 'Right!' but immediately lost sight of him. I don't know what happened to him. At that point, to my great surprise a hare ran along in front of me, its eyes bulging with fear, but I don't think it was half as frightened as I was.

Hoping that reinforcements would soon be coming along I just remained there, firing at the Germans, until, fortunately, either my efforts or other people's made them get down out of sight. Then I saw I had no one around me, that I was the only one left standing. I thought well, I can't carry on like this, so I got down in a shallow shell-hole and began to look around to see what was happening. I then realised that the wire in front of us was quite uncut, despite the intense bombardments of the previous week, and the Germans were firing at us through holes in their front line. I immediately replied by firing back at them – I had bombs but the distance was four times too far to throw them – and as I fired, they eventually got down out of sight and did not appear again.

I was hoping that reinforcements would be coming along so that we could attempt to go forward again but no one came. No one could get through that barrage.

Lieutenant Stefan Westmann
German Medical Officer

Then the British Army went over the top. The very moment we felt their artillery fire was directed against the reserve positions, our machine-gunners crawled out of the bunkers, red-eyed and dirty, covered in the blood of their fallen comrades, and opened up a terrific fire.

Captain Alfred Irwin
8th Battalion, East Surrey Regiment

They went forward shouting with such energy, kicking the football ahead of them. But so quickly Neville and his second in command were both killed plus his company sergeant-major. I picked up all the chaps I could and went over the parapet by myself. I stood well out in the open and said, 'Come on, come on, come on,' and they all came on quite smoothly.

Lieutenant W. E. Walters-Symons
Royal Garrison Artillery

Assaulting troops of the 32nd Division and the 8th Division left their trenches and walked up to within 150 yards of the barrage as formed on the ground. At zero hour the barrage proceeded into the enemy line in steps of 100 yards at a time. The assaulting troops followed the barrage and on reaching the enemy front-line trench descended into it and had hand-to-hand battles with the occupants.

The barrage crept forward and the assaulting troops followed it until the support line was reached, when similar hand-to-hand fighting took place. The barrage then crept at a slow rate of 100 yards per minute to the extent of gun range. At first the assault seemed to be going very, very favourably. One could observe the assaulting troops tackling the support and reserve lines. Such being the case, 'M' battery, which was near my observation post, galloped into no man's land so as to give closer supporting fire to the advancing infantry.

Unfortunately, during the heat of the attack the German troops had not been mopped up out of their deep dugouts, some of which were twenty-five to thirty feet deep. They recovered from the initial shock, came up into their trenches and quickly established frontal and rear fire; frontal fire to prevent any support troops helping the assaulting infantry, and rear fire to obliterate those that had been successful.

Captain Alan Hanbury-Sparrow
2nd Battalion, Royal Berkshire Regiment
I thought I saw that our front line had got into the German trenches and reported as such to the division. I said, 'I can't really see what's happening, I'm going forward.' I got a message to stay where I was and presently, as a barrage went forward, the air cleared and I could see. In the distance I saw the heaps of dead in no man's land, and the barrage bounding on towards Pozières, the third German line. I saw Germans almost standing up in their trenches, firing and sniping at those who had taken refuge in the shell-holes. I waited further, then I saw another brigade that was ordered to resume the attack. Providentially for that brigade the order was soon cancelled, and the realisation came that what had really happened was one of the most enormous disasters to have befallen the 8th Division.

Captain Philip Neame
15th Field Company, Royal Engineers
At Gommecourt, I was with the 56 London Division. We attacked successfully and captured the German trenches. The division on our left was mown down by German machine-gun fire – they never got into the German trenches at all – and the division on our right was stopped by

artillery barrages. The result was that we got in but were then isolated all day. We had captured our objectives but then had to withdraw at night.

Captain Alfred Irwin
8th Battalion, East Surrey Regiment

Eventually we reached the German third reserve line. We were so lamentably few that there was very little we could do that night, so I posted the men as well as I could and while we were heavily shelled we weren't attacked, and the next day we were relieved. We'd come down from 800 men to something under 200 in that attack, and it seemed to me a dreadful waste of life.

All my best chaps had gone. We buried eight young officers in one grave before we left. It was a terrible massacre. I think the attack should have been called off until the wire had been cut. I think they ought to have known what the condition of the wire was through their intelligence officers before we ever got to July the 1st.

Lieutenant Montague Cleeve
Royal Garrison Artillery

One thing I shall never forget was my first experience of dead bodies. On the first day at Albert the weather was very hot, and I was sent up to an observation post. I went with a marvellous officer who was later killed, a splendid young subaltern called Priddy. We found we literally couldn't walk along the trenches without treading on dead bodies, German and British. The stench and the flies were simply appalling. That was one of the most miserable memories I have of the Somme. It was pathetic really. Eventually one just got over it and thought nothing of it. We couldn't help it, we were alive and that's what mattered. And being alive, we jolly well had to get on with it.

Corporal Clifford Lane
1st Battalion, Hertfordshire Regiment

We took over a trench somewhere near Thiepval. It was very hot weather at the end of the summer, this trench was full of dead Germans and they'd been there some time. Some were sitting on the steps of these deep dugouts, which went thirty or forty feet underground, others were lying on the trench floor. We'd seen plenty of dead people before, but we'd never seen anything like this. They were all different colours, from pallid grey to green and black. And they were bloated – that's how a corpse goes in time, they get blown up with gases. We thought it was funny, really, which shows how your mind can get inured to such situations. We started making up the trench and had to tread on one of these blokes, who was partly buried. Every time we trod on him his tongue would come out, which caused great amusement amongst our people.

Private Arthur Baxter
51st Machine Gun Company, Machine Gun Corps
Some of our gunners, at night, they had to go out to no-man's land and stop there all night. We had an Irishman named Mick Flemand on one of our guns and he's out in no-man's land this night, two men with him, and a shell come that killed two and never touched him. During the night, he stuck that, alone, and a German officer and a German sergeant come creeping to steal a gun. They thought they'd killed all three, you see. Mick, he's got a revolver, that day, he let them get right onto him and he shot them both dead. He was still there when daylight came. Two pals laid out dead and two old Jerries. He got the Military Medal for that. Poor old boy, he couldn't neither read nor write. He'd come from Ireland and I used to read his letters for him. He come from Southern Ireland, they had a terrible job there in 1916, didn't they? When he had his leave from France, he daren't go home, you know. There was a place in London where the likes of him went. He told us he'd be killed if he went home, being in the British Army, you see.

Lieutenant Montague Cleeve
Royal Garrison Artillery
I came across a sergeant lying dead on the ground with his hand on an open bible. It was a Douai bible and from that I knew he was a Catholic. The shrapnel was pouring over our heads, but I closed his eyes, then closed the book and put it in my pocket before crawling back

to the front line. Later on I took his address from it and sent it home to his widow. I kept up with her for quite a long time.

Sergeant Charles Quinnell
9th Battalion, Royal Fusiliers
The shelling had eased off a lot when I spotted two khaki figures about fifty yards away. I tried to shout to them but by then my voice had dried up. I realised I'd never attract their attention that way, so I picked up a stone and threw it in their direction, and they looked up. An officer drew out his revolver and I thought, 'Oh, this won't do, I have no tunic on.' So I reached down and got my tunic and waved that backwards and forwards to identify myself and they came over. They were very sympathetic and asked me a few questions and then this officer said, 'Good Lord man, your regiment has been gone from here four days.' I said, 'Yes I know, I've been here for four days.'

Private Charles Taylor
13th Battalion, Yorks and Lancs
I started crawling towards our lines, and I had never seen so many dead men clumped together. That was all I could see and I thought to myself, 'All the world's dead – they're all dead – they're all dead.' That's all I could think as I crawled along. Everywhere I passed, to my left and right were dead men laying on the ground.

Corporal Reginald Leonard Haine
1st Battalion, Honourable Artillery Company
I saw the effect of the mines. I saw the crater at La Boisselle. It really petrified me, the size of it. I mean, it was as big as a cathedral.

Gunner Leonard Ounsworth
124 Heavy Battery, Royal Garrison Artillery
We saw some infantry transport come up, and there was a lieutenant quartermaster there. I went over and he said, 'How are you off for grub?' so I said, 'We've only got biscuits and bully.' He gave us some bread and butter, jam, tea and sugar. He was a chap who was getting on for fifty, I

Q912

Three soldiers show the camera the depth of the crater at La Boisselle after the gigantic explosion.

should think, a lieutenant quartermaster, not a fighting man at all, and yet he'd brought up all these rations. He was practically in tears. He said his lads wouldn't need it. You see when you lost men, it was a day or two before you could stop their rations coming up. The Army Service Corps would still be sending up the rations of so many men while you might have lost half of them. And what happened to all that grub? You'd live like fighting cocks on what was left for a day or two.

In the evening Noble and Robbins and myself went up to Trones Wood. There was no trees left intact at all, just stumps and treetops and barbed wire all mixed up together, and bodies all over the place. Jerries and ours.

Robbins pulled up some undergrowth and as we fished our way through there was this dead Jerry, his whole hip shot away and all his guts out and flies over it. Robbins just had to step back, and then this leg that was up in a tree became dislodged and fell on his head. He vomited on the spot. Good Lord, it was terrible.

Private Norman Demuth
1/5th Battalion, London Regiment

Sitting in the front line on a firing step was very uncomfortable, with nothing to do and not much to talk about. It made one sit and think much more deeply than one would have done otherwise. I think it made you consider life much more seriously, whatever age you were. I used to find myself sitting and thinking about God quite a lot, and I was never as afraid of dying, or being dead, as I was of being maimed. I was scared stiff of being maimed, but I didn't mind dying because I knew something was going to happen afterwards. I didn't know what it was properly, but I thought, well, we shall find out. I used to sit and think quite deeply about God and I felt perfectly certain that he existed, you see one very often felt something behind one. And I suppose my philosophy was that it was a very nice world to live in, and if we chose to muck it up it was our own fault.

From a practical point of view there was no religion in the front line, although our unit padre used to come and visit us quite a lot. But he was never allowed to stay in one place too long because he got in the way. Behind the line there were the usual church services and then there was a church parade on a Sunday, in which the whole battalion sang lusty hymns to a wheezy harmonium and the padre preached a sermon that you couldn't hear anyhow.

Then when you were on rest, the padre would come round to the billets – ours was very good indeed. And when I was wounded and got to hospital I thanked heaven for the padres, they were wonderful. They came round and took down your name and address and wrote your casualty postcards and generally looked after you. They never ranted, they never told you what a sinner you were or anything like that, and if they said a prayer it was a very short one.

Captain Herbert Sulzbach
German Artillery

One summer evening soon after the battle of the Somme had started, the guns were rumbling and there was a terrible noise of battle in our ears. Yet where we lay, just thirty metres from the trenches, there were mountains and peace, and hardly any shooting. We could see the French soldiers, and one night a Frenchman started to sing – he was a wonderful tenor. None of us dared to shoot and suddenly we were all looking out from the trenches and applauding, and the Frenchman said 'Merci.' It was peace in the middle of war, and the strange thing was, that just a few kilometres northwards the terrible battle of the Somme was going on.

Marjorie Llewellyn
Schoolgirl in Sheffield

Very soon we began to get the wounded arriving in the city from the Somme battle. The teachers' training college was turned into the Third Northern General Hospital and staffed by consultants from the other Sheffield hospitals. There were soldiers in some of the other General Hospitals, of course, but there were far too many of them coming in to be taken by those alone. As you can imagine, when the men got to the stage of being able to walk around a little in their hospital blue, they were made much of, and didn't lack for invitations out for tea. We were very, very proud of our boys.

Q660

Men of the Royal Fusiliers enjoy a rest after the attack on La Boisselle on July 7.

Gunner Leonard Ounsworth
124 Heavy Battery, Royal Garrison Artillery

When we came out of Manchester station I'd never seen anything like it. The crowd was such that they had mounted police to hold it back. The more seriously wounded were loaded into ambulances while all the walking cases went into civilian cars. I was in a 12/16 Sunbeam open tourer with a gentleman and his son in the front and sacks of straw filling the rear.

We drove through Manchester at a walking pace and the cars were mobbed. The chap with me was very small and the crowd thought he was a drummer-boy so he got all the attention, but I learnt afterwards he was a twenty-seven-year-old jockey and had two or three kids.

But you can gauge the hysteria when I tell you they were giving us such things as balaclava helmets in the middle of July. They gave us cigarettes, sweets, all sorts of things – enough to stock a shop – but balaclava helmets, I ask you! Of all the stupid things. The route was lined all the way to Rochdale, thirteen miles away, and when we arrived there were more people waiting to receive us. There were 690 of us that went into that hospital that day, and it only had beds for 200.

I had the time of my life at Rochdale. It was a civilian hospital, under the Second General at Manchester. When we were convalescing we used to go down in the town of an evening. We weren't supposed to, we were meant to be in at four, but the nurses never said a word when you came in late, just 'Naughty boy' or 'Get to bed.'

We used to come in through a back entrance. There was a tall iron railing fence, and we'd bent open a couple of the bars wide enough to get through. Well, a Dr. Scarr got to know about this and so one night he was waiting for us. There was four of us coming back and one of these chaps was an Irishman, Paddy. Scarr said something about where had we been, and Paddy started on him, 'Big fine man like you, you ought to be in the Army, etc, etc.' He didn't allow Scarr to get a word in edgeways, while we kept sidling further on and eventually disappeared. We never heard any more about it.

Captain Charles Carrington
1/5th Battalion, Warwickshire Regiment
This world of the trenches, which had built up for so long and which seemed to be going on forever, seemed like the real world, and it was entirely a man's world. Women had no part in it, and when one went on leave one escaped out of the man's world into the women's world. But one found that however pleased one was to see one's girlfriend, one could never somehow quite get through, however nice they were. If the girl didn't quite say the right thing one was curiously upset. One got annoyed by the attempts of well-meaning people to sympathise, which only reflected the fact that they didn't really understand at all. So there was almost a sense of relief when one went back into the man's world, which seemed the realest thing that could be imagined.

Private Norman Demuth
1/5th Battalion, London Regiment
One thing I found when I eventually got home was that my father and my mother didn't seem in the least interested in what had happened. They hadn't any conception of what it was like, and on occasions when I did talk about it, my father would argue points of fact that he couldn't possibly have known about because he wasn't there. I think his was probably the approach of the public at large They didn't know – how could they? They knew that people came back on leave covered with mud and lice, but they had no idea of what kind of danger we were in. I think they felt the war was one continual sort of cavalry charge; that one spent all day and all night chasing Germans or them chasing us. Had they realised the strain of sitting in a trench and waiting for something to drop on one's head, I don't think they would have considered it was just play. And of course the general idea was that England couldn't possibly lose.

Mabel Lethbridge
Munitions worker
When my father and brothers, uncles, relatives and friends came home on leave and were staying at or visiting our house, I noticed a strange lack of ability to communicate with us. They couldn't tell us what it was really like. They would perhaps make a joke, but you'd feel it sounded hollow, as there was nothing to laugh about. They were restless at home, they didn't want to stay, they wanted to get back to the Front. They always expressed a desire to finish it.

Private Edmund Blunden
11th Battalion, Royal Sussex Regiment
I became increasingly uncertain of the value of returning to England for periods of leave. Of course being welcomed back and sitting down again with one's own, and going for a little trot and seeing a few people left whom one knew, that was a great thing. Yet not being able to discourse about the things which were at the forefront of one's feelings, that was difficult, and perhaps we had, over on the Western Front, placed too much emphasis on certain things.

I felt a little disconsolate after the first excitement of seeing everything in its usual corner. And then I didn't feel very happy about being treated as if I was a man of means because I had a uniform on. But it was chiefly that I felt I might as well not have been there, in all that muck, for all the notice that was paid to me.

Such was the attitude in England, but I ought to have known. It was everybody for himself in a way. And I suppose there was no reason why any one of us millions – because there were four million in Flanders and France in the end – why we should have been favoured with a nod and a bow and a 'Thank you very much,' just for having got a bit muddier and more out of touch with good manners than we had been.

Private Norman Demuth
1/5th Battalion, London Regiment
Almost the last feather I received was on a bus. I was sitting near the door when I became aware of two women on the other side talking at

me, and I thought to myself, 'Oh Lord, here we go again.' I didn't pay much attention. However, I suppose I must have caught their eye in some way because one leant forward and produced a feather and said, 'Here's a gift for a brave soldier.' I took it and said, 'Thank you very much – I wanted one of those.' Then I took my pipe out of my pocket and put this feather down the stem and everything and worked it in a way I've never worked a pipe cleaner before. When it was filthy I pulled it out and said, 'You know we didn't get these in the trenches,' and handed it back to her. She instinctively put out her hand and took it, so there she was sitting with this filthy pipe cleaner in her hand and all the other people on the bus began to get indignant. Then she dropped it and got up to get out, but we were nowhere near a stopping place and the bus went on quite a long way while she got well and truly barracked by the rest of the people on the bus. I sat back and laughed like mad.

Marjorie Llewellyn
Schoolgirl in Sheffield
Schooldays were very different once the war had started. We had great maps in each of the classrooms and every day we used flags to mark the progress of the war on both fronts – in Gallipoli and then on the Somme when that started. There was a keen interest taken in this because we could see how it was progressing. We had evening assembly every night and special prayers were said for the soldiers. We always sang the last verse of 'Eternal Father' and then the hymn 'Holy Father in Thy Mercy,' and then said the prayer 'Lighten our Darkness.' This went on every night all through the war.

Mary Brough-Robertson
Munitions worker
Munitions workers were just about the lowest form of life in the eyes of the general public. We were supposed to make a great deal of money, and as other people didn't make so much they called us all sorts of things, even shouted things after us. If they knew what you were they had all sorts of nasty things to say to you.

I can't speak of what people made making shells, but I know the wage for filling them was only twenty-five shillings a week for a girl, which was not a great sum. In fact you couldn't manage with that amount, as you had to pay for all your meals, you didn't get any free. But when they finally went on strike the money was raised by 5/6d. a week and they introduced a bonus system. You filled so many shells, and after that you got a bonus for how many more you filled. This was a bad thing because it led to carelessness. The shells would come back to us as either too heavy or too light, and that was a very bad thing because they might fall short when they were fired.

The most depressing thing about the war was the casualty lists. Every time you opened a paper it seemed to be nothing but casualty lists, and you always found people in them you knew. Then everybody wore black, and that was depressing too, black, black, black everywhere. Boys who came home didn't try and depress you, they tried to be as cheerful as they could. But they came home dirty and tired and wouldn't tell you much about anything, your own brothers wouldn't anyway. Some of the others might tell you a bit more, and you knew how appalling all the mud and the dirt was, and you just felt that it was going on and on for ever, and that we never seemed to get any nearer the end of it.

Trooper George Jameson
1st Battalion, Northumberland Hussars

I'd give full marks to the Salvation Army. They had one place I used to drop into often. And it was a most uncomfortable spot to be in. It was at Vimy. The main road came through Vimy and down on to the plain that way. Well, you didn't take that main road if you could avoid it, it was under constant shellfire. At night it got even worse, as the Germans reckoned that transport used it at night, so they would keep strafing it the whole time. But tucked into the side of the hill was the Salvation Army. And they used to have tea and whatever going all hours of the day. How they survived there I don't know. Wonderful people. In the middle of nowhere to suddenly walk into a place and get a piping hot pot of tea, it was a great reviver.

1916

Howard Marten
Conscientious objector

The ranks of the No-Conscription Fellowship were made up of men from every conceivable walk of life. You had all sorts of religious groups, from the Salvation Army to Seventh-Day Adventists, Church of England and Roman Catholics. Then you had the more politically minded: the Independent Labour Party and different degrees of Socialists. Then a very curious group of what I used to call the artistically minded – artists, musicians, all that. They had a terrific repugnance of war.

One or two of the officers and NCOs were quite reasonable men. There was a little Scottish regimental sergeant-major, and he almost had tears in his eyes. He said, 'You don't know what you're up against. You'll have an awful time.' He was genuinely concerned at the trouble that we were going to meet.

We were forever being threatened with the death sentence. Over and over again we'd be marched up and read out a notice: some man being sentenced to death through disobedience at the Front. Whether they were true cases I don't know. It was all done with the idea of intimidating us. But we wouldn't have taken that line unless we were prepared to face that situation, we realised that it was sufficiently serious.

Finally we had the second court martial, which took a whole day. It all had to be gone through all over again. Eventually we were taken out to the parade ground. There was a big concourse of men lined up in an immense square. Under escort we were taken out, one by one, to the middle of the square. I was the first of them, and until my verdict was known nobody knew exactly what was going to happen. Then the officer in charge of the proceedings read out the various crimes and misdemeanours – refusing to obey a lawful command, disobedience at Boulogne and so on. Then: 'The sentence of the court is to suffer death by being shot.'

There was a suitable pause, and I thought, 'Well, that's that.' Then he said, 'Confirmed by the Commander in Chief,' which double-sealed it. There was another long pause – 'But subsequently commuted to

Howard Marten, Conscientious Objector.

penal servitude for ten years.' And that was that. The thing that interested me particularly was that penal servitude meant your return to
England, into the hands of the civil authorities at a civil prison.

It was all very strange. You had a feeling of being outside yourself, as
if it wasn't affecting you personally, that you were just looking on at the
proceedings. It was very curious.

Captain Graham Greenwell
4th Battalion, Oxford and Buckinghamshire Light Infantry

When we were out at rest behind the line during the battle of the
Somme, I was told one morning that a private in my company, who had
been out since the beginning of the war, was unfit to go on parade. But
the doctor had passed him fit and said he should be on the parade.
When I went to see him I came to the conclusion that he was in a very
serious mental condition. I told him he was not to go on parade and I
reported the matter to the commanding officer. He told me that it was
not for me to decide, only the medical officer, and that he should be
made to get up and go on parade. Later in the morning this chap shot
himself.

This incident shook me very much. Here was a case where undoubt-
edly the battle had been too much for the man. But if everybody had
behaved like him, the Army would have disintegrated.

Corporal Sidney Amatt
7th Battalion, Essex Regiment

They never asked for volunteers, they'd say, 'You, you, you and you,'
and you suddenly found yourself in a raiding party. They went over at
night, in silence, and the parties were always arranged in the same way.
Number one was the rifleman, who carried a rifle, a bayonet, fifty
rounds of ammunition and nothing else. The next man was a grenade
thrower and he carried a haversack full of Mills hand bombs. The next
man was also a bomb-thrower, he helped the first man replace his stock
when it was exhausted. And the last man was a rifle and bayonet man,
and all he carried was a rifle and fifty rounds of ammunition in a ban-
dolier slung over his shoulder.

The idea was to crawl underneath the German wire and jump into their front-line trench. Then you'd dispose of whoever was holding it, by bayonet if possible, without making any noise, or by clubbing over the head with the butt. Once you'd established yourself in the trench you'd wend your way round each bay. A rifleman would go first, and he'd stop at the next bay, which was normally unoccupied. The bomb-thrower would then throw a grenade towards the next bay, and when that exploded the rifleman who was leading would dash into the trench and dispose of any occupants that were still left. And so we'd go on until we'd cleared the whole trench.

Two or three other parties would be doing the same thing until we'd cleared about a hundred yards of trench between us and brought back some prisoners. Anybody that had survived any grenades would be more or less stupefied, so we'd disarm them and get them back so they could identify which regiment they were with. They'd be taken, first of all, to the unit's headquarters to be interviewed by one of the officers. Then they'd be taken right back to brigade and divisional headquarters to be questioned by interrogating officers hoping to glean whatever information they could about who was holding the line in front of us.

It was usually the biggest man in the raiding party who was chosen to lead, because he had the best chance of fighting the Germans, who were nearly all much bigger than us. All the other smaller chaps were used to throw grenades. But the raiding parties were rarely successful because by the time we got halfway across no man's land and come up against the Jerry wire, the Germans had usually realised something was going on and opened up their machine-guns on that area. So we'd have to scuttle back to our own lines before we all got killed.

I got in several German trenches but only one that was manned. The Germans nearly always held the higher ground and so had constructed dugouts, which they retired to after any strafing by our artillery, leaving the trenches more or less vacant. But if one of them was occupied, once you'd got in the trench amongst them the Germans nearly always put their hands up and shouted 'Kamerad!' without any opposition at all.

Lieutenant Montague Cleeve
Royal Garrison Artillery

It was a complete and utter surprise to the Germans that we had ever devised such a thing as a tank. They were so shattered when they first appeared on the Somme that all resistance in the German section where they were used collapsed. The mistake we made then was not to have prepared for this lack of opposition. We should have had our cavalry all ready to take over from the tanks and wipe the whole thing out. We could have turned the flank of the Germans in no time. But the success of the tanks took us by surprise and we were so ill-prepared that nobody followed them up.

The German resistance collapsed until they began shooting at the tanks when they were miles ahead of the former British front line. Then they had to come limping back, one by one, and that was an end to the thing.

The tanks had a complete walk-through. I remember seeing one moving at Pozières, it just crawled on and on – bumping into shell-holes, nose up, then climbing out, then diving down into another, then diving up again and not quite making it. That gave the Germans the opportunity they needed to direct their machine-guns at it, and it soon became a complete wreck by everybody shooting at it.

I don't know what happened to that crew, but the tanks represented a missed opportunity. Had we only followed them up with cavalry, or any mobile troops, we could have got fifteen miles or so behind the German lines under their protection, then captured the German head-quarters and turned the whole result of the Somme.

Lieutenant Wilfred Staddon

The commander opened the door of the tank behind the port gun and called out to me for directions. I told him to go straight up the main street of Flers and bear right for Gueudecourt. I mentioned I didn't know where the flanks were, but I don't know whether he heard because the door was soon closed.

My attention was then diverted by a group of Germans coming out of a cellar. There were quite a lot of them and my imagination turned

A tank is guided across an old trench.

Q3544

them into an army corps. Anyhow, I saw almost at once that they were unarmed. I went along to them and as a platoon officer soon formed them into a platoon of exactly eight times four, then reluctantly spared a corporal and sent them back.

My attention then was diverted by a slow-moving biplane coming in the direction of Thiepval. I was the only man who had a red flare in my pocket, so I put it on a wall and it ignited at once. The observer in that plane could hardly help seeing it and I've no doubt he saw the tank, so in spite of all the smoke and brick dust, he probably saw this group of Germans and he put two and two together and made five.

I found myself approaching the wire protecting Flers about an hour after zero hour. There were very few company officers left – I think only two of us who actually reached the wire. The wire was only half cut but my companion, Lieutenant Chesters, urged his men forward with conspicuous gallantry, really. But he paid the penalty – he was too conspicuous and I saw him die in the wire.

The method I adopted to get through the wire was to pull it over me. Much of the time I was on my back. We got through the wire and found the approach to the Flers trench was actually a sunken road. We gathered together and rushed it. I'd already seen a white handkerchief, so perhaps that gave us a little courage. Anyhow, we got there.

There was not a little slaughter in the village – mostly it was the Germans. You could understand that we felt a bit pleased, what with all the casualties we'd lost on the way. Anyhow, it was soon got into some sort of shape, and I found myself chasing the commander. He'd shed his equipment and only had a revolver in his hand. I took aim but he spotted me, dropped it and ran. He made for a dugout and dived into it so I threw a phosphorus bomb after him. But I'd forgotten the exit so he got away and I saw him dodging behind walls again.

At that moment, a shout went up that a tank was proceeding up the high street of Flers with a group of laughing Tommies behind it. It wasn't laughing Tommies though, but a group of Germans with chattering teeth. I'd never seen chattering teeth before, but I did then. The tank, meantime, had gone farther up the road. Of course, he'd got a nice steel waistcoat, we hadn't, we were still peering behind walls. We didn't know what we were going to meet, so we were rather slower, and when we eventually got to the exit of Flers, there was nobody there but the little group who were with me.

All of a sudden a Lewis gunner shouted, 'Look Sir!' and there was my opposite number again, walking along back home with his sergeant-major. I took aim but missed them both, and they fell into a ditch. I advised my Lewis gunner not to be too lavish with his ammunition and thought no more about them.

Captain Philip Neame
15th Field Company, Royal Engineers

We were one of the first brigades ever to see a tank, because we were earmarked to go in on the second or third attack in the Somme. It was towards the middle of September and we were allotted one of the first ones to land in France, to do some training with. Everybody was staggered to see this extraordinary monster crawling over the ground.

But there was only a limited amount of training you could do with one tank, so all it really came down to was learning a suitable formation for the infantry to follow behind it. We knew it had to make gaps in the enemy barbed wire and a little column of infantry had to follow through the gap.

Everyone thought it was a terrific thing until the first battle when we actually had to do it, and then we rather lost faith because it broke down before it reached the German front line. During the exercises it had been all right, it was on decent ground at Leuze Wood (known by us as Lousy Wood) and just why it broke down I don't know. I think perhaps the track was worn out by then.

Captain Tom Adlam
7th Battalion, Beds and Herts Regiment

We'd been in the reserve when our battalion was called in to try and straighten out the line. Then just before we went up, my CO was called away so I was put in charge of the company. I was briefed at headquarters and it was impressed upon me that we had to do this at night, because they'd already tried several times in daylight and been held up by various strongpoints. So we had to get into the trench at night, then try and bomb our way to these strongpoints.

Luckily, just before we started the attack my CO came back and took over. But by then it had taken us so long to get into position it was almost daylight. I knew we weren't supposed to do this in daylight but the CO said, 'We'll get over.' The section of trench my platoon faced was only about a hundred yards away, so we did get quite a long way before the machine-guns started up.

We dived into shell-holes and I thought, 'We've got to get into this trench somehow or other.' So I went crawling along from shell-hole to shell-hole till I came to the officer in charge of the next platoon. I said, 'What do you think, father?' (We all called him Father, it was his nickname.) He said, 'I'm going to wait till it gets dark then crawl back. We can't go forward.' I said, 'Well, I think we can. Where I am, I'm not more than fifty yards from the trench.'

He shook hands with me solemnly and said, 'Goodbye, old man.' I said, 'Don't be such a damn fool. I'll be back all right.' I got back to my platoon and said to them, 'Get a bomb in your hand, pull out the pin and hold it tight. As soon as I yell 'Charge,' stand up, run two or three yards and throw it. And I think we'll get into that trench, there's practically no wire in front of it.'

And they did. They all got up and ran, and we got into our bit of trench. In it, we found bags of German bombs that looked like condensed milk cans on the top of sticks. On them was written '5 secs,' so I experimented with one. I pulled the string and said, 'I'm going to count one, two, three, before I throw it.' My servant was beside me looking over the top of the trench and he said, 'Bloody good shot, sir, hit the bugger in the chest.' I think when the Germans found their own bombs coming back at them it rather put the wind up them.

So the men brought armfuls of these bombs along, and I just went gaily along, throwing these bombs and counting 'one, two, three' each time. It was most effective. Then we got close to where the machine-gun was, and got a whole lot of bombs ready. I started throwing as fast as I could until my servant said, 'They're going, sir, they're going.' So I yelled, 'Come on, chaps, run in,' and we charged up the trench. We never caught the Germans, but we drove them out.

Eventually we got to a certain point and the CO saw two trenches leading up towards Schwaben Redoubt. And he said, 'It would be a good idea to get an advance post up there.' So they started off and a man got killed straight away. I said, 'Oh, damn it. Let me go, I can do it.' So I went on with some men and we bombed up the trench. We took more prisoners in dugouts and got our advance point out towards the enemy.

Then we went back for the night. Some grub came up and we sat down and had a meal. Then another company came up and took over from us, and we moved a quarter of a mile back. We were able to rest, then lined up again next morning. The attack on Schwaben Redoubt was going to be at 1 o'clock, and as our company had done most of the fighting the day before they put us in the last line of the attack, with three other companies in front. We got in position at twelve, and chatted away to keep our spirits up. Told dirty stories and made crude remarks. There was a nasty smell about and of course we all suggested somebody had had an accident. But it wasn't that, it was a dead body I think.

Then the shelling started and we went forward. You wouldn't think anything could have lived through the bombing that went on at Schwaben Redoubt. By the time we got close to it there was a huge mine crater there about fifty feet across. It was lined with Germans popping away at us. So I got hold of the old bombs again and started bombing them out. After a bit we got them out and started charging the trench, all my men coming on behind very gallantly. We'd got right to within striking distance of Schwaben Redoubt itself when I got a bang in my right arm and found I was bleeding. But having been a bombing officer who could throw with both arms I was able to use my left one for a time. I found I could bomb pretty well with it.

We went on for some time, holding this position and working our way up the trenches as far as we could. Then my CO came up and said, 'You're hurt, Tom.' I said, 'Only a snick in the arm.' He said, 'Let's have a look at it,' and he put a field dressing on it. He said, 'You go back, you've done enough.' So I sat down for a time, and the fighting went on.

Captain George Jameson, Royal Field Artillery, also proudly served with the Northumberland Hussars.

It was a surprise when I got the VC for my actions, because I just did a job out there, I'd never realised there was anything unusual about it. I'd been more frightened when first going to the trenches, sitting there, waiting for it all to start. But when it gets going, you remember you're in charge of a group of men, and we were taught we had to be an example to them. So you lost your sense of fear thinking about other people.

It was funny how I heard about it. I'd gone back to Colchester and had been in town for an evening out. When I got back to the mess the orderly room porter said, 'There's a lot of telegrams for you, Sir,' and there were about a dozen of them. 'Congratulations!' 'Heartiest congratulations!' 'Congratulations from all at home!' 'Congratulations from the regiment!'

So I said, 'Can you get a wire off to my father for me?' And I wrote, 'Why congratulations? I know nothing!' and sent that off. And my father wired back, 'Have heard papers are asking for a photograph of you, as you've been awarded VC.' And that's how I heard. The papers had heard on the Saturday so it could come out in the Monday papers. And on the Monday there were photographs of me all over the papers.

Gunner George Cole
3rd Northumbrian Brigade, Royal Field Artillery
I can remember going past the church in Albert, with the madonna. There was a legend that on the day this madonna fell, the war would finish. I was a bit of a comic, like, so I said, 'Let's knock it down now and the war will finish.'

Captain George Jameson
1st Battalion, Northumberland Hussars
I hung my Thresher and Glenny coat up at the door. Later on the weather switched to freezing. The ground got iron hard. And I didn't see my coat for at least three weeks. But when I went back for it, it was so frozen that it broke into pieces.

Lieutenant Montague Cleeve
Royal Garrison Artillery

After my first training in the Army I looked on myself almost as a machine in charge of so many lesser machines, which I had to connect up with to make them function. But then as I got into closer contact with both officers and men, in the hubbub of war, and the tragedies and the successes of it, we found ourselves thinking more and more in terms of a family. I know in 35 Siege Battery, more so than in any other, the family spirit was perfectly extraordinary.

My batman was also my friend. Batmen were very carefully chosen, a lot of them had been in service, as footmen and other things. They knew what it was to serve somebody, and they served magnificently. I remember the major's batman was a gunner called Hampshire. And when the major was invalided home in October 1916, he handed Hampshire over to me, which was very kind of him. Hampshire was a marvellously attentive person who sought my every comfort. He always saw to it that when I came home all covered with mud from the forward observation post, he would take away my uniform and next morning it appeared again, and it would be quite smart, with polished buttons and all that. He kept me marvellously tidy, and we became great friends. That was often the case.

I was forward observation officer throughout the Somme, and coming back one night after doing my tour of duty at the observation post, I found the conditions in the trenches simply appalling. You often had to wade up to above your knees, sometimes right up to your waist to get anywhere, and it was an awfully slow process because your feet had nothing to tread on. That night I was in the process of trying to get back to the battery when I stumbled and lost my gas-mask in the slush.

Of course that was the very night when they chose to use gas. The smell of it was horrid. Somehow or other I struggled back. Fortunately, I think it may have been only lachrymatory gas at that time, but there was a lot of mustard gas about and we had to be awfully careful. We were constantly having gas-mask inspections, but we didn't have to wear them unless there was a gas alert. But it was very nasty, and it lingered in the ground unless there was a wind to blow it away. I don't think mustard gas affected the artillery quite as much as it did the infantry, they got the worst of it, as they did most of the trouble.

Sergeant-Major Richard Tobin
Hood Battalion, Royal Naval Division

Colonel Freyberg said, 'Hello Tobin, how are you?' and I said, 'All right, sir.' He said, 'We'll get a VC today,' so I replied, 'You can have mine as well.' He got his. Our final objective was the village of Beaucourt, but we hadn't sufficient men to take it so we dug in and waited for reinforcements to come up. The colonel sent me out on battle patrol. That's when you go ahead of your trench with just twenty or thirty men. You're there to hold up a counter-attack as long as you can. Well, that's a posh way of putting it. You're really there to do as much damage as you can, and to warn the front line while they're getting ready.

However, there was no counter-attack that night so we came back from our battle patrol all right. One of our men went out and came back in great glee. He'd seen a German wagon going along bringing their rations up, so he climbed over the back, bayoneted the driver and pinched the mail. He brought it back to the line and that night we had schnapps. In the mailbag was a box of cigars that had been coming up for the German commander, so Freyberg sent it back to our general. There was a jumping-off trench halfway across no man's land and the brigade was sent out to line this trench. We were assembled at one or two in the morning but then had to wait until quarter to six. We stood there in dead silence, you couldn't make a noise, and the fellow next to you felt like your best friend, you loved him, although you probably didn't know him a day before. They were both the longest and the shortest hours of my life. An infantryman in the front line feels the coldest, deepest fear.

Then, it was just five minutes to go – then zero – and all hell let loose. There was our barrage, then the German barrage, and over the top we went. As soon as we got over the top the fear and the terror left us. You don't look, you see; you don't listen, you hear; your nose is filled with fumes and death and you taste the top of your mouth. You are one with your weapon, the veneer of civilisation has dropped away and you see just a line of men and a blur of shells.

Then came the mist of dawn – a November dawn – and a burst of shells which gave a dirty orange colour and left horrible fumes. We saw a gap in the line and closed in. Finally we reached the Germans' front line and saw some figures rising from the ground with their hands up.

Other Germans were still down their dugouts, so the bombers attended to them and we went on. We were soon across the second line and then the third, which was deserted, so we rested there a bit. I discovered my battalion was down to less than three hundred and out of twenty officers there was just one left – a captain. He was a very good chap, but he'd never been in a battle before. I was a sergeant-major so I knew what was to be done, but could I tell him, and could he do it if I did? It wasn't for me to do it, and I felt very lonely.

Corporal Reginald Leonard Haine
1st Battalion, Honourable Artillery Company

I think Beaucourt was the most intense battle I was ever in, it was really grim. On the first day we had to get through the wire, which made a lot of casualties. Then there was a very complex trench system. And when you got through the first trench system you had a bit of open country and then there were these redoubts and things that the Germans were holding on to. The Germans were very good at that time, they hadn't lost their nerve. And it was astounding to me that on the second day we did take Beaucourt, because we were very thin on the ground for that attack and the Germans had brought up reinforcements. I think, luckily for us, their reinforcements hadn't been on the Somme before and they panicked. Otherwise we shouldn't have got through. The barrage put a curtain of shells over you, that was the theory, and you advanced. Of course you're bound to get casualties from your own shells, you were bound to get quite a lot of casualties when you were on a big show like that.

General Freyberg was wounded just near me on the second day. He stood out in the open and we said, 'For God's sake get in, Sir!' But he was like that and he paid the price; he went down. A chap who'd got about seventeen wound stripes over his arm.

We had a most gruelling time that second day. When we got beyond the village and there were no trenches, we went into shell-holes as deep as we could get. But they gave us the most almighty pasting that day with really big stuff. I think they were 11-inch howitzers, chiefly. It was a very grey day and you could see things coming towards you before they hit, it was a most unnerving experience. They came in salvoes of four over. That was only one part of the shelling. Of course there were all the ordinary field guns and that sort of thing, but I particularly remember those big guns and seeing these little black balls getting bigger and bigger until they came in the most almighty roar round you.

After that show we were lugged out of the line for a while. Well, we'd got nobody left. I went in as a platoon sergeant on the first morning and within the first quarter of an hour we had our company commander killed and two out of three subalterns wounded, with the result that I became the second in command because there was nobody else left.

Artillery was the predominant thing in the later years of the war – the massed artillery. On one occasion when we were at Beaumont-Hamel in November 1916, we had a thousand guns massed on a mile front behind us. Well, you can imagine all this stuff coming over you, and with the German stuff coming the other way, you couldn't hear a word. The noise of battle when you're out in the middle of it is so terrific that you can't hear any individual shots.

Corporal Clifford Lane
1st Battalion, Hertfordshire Regiment
The winter was so cold I felt like crying. I'd never felt like it before, not even under shellfire. What I had felt under shellfire, especially during the first two years, was a wish for a wound, a 'Blighty wound' we called them, to get me home. You thought a Blighty wound was the most fortunate thing that could happen to you.

But there were times, after being shelled for hours on end during the latter part of the Somme battle, that all I wanted was to be blown to bits. Because you knew that if you got wounded, they could never get

Q1340

An exhausted soldier rests and contemplates during his time on the Somme.

you away, not under those conditions. You'd see other people with internal wounds and you thought your only hope was to get killed outright, your only relief. It wasn't only me who felt like that, it happened to lots of people.

I suppose we were despondent because after two years the strain was terrific. The luckiest person in the war was the man who went out and the first day got a nice flesh wound that brought him home again. I've known men to be wounded three or four times soon after they'd got to France. They'd go in the front line, be wounded, come home, go out again, be wounded again within a few days – the finest thing that could happen to you. If it was a slight wound you didn't suffer much and you were out of it. The worst cases were those who – and there were quite a few of us – went on and on and on, without getting any relief at all.

But of course you had to take the chance of whether the wound would be a nice one or not, and there was a further danger of infection. A third of those wounded, even with fairly slight wounds, died of an infection. The soil in France and Flanders was absolutely contaminated. I was at Rouen hospital after I finally got my first wound and this old soul said, 'Yes, you've got a jolly nice wound there, mate, it'll get you to Blighty all right. But the only thing is, it's infected.'

Well I knew what that meant. I had a tube in here, and a tube in there, and every day the nurse had to take them out and start again. I was on my back for about six weeks, but it was the finest six weeks of my life because I could sleep and sleep and sleep. I had to lie on my back, but I really enjoyed it and the infection cleared up. That wound just about saved me I think – yes, it was a lovely wound.

Sergeant Ernest Karganoff
French Army
War being a tough game, soldiers needed some compensation, and during that time we had the *marraines de guerre*, 'wartime godmothers' – pen friends. We got in touch with them by advertising in an illustrated weekly newspaper called *La Vie Parisienne*. We received many friendly letters, some with a picture of the girl. Even a married woman could have a *fils de guerre* a wartime godson.

Exhausted men of the Worcestershire Regiment rest in the mud.

They would send us packages – they usually asked what we needed and then sent tinned food, chocolate and woollen socks, sometimes hand-knitted. One of my *marraines* sent me flowers, perfume, cigars and a stocking to make a scarf of. That was a very nice souvenir. When on leave I used to visit my *marraines* and we'd go to the theatre together, or to a restaurant or the movies, having as good a time as we possibly could during a war. I corresponded with seven *marraines de guerre*, and as I had ten days' leave, I had time to meet them all.

Captain Tom Adlam
7th Battalion, Beds and Herts Regiment
We always felt that someone up above was ordering things, and that they probably knew more about it than we did. We just carried on. I mean, we used to criticise them, saying, 'What the hell are they doing this for?' or something of that kind. But we always took it. It was being good soldiers, I suppose.

Captain Philip Neame
15th Field Company, Royal Engineers
I think what we all thought and hoped was that the war was bound to end with some form of open warfare. It could never go on for ever with this trench warfare.

1917

To see men sinking into the slime, dying in the slime –
I think it absolutely finished me off.

By the end of 1916 the British Expeditionary Force had expanded to fifty-six divisions, and for its planned offensives in 1917 it would have twice as many heavy guns as were assembled for the Somme. In the British sector Haig launched a succession of minor attacks on the Somme to suggest to the Germans that he planned to resume major operations there once the weather improved. Local attacks began on January 10 and there was a three-division assault on February 17.

German strategy for 1917 was to remain on the defensive in both East and West. The German army abandoned many of the positions it had expended so much blood to defend and withdrew in early 1917 to pre-prepared defensive positions built the previous year, the *Siegfried-Stellung*, known to the British as the 'Hindenburg Line.' It began near the British front at Arras and ran through Saint Quentin to Laffaux, six miles north-east of Soissons. These lines incorporated every lesson learned in defensive warfare, masses of wire protecting concrete strongpoints that formed a deep outpost line designed to absorb most of the weight of an attack forward of the main trenches.

On April 9 the British attacked at Arras. Fourteen divisions including four Canadian divisions supported by 2,817 guns and forty-eight tanks tore into the defences to a depth of over three miles. The Canadians captured Vimy Ridge and some ten thousand

Germans were taken prisoner. Further attacks continued to gain ground and a major German counter-attack on May 6 was driven off with severe casualties. In the last week of May the British VII Corps broke into the first part of the Hindenburg Line in a sector held by depleted divisions stationed there for a rest.

On April 16 the new French Commander-in-Chief General Nivelle launched an offensive on the Chemin des Dames. He staked everything on a quick breakthrough but failed to achieve it. The first large-scale attack by French tanks failed tragically; most of the eighty-two Schneider tanks were destroyed. The new German defences proved effective. The sheer weight of the French attack, fifty-two French divisions against thirty-eight German and a greater preponderance of artillery, captured a few miles of ground and twenty-thousand prisoners in the first four days. Yet by the end of April there was no sign of a breakthrough, and French losses were soaring: it was all very familiar, and to soldiers who had been promised a victory after three years of suffering it was too much. On April 29 the first mutinies began. Over the next few weeks sixty-eight of France's 112 divisions reported 'acts of collective indiscipline,' essentially strikes. Soldiers refused to go back into the line or to make attacks. Pétain was appointed Chief of the General Staff; he restored order in due course, but it was plain that the only Allied army left in the field was that of the British Empire. Russia had disintegrated into revolution and the United States, which had entered the war that summer, was at least a year away from fielding an army of European size.

British attacks on the Somme in January–February 1917 were intended as no more than diversions. Haig's true objective was to break through to the Belgian coast and capture the ports of Zeebrugge and Ostend, used as bases by German coastal U-boats. One division (with special tanks) was prepared for an amphibious assault behind the German lines. The first stage of the plan was to attack the southern end of the ridge that dominated the Ypres salient, Messines Ridge. On May 21 British artillery began to bombard the area, their fire increasing from June 2 until 2,266 guns were involved. Mines had been dug under the German front line in a tunnelling operation of unprecedented ambition. They contained a total of about 450 tons of high explosive and their detonation at 03:10 on June 7 reverberated across the Front and was heard on the southern coast of England. The German front line vanished in an apocalyptic blast, and seven British divisions, one Australian and one New Zealand, stormed the Ridge.

On July 31 the offensive known to history as the 'Third Battle of Ypres,' 'third Ypres,' or more commonly 'Passchendaele,' began. An artillery bombardment had been under way since July 18 and air battles raged overhead as the British and French air forces sought to make the task of the German gunners impossible by destroying their observation balloons and shooting down their reconnaissance aircraft. On the night of July 31 it began to rain.

The rain that summer was the worst for forty years, a near constant drizzle that filled the craters with muddy slime. The drainage system had been shattered by the weight of the bombardment, and even when it stopped raining, it remained overcast with never enough sunshine to dry out the ground. Soldiers of both sides fought and died in a man-made swamp. In the brief periods of good weather, General Plumer's Second Army consistently managed to make modest advances, inflicting heavy casualties on the enemy in what were known as 'bite and hold' tactics. German counter-attacks were smashed by British artillery. Haig continued the battle through October and into November when the ruins of the village of Passchendaele came to form the immediate objective. He had reports on his desk suggesting German morale was about to crack, but his own army was sorely tried too. Both sides lost approximately a quarter of a million men at Ypres.

As the Passchendaele offensive petered out the British launched a surprise attack on the German lines near Cambrai. It was spearheaded by 378 tanks, the first mass tank attack in history. Its instant success was the product of new artillery methods pioneered by the British that did away with the need for a lengthy bombardment that gave the enemy time to bring up his reserves.

As the battle of Cambrai was under way, the Bolsheviks seized power in Petrograd (St. Petersburg) and Russia sued for peace. One of the German divisions at Cambrai had recently been transferred from the Russian Front. Over the winter of 1917–18, as Russian troops laid down their arms, up to forty more German divisions would be available to face the Allies on the Western Front. The American Army would not be available in force until later in 1918; Germany had one last opportunity to win the war before the odds became insurmountable.

Corporal Clifford Lane
1st Battalion, Hertfordshire Regiment

We were so thirsty that we actually drank water out of shell-holes, and God knows what a shell-hole contains. It could hold anything – very often parts of a human body. But we were so thirsty we drank it cold and without boiling it, because you couldn't get a fire very often.

Mrs. Scott-Hartley
Voluntary Aid Detachment

I was working as a VAD in a hospital in Bulstrode Street, in West London. It was a big house taken over by the authorities, and all the cases were shell-shocked, which meant they couldn't keep their hands or their heads still. I had to hold them gently behind their heads and feed them, and I also used to write their love letters. Many couldn't say what they wanted to say, or they were probably too shy to tell me, but I used to write them for them, and let them read them back. I used to say, 'My dearest darling,' you know, and 'Forever yours.'

Lieutenant Ulrich Burke
2nd Battalion, Devonshire Regiment

Our own Expeditionary Force canteens, as they called them, were far back behind the lines. But the Salvation Army and the Church Units were well up. If they could find a place where they could set up, then they'd scrounge some wire netting from the battalions and a piece of wood to make beds, and they'd soon have some tea to give you. One day there might be a Catholic padre on and the next day a Protestant, a Jew or a Presbyterian. They all took turns, and it was close to the line. You could always go into the canteen. Sometimes troops couldn't keep up, they were more exhausted than the others, but you didn't wait for them because you knew damn well they'd find their way home. But on the way they'd go into these places and were given a rest and a hot cup of coffee, and then told exactly how much further they had to go. They were marvellous, those people, especially the Salvation Army.

Private Raynor Taylor
Welch Regiment
I was just eighteen years old and I'd been doing a bit of courting. My girl worked at the cotton mill, same as me, and lived nearby, so after I'd been home for dinner we'd walk back together. I thought she was wonderful and when I went in the Army I used to get some very nice letters from her. When I came on leave I'd go out with her every night and I was even invited to their house for my tea, which was a step forward. I think it was because I was in uniform.

I thought I was in love with her, I really did. I treasured those letters. I was so sentimental I felt like a music hall star. Try and imagine this: a full moon. Not a sound. You're on sentry duty in the front line. It's peaceful. You're thinking about home. Thinking about this girl. I'm thinking that the same moon will be shining on her. I can remember this, I was really moonstruck.

We came out of the line and I got a letter from her and one from my mother. I remember I didn't open my mother's, I opened hers first to see what she had to say. It was devastating. In the nicest possible way she said she didn't want to go out with me again because she was going out with somebody else. It was a lad I knew, who I thought was a good friend, but he wasn't, he pinched my girl. Honestly, my world fell apart. I was eighteen and this was the first girlfriend I'd had, and she ditched me. Of all the experiences that I've had, even today, I can't think of anything that upset me more than that did.

When I was wounded I was sent home, and arrived with my hand in a sling and limping. I didn't look very well. Then I was coming up the road when I saw this girl coming down it – it was the first time I'd seen her since she ditched me. We passed one another and her face was the colour of beetroot. I never ever saw her again. She married this bloke. He was a bit of a boastful character and had a job which put him into a reserved occupation, which meant he wasn't called up. I was very bitter. I met him years afterwards but I never mentioned his wife.

Corporal Sidney Amatt
London Rifle Brigade

We were always cold. In the winter we had thick woollen underwear and woollen shirts – well, not woollen but a similar material – and a cardigan or pullover. Then we had our uniform and on top of that we had our overcoats. During the winter of 1917 sheepskin coats were issued for the troops who were manning the front line. It was a sheepskin leather coat with the fleece still on it, and you put it on so the fleece was outward. You wore that over the top of your overcoat.

If you were at the front line you also had large gauntlets, otherwise you were issued with woollen gloves. And you had a woollen scarf, which acted as a cover for your head after you'd taken your steel helmet off. You weren't allowed to go about unless you had a steel helmet on and your respirator fixed round your chest. These respirators came in 1916 with the advent of the Lewis gun, and you had to wear them all the time.

Heinrich Beutow
German schoolboy

Black and white posters went up showing a man putting a hand to his lips and saying, 'Be careful, don't talk too much, the enemy is listening in.' Nobody took them very seriously. Not we as schoolchildren, anyway.

Food was getting scarce, queues were getting longer and soon going to a soup kitchen became one of the features of everyday life. Meat was particularly scarce. Butter was quite scarce and we had the famous German turnips again and again because there were so few potatoes. The winter of 1917 to 18 was called the Turnip Winter.

Schoolboys were taken out of school, and we had to go into houses and count everything – rabbits, for instance, and goats and sheep. Everybody seemed to be keeping rabbits because of the shortage of meat. Then they took us out in whole classes and sent us into the country to help the farmers. We liked that, but it meant we didn't get much teaching. All the teachers were out as soldiers anyway, and generally the whole life of the country was becoming grimmer.

There was a strong sense of people saying, 'This war is lasting too long.' Some became quite outspoken. The feeling was that the war was lasting too long and that Germany didn't have much chance of winning it, because the conditions within the country were getting so very difficult.

Lieutenant E. W. Stoneham
Royal Artillery

The comradeship among men was really most extraordinary and very difficult to describe. On one occasion I was offered a safe job behind the lines if I would care to join Brigade Headquarters. It was very tempting but I didn't want to go. There was something about the relationship with the men that one didn't want to break. One would somehow have felt rather a traitor to them, so I refused it and stayed with them. Somehow one had a very strong sense of belonging – to the men and to the job. Even when I got back to England on leave, it seemed to me that I really belonged at the Front, that the leave was only an interlude. In a way I was quite ready to get back. That was reinforced by the fact that my family didn't understand what was happening out there, and I didn't really want them to know about it. So when I was talking to my parents or my sisters, I had to pretend that it was all very nice out there, and I had to describe a world that wasn't real at all. The real world was the one that I had to get back to, and I felt no compunction about getting away when the leave was over.

Private Shuttleworth
Army Service Corps

After being wounded I was given the job of supervising a gang of Chinese labourers unloading ships. In the morning they would parade, and goodness only knows what they would wear – ladies' blouses, black satin trousers, old coats, soldiers' tunics – anything they could borrow. I mean steal really, because they would steal anything. I remember one incident where a coolie was trying to leave a ship with the top of a pick-axe in his satin trousers, but he was laughing too much – they were always laughing, they were a jolly lot. You had to treat them firmly but kindly. I believe one of the sergeants who got on the wrong side of them was later found with his throat cut. They did occasionally send out these black-hand gang notes to people. It was the custom to send any NCO back to England immediately if they received one of these notes, just for safety.

Private Robert Poustis
French Cavalry

The French soldiers were a little too familiar with their officers, especially in the infantry. In the cavalry perhaps not so much. In some regiments in the French Army, the poor infantry soldiers said, 'Well, you promised us that once we'd attacked we'd be relieved, and yet we stay here in the lines. It is always us that are killed.' They also said, 'Well, the food is not good, the billets are not comfortable, we want to go and see our families,' and so on. And we, as cavalrymen, were on the front line, so we knew when there was bad feeling among the soldiers. This was not in all the regiments, but in those that had attacked too often, or when there were heavy casualties, they were somewhat discouraged. They refused to obey their officers. I saw the poor officers walking here and there sadly and men not saluting them.

Corporal Sidney Amatt
London Rifle Brigade

The Germans adopted a tactic that we copied afterwards. They'd pick out big, strong, physically fit men and arm them with clubs – long-handled clubs about twice as long as policemen's truncheons and with weighted ends. They'd black out their faces and crawl through our wire. Then, without making any noise at all, two of them would bodily lift out one of our sentries – lift him out the trench and drag him over to their lines without anybody noticing anything at all. When we got wise to that sort of thing, we doubled the sentries. We lost several of our men like that. You'd look around and say, 'Oh, where's so and so?' and he'd gone, and we never knew anything about it.

Private Reginald Leonard Haine
1st Battalion, Honourable Artillery Company
It was an extremely severe winter. The gunners behind us told us there were forty degrees of frost. It made things almost impossible, because a shell bursting a quarter of a mile away could kill you. Now usually if you were in luck a shell could burst within a few yards of you and if your number wasn't on it you were all right. But at that time these shells they just hit this solid ice and they scattered. We had our colonel killed there during that February. He was a wonderful chap: Ernest Boyle. He was fifty-six years old, which for a front-line soldier was very old. He'd been severely wounded at Hooge in 1915 when we did a show there. But he was one of the few real fire-eaters I ever met. There were a few; most were unintelligent people; they hadn't got the imagination. But Ernest Boyle was a complete and utter patriot, and I remember he used to say, 'My ambition is that my bones shall be buried in Flanders' – and they were, poor chap. He got just a thing from a shell which landed, oh, two or three hundred yards away I suppose; killed him. He was taken down the line to a little village called Hamel. He was a very well-known chap because he'd got such a wonderful career, and several generals and people turned up for his funeral. But they couldn't dig a grave because the ground was completely solid.

Lieutenant Henry Williamson
Machine Gun Corps
One night when we weren't being shelled we heard that the old Hun, as we called him, had pulled out his heavy howitzers and gone. Then we saw the Bengal Lancers trot past us, and it was a wonderful sight. Rumours then went around that the Hun was packing up altogether. He was going into the Siegfried Line, and bit by bit we followed. Our

patrols went out but a very good rearguard action delayed our advance. But at last we got to green fields and roads that weren't shelled. All the railway lines had been picked out, and all the buildings had been blown up, but it was almost virgin country and we could gallop on the downs and see hares and larks. After months and months of brownness and chaos and everything going to ruin, to see that open country again was marvellous.

Private William Holmes
12th Battalion, London Regiment
We were getting new recruits from London, and one day we had these two youngsters, between sixteen and seventeen years of age, who had only been with us for two weeks, when all of a sudden we had to do this attack. The commanding officer came out and told us to get ready quickly. We'd been laying in reserve to a regiment in front of us, and the previous morning the Germans had come over under a barrage of smoke and captured a whole battalion. The two English battalions on either side couldn't get in touch with each other, so we were to make an attack against those Germans.

These two youngsters, when they knew we were going to be doing this attack, were literally crying their eyes out: it was such a shock for them to go on an attack so soon. When we moved up to the attack we lost sight of them, but they had actually cleared off and been caught by the redcaps about three or four miles from where the action was taking place. They were brought back and charged.

On the Sunday the whole battalion was paraded. The two young men were brought in and stood right at the end, near the officer. Their caps were taken off, every insignia of their regiment was torn off, to disgrace them as much as they could. Then, the verdict of the council was read out, which described how these two young men had deserted and, by their desertion and for letting their mates down, they were going to be shot next day at dawn.

As these two young men had been in my platoon it was decided that we would draw lots. Those that were drawn out – four of them – knew what they had to do at 8 o'clock the next morning. They felt as I would have done – terrified. Almost sick with the whole thought of it. They were going to go and shoot their own mates. But there you are, we had to have discipline.

So next morning the two young men were brought out to a yard and blindfolded. The four men from my battalion who were going to shoot them, each had been given their bullets. And each pair were told to take one of the boys. One was to fire at the head and the other one at his heart. So that the chances were that they would be killed instantly, as of course they were.

The terrible thing was, the parents were never told, they were simply sent telegrams to say that their son had been killed on active service. The four men who had had to shoot them were sick with it all. There was sympathy in the platoon for the boys – but more sympathy really for the parents. We lived with it all for days, weeks – I can see it all now.

But the point was this: every soldier, directly he arrived in France, was read out the war facts. Every man had come out to fight. For the mere disobedience of an officer you could be shot. So we knew that. And so we took punishment as a fact of life.

Private Shuttleworth
Army Service Corps

After I was wounded I was given a job in a hospital. A lot of the patients were badly wounded German prisoners of war. If one of them died they were placed in a rough box and we engaged what the French called a funeral director. He was just a driver who turned up with one horse, a rough old hearse, and wearing a dirty old coat and black satin hat, all battered, and a red scarf round his neck. As we went through the villages the children shouted, 'Allemands! Allemands!' and spat and threw stones and sometimes they got a bit rough. Everybody knew they were German prisoners being buried. When we got to the cemetery the ceremony was carried out as quickly as possible: the parson would read the service, the soldiers lowered the box, then the Last Post and home we came. The soldiers got rather fed up with doing this every day.

British troops celebrate the capture of Monchy-le-Preux on April 11 alongside the London omnibus, now reinforced with wooden panels, that brought so many to the front in 1914.

Gunner Philip Sylvester
Royal Artillery

We moved forward, but the conditions were terrible. The ammunition that had been prepared by our leaders for this great spring offensive had to be brought up with the supplies, over roads which were sometimes up to one's knees in slimy yellowish-brown mud. The horses were up to their bellies in mud. We'd put them on a picket line between the wagon wheels at night and they'd be sunk in over their fetlocks the next day. We had to shoot quite a number.

Rations were so poor that we ate turnips, and I went into the French dugouts, which had been there since 1914, and took biscuits that had been left by troops two years previously. They were all mouldy but I ate them and it didn't do me any harm. We also had crusts of bread that had been flung out of the more fortunate NCOs' mess at a previous date, we scraped black mud from them and ate them. One could make two biscuits last for about three-quarters of the day.

As we went forward the weather was very biting. They called the advance on Vimy Ridge and Arras the Easter Egg – because it took place on Good Friday and Easter Monday. We were elated at the beginning because of the terrific bombardment that was going on, with very little answer from the Germans. The roar was of such a nature that one couldn't help but feel that the Germans had been overwhelmed, that they hadn't got a chance. We felt as secure as we would in our armchairs at home, even when we were sitting in the saddle.

However, then we advanced through the barbed wire and found there were no roads, and we had to use our horses like pack ponies. We were issued with shell carriers for 4.5 howitzer shells, and making two journeys from an ammunition dump meant a considerable number of shells were getting up, but it was a very hard day's work walking through the mud, because you couldn't ride while the shells were on there. You'd be at it the whole time, taking these shells up to various positions.

I belonged to the Lewisham Gunners, an army brigade that served with twenty-three divisions during the two years or so we were in France. They were in every action. An army brigade is a force that is for storm purposes or repelling an assault, and whenever a division was in trouble or required assistance we were put into action. One instance was the storming of Infantry Hill. It had changed hands about three times, and at an hour's notice we were brought down from one section of the line and put into action. Next morning, after pouring shells at the enemy, our infantry captured the particular position and then were pulled down to another part of the line, resting in between when we weren't wanted. While we were resting things were quite happy and we enjoyed life. We rather got used to it, and it became an everyday existence, like going to work in the city – until there was a battle.

We went off to other parts of the Front, then to a place near Arras to have a rest. We were fed on double rations – as were the horses – to strengthen us as summer was coming. It was rather nice, and although we were quite a distance away from Messines, when I was on picket duty I heard the terrific roar of the mines going off. Eventually we heard we were going to go to Passchendaele. The 51st Division had just come out and I used to hear their bagpipes in the morning. I remember their buttons were polished, and they were always marching up and down, and above our heads the Richthofen circuses would have their dogfights going on at various times. Occasionally you would see a plane turning round, spiralling and then coming down, then inquisitive onlookers would go to get some souvenirs. But when we heard we were going to Passchendaele I was not at all displeased, because I wanted to see it.

Private George Hancox
Princess Patricia's Light Infantry, Canadian Army

At Vimy Ridge the weather wasn't too good, it was threatening rain and we had a certain amount of drizzle. The trenches themselves were nothing but unconnected ditches, there was no traversing and no revetment, and just a sandbag parapet in front with loopholes. There were a number of flares going up, which gave a very eerie effect, and quite a bit of rifle fire, but not too much machine-gun fire. On the whole we found it more depressing and disillusioning than frightening. We weren't so much frightened of being killed and wounded as we were

Soldiers fix scaling ladders the day before the battle of Arras.

depressed by the conditions. We had thought we were going to fight a glorious war, but the reality was so different.

Captain Reginald Leonard Haine
1st Battalion, Honourable Artillery Company

Right after the retreat of the Germans took place, we were marched up from the Somme – we'd finished there – and marched up to Arras. To my mind it was astonishing, because we didn't march straight up; you had to march right back to clear the path for the people who were fighting and get right in the back area. Once we got to Arras they put us into very strict training. We came straight out of the Somme to do training!

During the middle of April we pushed forwards through a little village called Bailleul. We sort of dug in in front of the Hindenburg Line as near as we could. Our instructions were to get as near as we could to the German wire. Well, that was terrifying enough, because you could not see anything for this wire; there seemed to be acres and acres of it.

Then we were lugged out of the line practically back to Arras for a day or two. Then on the 23rd of April, St. George's Day, the division was put into the attack of Gavrelle. If you took Gavrelle you'd taken that part of the Hindenburg Line. There I had one of the worst days of my life – in support. Three of our companies went up early in the morning. They did the first attack, and then company by company we were sent up to the attack. And I waited all day with my company lying in a sunken road, and believe me, you sweated blood.

Gunner J. G. Shone
Royal Artillery

When we broke out of the catacombs at Arras we were bombarded by gas shells. I walked back to a first aid dressing station and inside was a doctor, surrounded by the dead and the dying. I tried to tell him what I wanted but he didn't understand me as I couldn't speak, so he pinned a label on me saying Laryngitis. I ended up at the No. 7 Canadian General Hospital at Étaples in a surgical ward. Not being wounded but just sick in the chest, I had to go to the bottom of the ward to see the doctor one morning. He was a Canadian major and as he was examining me he put

This is part of the barbed wire entanglement in front of the Hindenburg Line.

something down my throat and nearly choked me. I snatched his hand away and he said, 'Do you realise what you are doing?' I said, 'Yes, Sir, but you were choking me.' He said, 'How long have you been out here?' I said, 'Since 1914, and I'm still here. But what you're treating me for is gas, not laryngitis.'

Sergeant A. Wilson

Weeks before the attack each platoon was given a photograph of the line in front of us between Bullecourt and Écoust, so every man was rehearsed as to which corner he had to go to. So as far as our authorities were concerned it was such a cut-and-dried affair we were going to eat the place.

On the morning of the attack the artillery bombarded the German line at Bullecourt with all they'd got. There were at least two hundred yards of barbed wire in front of the German lines as far as the eye could see. As our shells fell dirt was flying and the barbed wire twisted and was thrown all over the place. It looked impossible for even a blade of grass to exist, never mind a German machine-gunner. At 4 a.m. on the third day we all had to go over. I had a Lewis gun, and it was quite a work of art to carry it over conditions like that. I was right opposite a hundred-yard gap in the wire, and I got through without much trouble and quickly installed my machine gun in one of the trenches. But everyone followed through the same gap until there was such congestion there that the Germans just opened up with their machine-guns. Such a slaughter went on that at the end of it there were only a handful of my battalion left.

Private James Hills
Sniper

There were German lookouts that we couldn't see from our trench. So I lay in no man's land and carefully parted the grass with my .303 and the only thing that stopped me firing straight away were the bits of grass and poppies that blew in front of my rifle. I drew a bead on the first one and as I'm a good shot I was positive I could hit him. But just as I was going to fire a poppy blew in front of my eyes and I hit the second one

Q862

Australian troops of the 3rd Division wait in the trenches the day before their opening attack in the Third Battle of Ypres.

instead. It was a beautiful shot and I was tickled pink by that. I put my head back down in the grass and lay there without moving for half an hour. I wasn't going to stick my neck out for some retaliation.

As I lay there all sorts of funny things crawled up my sleeves. It's a strange feeling to have your head down in the grass and you daren't move no matter what happens. Eventually I moved my position back another fifty yards, which took about two hours, because I had to work backwards on my elbows and toes, at the same time hauling two rifles and all the ammunition. I couldn't move straight backwards, because when the sun shone it would show up a trail of flattened grass that could easily be seen, so I had to move in a sort of zigzag. Well, I stuck it out and at midday I carefully put my hand in my pocket and took out a bit of crumbly biscuit and stuck it into my mouth to chew, and I thought to myself, 'Cor, what wouldn't I do for a cup of tea.'

Lieutenant Charles Carrington
1/5th Battalion, Warwickshire Regiment

The Australians suggested that as we were having a few days without any particular battle going on, it was surely the moment to have a test match. They found a bit of unshelled ground within reach of their positions and ours, we got some bats, balls, bales and stumps – and we played cricket. What the Germans could have thought was going on I can't imagine. But it must have been reported by some German because unfortunately next morning, when the Australians were assembling on the pitch and we were on our way, they were heavily shelled. Some were killed and others were wounded and the ground was ruined. There was never going to be a return match.

MESSINES

Major Bryan Frayling
171st Tunnelling Company, Royal Engineers
We were to observe what happened to Spanbroekmolen, a mine called Ontario Farm and the group of mines called Kruisstraat. We had placed the mine ninety-two feet down, or one hundred and ten feet if you added the rubble we put on top. I had two subalterns with me and we put out our sliding sticks on the correct bearings then waited in the pitch dark. When zero came, my anxiety was that some of the mines had been sitting in extremely wet ground for nearly a year, and that the explosive was Amatol, which doesn't go off when it's wet. It was in soldered water-proof tins but we wondered how they would fare. The first thing we felt was a terrific tremor through the ground – it was quite fantastic. After that we saw the flames. Kreuschadt was the first, then Spanbroekmolen was almost simultaneous with it. In all, of the twenty-four mines I counted twenty, some of them so close together they looked like one, but over a range of miles from east to west there was all this lot going up.

Captain Cyril Dennys
212 Siege Battery, Royal Artillery
We built for each of the four howitzers a platform. In a normal battle you would have the gun in a pit, but at Ypres you often couldn't do that, because the water level was too high. So we used to make a sandbag, or double sandbag, wall around the edges of the gun pit. In the Ypres salient, sometimes the ground was so devastated and wrecked that the usual camouflage netting might give you away. So we would make the position look as untidy as the surroundings. We used to throw around bits of old sackcloth, sandbags, half a rum jar – and instead of putting the implements, the battery hand spikes and levers and things in neat order, we used to throw them about. We were told to do this by the RFC pilots. They said, 'For God's sake don't have any kind of order. Have your battery positions as untidy as you can and never allow your men to approach the guns along the same track, or they'll make a path that will be visible from the air.'

The British cavalry advances over newly captured ground in April.

Part of a Lewis Gun team awaits the enemy on a canal bank near St. Venant.

Sapper Roll
1st Australian Tunnelling Company, Australian Engineers
The whole hillside rocked like a ship at sea. The noise from the artillery was deafening and the thunder from our charges was enormous. The infantry dashed forward under a barrage and kept sending back thousands and thousands of prisoners. They came back through our dugouts and they were absolutely demoralised. We were all so happy we didn't know what to do! Then, when we got a look at the craters, we saw there were lumps of blue clay as big as small buildings lying about. Our Hill 60 crater was a hundred yards across from lip to lip and forty-five yards deep, although a lot of the stuff had naturally fallen back into the crater. We thought the war was over.

Private Frederick Collins
Royal Tank Corps
At 4 o'clock in the morning we stood there in our overalls with our revolvers. Our officer made us get out of the tank and get in a little slit trench at the side of the Australians. Then the bombardment started and the mine went up. It was a tremendous crash, we saw all the flames. We jumped in the tank and off we went and as we went along the mist got lighter and there was no holding the Australians, they were gone. But we caught them up.

We were sailing along nicely when all of a sudden there was a tremendous thump right in the belly of the tank. A shell had hit our tank. I was the second driver so I sat there pulling the gears in for when they wanted to turn. The place was full of smoke and gas but the shell didn't come through. The bottom of the tank was steel and it bent that up about two and a half feet.

This chap on the 6-pounder had got hit – it fetched two great lumps out of his hand, and the leg of the next chap, who had been standing with the machine-gun, was black. The officer shouted, 'See if you can get any stretcher-bearers!' We didn't even know where we were, it was all smoky inside the tank and we didn't know who else was hit.

Then we found that we couldn't open the door, we were trapped inside until another man came and opened it. There happened to be stretcher-bearers nearby and they came and took these two chaps out. We closed the door again and the officer said, 'See if we can start the engine, we're going to carry on!' They managed to start the engine again. I was as white as a sheet, they told me afterwards. I should think I was as well! We carried on, quietly. The Germans had run like rabbits when the mine went up.

At last we came to within twenty yards of the mine. Everywhere was quiet. Thompson said, 'We'll get out and have a look,' so we got out of the tank and walked over to this huge crater. You'd never seen anything like the size of it, you'd never believe that explosives could do it. I saw about a hundred and fifty Germans lying there dead, all in different positions, some as if throwing a bomb, some still with a gun on their shoulder. The mine had killed them all. The crew stood there for about five minutes and looked. It made us think. That mine had won the battle before it started. We looked at each other as we came away and the sight of it remained with you always. To see them all lying there with their eyes open.

Captain J. C. Hill
Special Gas Company, Royal Engineers

The German gas attacks were giving us great concern, they caused eight hundred casualties at least at Ypres. It took us away from the offensive on to the defensive, I was sent as chemical adviser to the 8th Corps. One morning we found a thousand casualties from a new type of gas shell. It was mustard gas.

The men were blinded and couldn't see at all, and they were choking – thousands had to leave the line. Fortunately, one or two of these shells hadn't exploded, so I got one of them and nursed it on my knees all the way back to the research station. But it took our best chemist weeks to find out what this new substance was. It was a dreadful oily liquid called dichlorodiethylsulphide that evaporated very slowly. Because it had such a faint smell the troops tended to take no notice of it, then when they finally did feel their eyes smarting, it was too late. If they got it on the soles of their boots it would go through and burn their feet. And if they got some on their boots then went into a hut or a dugout and slept there, they would gas everyone else in it too.

THIRD BATTLE OF YPRES

Major Richard Talbot Kelly
Royal Artillery
It rained absolutely continuously, one was as afraid of getting drowned as of getting hit by shells. Actually the extraordinary quagmire nature of the Passchendaele battle masked much of the effect of the shells, which sank so deeply into the mud that the splinter and blast effect was to a large extent nullified. But half the men in my battery were suffering from ague. I had only one sergeant left on his feet and I was the only officer left at the guns. But it was the weather, more than anything else, that got one down. When one woke in the morning in the little scrape you'd scratched out of the ground to get out of the way of the worst of the splinters, you felt the water bubbling and oozing in the small of your back.

Private Frederick Collins
Royal Tank Corps
Our objective was the Menin Road, and we were sailing along when all of a sudden we were hit. A shell had struck the track and broken it, so we were finished. We were under terrible gunfire. You wouldn't believe the shells going over the top of the tank – whizz-bangs and big ones. The state of the ground was terrible, there were great pits of water full of dead mules and the stench was indescribable.

The tank commander got out and tried to find another tank. We stayed where we were, because we should only have been killed if we'd gone outside. As it got towards dawn, the officer, Lieutenant Thompson, said, 'Well chaps, we shall have to make a run for it. If they catch us here when it's light, we're done!' He explained where we were going to be safe and we ran out two at a time while the German planes came swooping round and firing at us. We were very, very lucky not to be hit – you could see the bullets going round Thompson and his shell-hole. In another shell-hole we found two dead men. I knew them – it was an officer and his driver, and the officer's brains had been blown out. There was also an old priest there, dressed in a black cloak and a round hat, who was giving them the Last Rites.

Captain Horace Birks
Royal Tank Corps

This was the first time I had actually commanded a tank in action, and I was petrified. I hoped I'd sprain my ankle or the whole thing would be called off or something like that. The ghastly hour got nearer and nearer, and the worst moment was when we started up our engines and they backfired and you got a sheet out of the exhaust and everybody called each other a bloody fool as we waited to know what was going to happen.

We climbed into the tank, the gearsmen got into their places, the sidegun was put in, the driver got in and then the officer through the top, and we started off. We soon had to close down, though, because we were within comfortable machine-gun range, and once we'd shut down we were completely isolated from the world, we had no means of communication at all.

Inside it got hotter and hotter, as the only ventilation was for the engine and not the crew. If you wanted to see outside you had to look through a steel periscope which gave everything a sort of distorting, translucent glow. Inside it was hot and steamy and steeped in a Stygian gloom. And the noise was such that you couldn't hear anything else at all, so people made little gestures at you – rude or otherwise – and that was your sole means of communicating. My particular tank never went until the engine had boiled, although once it was boiling and you kept it going it went quite well after that.

You could easily tell when the barrage came down because any shell bursting within a few yards of the tank gave such tremendous back pressure you felt it all the way through. In fact a shell bursting between the horns of the tank would almost lift it up in the air. Then the machine-guns were easy to discern because they were just like peas rattling away on a tin can.

Captain E. W. Stoneham
Royal Artillery

I suddenly received orders from a staff officer to meet him at a certain map reference in order to tell us where to fix up a new battery position.

When I looked up this reference on the map I found it was the village of Westhoek, but when I got there there was no village to be seen at all, there wasn't a wall standing, you couldn't see any buildings, and even the roads had been obliterated, but it was a place where the troops had to build a special road in order to take ammunition and other stores up to the Front, and they had built a long road; planks laid side by side, a road which we then called, which was generally known as the Corduroy Road. The ammunition and stores were brought up mostly in wagons drawn by six mules each, these were general service wagons, we called them GS wagons. And it came to be known as GS Avenue, because the road was shelled so often day and night that many of these wagons, of course, had been blown off the road, and were lying along the side as if it were an avenue.

Of course, there were great dumps of ammunition, boxes of food and so on. It was a terrible place for the mules, and it was not very unusual to see a shell fall in the middle of a team of six mules and the mules lifted right and clear and blown right off the road, so that in many places there were dead mules lying.

I met the staff officer and he pointed to a place about forty yards away from this Corduroy Road and said, 'Put your guns there.' Then he went away and I was left to figure out what seemed at first to be an absolutely impossible position, because immediately off the road there were huge shell-holes full of water, and anything may have fallen into that water. The particular place we would have to get to was full of huge craters – there was a mule in the first one and after this there were plenty of others and it seemed at first impossible to get there at all.

However, we had to carry out our orders, and when I was able to bring up some men, we started to fill in the first of these craters. We threw in a lot of boxes of stores and ammunition – we didn't know what was inside them, but we found a lot of boxes about. We found some bricks and so threw those in on top and then more of anything we could find, until eventually we were able to lay planks over the top. Then we brought up a gun and with great difficulty, because of course these were heavy 6-inch howitzers, got it off the road onto the first part of the route.

Then we had to get it from there past other shell-holes, which we had to fill in, and it took us a very long time but we did eventually get one of our guns about thirty yards from the road. But it was a very foolish place to choose for a battery, because apart from the effect it had on the spirit of the men, it was impossible to carry out. We managed to get three guns there, but they were all knocked out and we lost fifty men. Then, having suffered that, we were told to pull out, which was more easily said than done. It took us several weeks to get these guns away. We sent up detachments of men, and time after time they toiled with these heavy guns which kept slipping sideways and getting caught in the mud, and it was a very long time before we were able to get any of them back onto the road and away.

Corporal Clifford Lane
1st Battalion, Hertfordshire Regiment

We went over the top. It was all quite nice, we didn't have anybody firing at us, not for the first quarter of an hour or so anyway. We were getting strung out in what we called open formation, a couple of yards between each man, and eventually we came under long-distance machine-gun fire. As we were going along the man on the right of me was hit in the heart and died. He probably died, but we weren't allowed to stop anyway. It missed me altogether, and that was just the luck of the war.

We were told that we'd got to get a stream called Steenbeek. We got there and were told to lie down prone. We were all lying there when suddenly I felt an object fall at my side. I looked around and it was a tin of Woodbines. I looked again and there was a padre. I'd never seen a padre taking part in an attack, and whoever he was he was worthy of the very highest praise, because he was in a very dangerous position.

We hadn't had too many casualties at that time, and then we saw a pillbox not far away, about a couple of hundred yards. We were told to make for that. We got up and got about fifty yards towards it, then we were told to get down again. Then we were told to get up. As we got up we came under very heavy machine-gun fire from quite a distance away and practically the whole of our platoon was wiped out. It got most of them in the heart. The one that hit me caught me in the shoulder joint.

Private Harry Patch
Duke of Cornwall's Light Infantry

At Pilckem Ridge I can still see the bewilderment and fear on the men's faces when we went over the top. C and D Company was support, A and B had had to go at the front line. All over the battlefield the wounded were lying down, English and German all asking for help. We weren't like the Good Samaritan in the Bible, we were the robbers who passed by and left them. You couldn't help them. I came across a Cornishman, ripped from shoulder to waist with shrapnel, his stomach on the ground beside him in a pool of blood. As I got to him he said, 'Shoot me,' he was beyond all human aid. Before we could even draw a revolver he had died. He just said 'Mother.' I will never forget it.

Lieutenant Ulrich Burke
2nd Battalion, Devonshire Regiment

When you get out on top you try and keep in as straight a line as possible. You're spaced at three to four yards intervals and you go forward at the high port, that is, with the rifle diagonally across your chest and the bayonet pointing upwards towards the sky.

We reckoned to do a hundred yards in a minute to a minute and a half. I know one can run it in ten seconds. But with the men having to go round the shell-holes, and at the same time being fired on and trying to keep their distance between one another and keep their alignment, it was only when you got to within twenty yards of the trench that you said, 'Charge!' They then brought their rifles down, charged into the trench and killed and bayoneted the enemy.

We then headed for Lake Farm. There our commanding officer was killed. The second in command took over and we went on a bit further. When we got to the enemy trench we jumped in. This German put his bayonet up and I caught it in the right shoulder, right across my back. It just missed my spine but I was impaled on it. My great fear was that he would press the trigger, which would have made a hell of a mess. But my sergeant, who was nearby, saw this, came in close, shot the fellow and then hoisted me off the bayonet with the help of another man. I was on top of this dead German and it wasn't pleasant. A bayonet wound hurts directly it goes in and the withdrawal is even more anguished than the putting in, because at least the putting in is instantaneous. If you get hit by a bullet or bomb splinter it's so hot that it cauterises the wound and you don't feel anything for a minute or so.

Gunner H. Doggett
Royal Artillery

Our ammunition wagon had only been there a second or two when a shell killed the horse under the driver. We went over to him and tried to unharness the horse and cut the traces away. He just kneeled and watched this horse. A brigadier then came along, a brass hat, and tapped this boy on the shoulder and said, 'Never mind, sonny!' The driver looked up at him for a second and all of a sudden he said, 'Bloody Germans!' Then he pointed his finger and he stood there like stone, as though he was transfixed. The Brass Hat said to his captain, 'All right, take the boy down the line and see that he has two or three days rest.' Then he turned to our captain and said, 'If everyone was like that who loved animals we would be all right.'

Lieutenant Colonel Alan Hanbury-Sparrow
2nd Battalion, Royal Berkshire Regiment

The crucial attack of the division on the right had completely failed and we were in rather a precarious position. The brigadier came up, and whilst he was there there was a sudden stampede of our men as they were driven off the hill and they fell back. We fell back from where my temporary headquarters were and took refuge behind an old parapet that I think had been built in 1914 – it was not thick enough really to be bulletproof. But, providentially, it was facing the right direction and about fifty of us took refuge there.

An attack started forming up against us out of Polygon Wood. At the same time there was a gun ranging on this particular trench. It had obviously seen us go there and I imagine it was one of four guns in a battery. I knew that once that battery got the range and opened fire we were done for. At the same time a machine-gun, which seemed very much closer than I liked, swept the top of our parapet and killed three in the process. They'd got the position exactly. We were in a very parlous situation.

I sat down as there was nothing to be done, and I did what I generally did on those occasions – I played chess with my adjutant. I always had with me a little chessboard with pegs. We played on, rather aimlessly it's true, but it steadied the men. Then suddenly a shell fell into the trench. I thought to myself, 'Now our time has come, you've had a long run for your money and I wonder what it'll be like to be dead.' At that moment I realised that whatever happened I wasn't going to be killed. It's impossible to describe this consciousness. It's not like ordinary consciousness at all, it's something like a prophet of old when the Lord spoke, something quite overwhelmingly clear and convincing. I wasn't very proud of myself because I didn't care what happened to the others – I was going to survive. I took a rifle and began shooting. I hit two Germans at six hundred yards and made a third skip for his life. The extraordinary part was that the machine-gun never fired again, that was the last shell that it fired, yet there was no reason why it should have stopped. It was as though for a moment I got a glimpse of time coming towards me.

Lieutenant Edmund Blunden
11th Battalion, Royal Sussex Regiment
One or two signallers and I had to walk in the open straight in front of the Germans, who were perhaps two or three miles off. But they could see us all right and they did some beautiful shooting, they made rings round us. One of the lads, a tall handsome youth, said, 'I never did see such shelling!' It was exactly like applauding a conjuring trick, or something in the halls, or a piece of fast bowling in a test match. It struck me even then, what self-control. But he was really looking at a remarkable feat of skill on the part of some other human being, and I thought a lot of that.

Lieutenant Edmund Blunden, a proud member of the 11th
Battalion, Royal Sussex Regiment.

Corporal Andrews

All of us going to Étaples had combat experience. But when we got there we found the discipline was literally Prussian. After three years of war the troops were in no mood to be messed about by base wallahs of all ranks and regiments. The bullring was the parade ground where our transformation was to take place from cavalry to infantry. It comprised of acres of sandy waste near the Boulogne–Étaples railway. Here we were kept on the move from early morning to late afternoon, harassed by sergeants with yellow bands round their arms, who were known as canaries.

Thousands of men of all regiments performed in the arena until they were thought competent. I remember a colonel who stood mounted on a high rostrum until he'd inspected every detachment as they marched past him. If he didn't like the marching of a particular group, he sent them to the rear of the column like a lot of naughty schoolboys. Being cavalry, we hadn't been used to marching, so we had a lot of that. At midday we used to march back to camp for our meal, then march to the bullring again. Lady Angela Forbes, who ran canteens at the time, introduced some wooden huts in the bullring so the troops could have a cold meal of bully instead of having to march all the way back to camp. That was kind of her, but she didn't realise we weren't allowed to make our own use of the time saved. Additional drills were imposed on us. It was in this oppressive atmosphere that the fire of resentment smouldered, and it only needed a spark to touch off an explosion.

Well, that soon came. In the depots were imperial troops – English, Welsh, Scots and Irish as well as Canadians, Australians and New Zealanders. The town of Étaples was out of bounds. Nobody was allowed into it without a pass and the route lay over a railway bridge that was guarded by a redcap. One evening, a Jock wanted to go into town but he hadn't got a pass so the redcap told him he couldn't go. There was a skirmish and the redcap pulled out his revolver and shot the Jock dead. That was sufficient for the Scots, and quite enough to set the Australians alight, who were against any form of discipline imposed by Imperial officers. Then the Canadians followed, and that night the whole town was ablaze with rioting troops. Law and order disappeared as the troops went berserk. The major in charge of our infantry base depot came to us and said, 'Please don't go down into the town tonight, boys.' We didn't go, but an hour later we were paraded with trenching tool handles and topcoats and were marched into the bullring, where a picket was posted over the ammunition.

Next morning at daybreak we were marched back again to camp and we got down between the blankets. Soon after reveille went a sergeant came round shouting, 'Show a leg.' Somebody shouted something unrepeatable back at him and we didn't show a leg. He came round half an hour later and the unrepeatable was repeated. We finally got our breakfast at about 9 o'clock. Nothing more was said about it and as a result, all redcaps were withdrawn from the sight of the troops. Almost all the troops were cleared and sent up the line to their units. Eventually, the deserted bullring became a training ground for message dogs and the camps became convalescent depots. What happened there was not a mutiny. The troops were simply lawless. It was a riot – a prolonged riot.

Private Harry Patch
Duke of Cornwall's Light Infantry
They wanted a number two for C Company's Lewis gun, as he had been sent home on compassionate leave. Somebody said, 'Well, here's someone who's had training for the Lewis gun. Here's your number two.' That's how I got to be number two. And whatever I didn't know, Bob, the number one gun, taught me.

There were five of us in a Lewis gun team. Number one carried the gun and the revolver. He couldn't manage a rifle and the Lewis gun – it weighed twenty-eight pounds. The easiest way was to carry it on your shoulder, on the centre of gravity. The only cover we had for it was our waterproof sheets. It was up to us to keep the gun and magazines ready. I had a bag lined with all the spare parts, which went over my shoulder. This bag of spares, which we could almost build a gun from, weighed about the same as the gun. You had that to struggle along with as well as your full pack. The gun had a tripod, which folded up for carrying, and which I also had to take. This had three cast-iron legs with a place for the Lewis gun to fit on. You could swivel it a bit, but not much.

Number three, four and five were loaders. As number two I had a revolver as well. Three, four and five had the Lee-Enfield rifle. They had a few pouches with spare ammunition for the rifle, and the Lewis magazines. These three carried four loaded magazines, even when we left the front line to go into reserve. They had two hundred rounds each, fully loaded, ready to be called upon. They carried these magazines in pouches, on a strap on the shoulder, over their other equipment. Two in the front and two on the rear, at the side of their pack. They were made of webbing, as you couldn't use leather in the front line, the rats would gnaw it to pieces.

I used to lie down on the left-hand side of the gun, and when Bob had fired the magazine I would take it off with my right hand and hand it back to number three. He'd then hand it back to be reloaded. The three people behind you would be reloading with fifty rounds again. Number five would pass up a new full magazine to me and I would put it on and wait for Bob to use it. The magazine was designed so that it would only go on in one way. There was a pin in the gun we put the magazine on, it went in on a seat, ready for the round to go in. As far as I remember there was a spring of some sort, and you had to press something to pull it off.

The gun could fire fifty rounds a minute. Bob was expert at it, he was so light-fingered he would fire a round and finish, or he would fire two as was needed. I managed to get down to three and never got down to one. Bob could fire from the hip, he would pull the gun from his shoulder, one hand on the trigger, the other on the barrel. He pulled the trigger and it was away. If you looked under the magazine you could see the cartridges. If any of those brass cases were dented at all, the piston, when it came around, wouldn't throw it out and the gun would stop. If you had a dirty cartridge or magazine the round you used wouldn't come out and the gun would stop. You'd have to get it out and pull the lever back by hand to get it going again.

The biggest cause of stoppages was heat caused by the discharge flames. The gun was air-cooled by air being pulled in. Later on they improved to the Maxim, which was water-cooled, but the Lewis gun was air-cooled. After you had fired two magazines you could not hold that gun, it got too hot to handle really. That's why Bob would never fire a whole magazine if he could help it, because of getting the gun too hot. It took a couple of minutes to cool down. If the gun stopped it was my job to get out whatever part it had stopped for. Bob and I between us could strip down that gun in a matter of ten to twelve seconds.

BATTLE OF MENIN ROAD RIDGE

Lieutenant Douglas Wimberley
232nd Machine Gun Company, Machine Gun Corps
I spent the night before the battle in a concrete pillbox, Ferdinand Farm. It had very thick concrete walls but it was a curious sort of place to have a headquarters. It had been built by the Germans, and so the entrance faced the German lines. Inside it was only about five foot high and at the bottom there was about two foot of water. This water was simply horrid, full of refuse, old tins and even excreta. Whenever shells burst near it the smell was perfectly overpowering. Luckily, there was a sort of concrete shelf the Boche had made about two foot about ground level. It was on this shelf that four officers and six other ranks spent the night. There wasn't room to lie down, there was hardly room to sit upright, and we more or less crouched there. Outside the pillbox was an enormous shell-hole full of water, and the only way out was over a ten-inch plank. Inside the shell-hole was the dead body of a Boche who had been there a very long time and who floated or sank on alternate days according to the atmosphere.

Captain E. W. Stoneham
Royal Artillery
One morning, on the day that the battle was going to begin – about 5 o'clock – I found myself in the middle of the night – about 3 o'clock in the morning – standing in a trench with another artillery officer, and his duty was as soon as zero hour started – as soon as the barrage opened up – to go forward with a couple of telephonists and try to lay out a telephone line, go right into the barrage with the infantry and if he wasn't

These are some of the men of the Durham Light Infantry before the Menin Road Ridge battle on September 20.

blown to pieces, to try to get messages back to say where the infantry were, in order that the artillery could choose their targets. My job was simply that if the telephone line failed – if I heard no more from him it would be assumed he had been killed – I had to go out, try to lay the line and do the same thing. While I was talking to him he had to explain to me exactly what he intended to do so that I should understand his plan, and while he was talking to me he was ashen pale, and it was extremely difficult for me to follow what he wanted to do, because he was in such a state that his jaw had dropped and he couldn't lift his jaw, he couldn't shut his mouth, and his words were very indistinct and I had quite a difficulty in understanding what he wanted to do.

Zero hour came. He climbed out of the trench as calmly as anything, and he went forward and he did a magnificent job. It is curious how, it was a case of imagination. I imagined him to be very imaginative, and usually of course the only way you could carry on was to keep the lid tight down on your imagination, but sometimes you had to do the opposite, at least so I found I had to do when this sort of thing would happen. For example, one day I was crossing the battlefield and I suddenly heard shouts and I saw not far from me a man had fallen. He had obviously been hit and he was yelling out in great pain. Of course I ran in his direction, but as I ran I had a horrible fear that I was going to lose my nerve and not be able to help him at all, and so what I did was to imagine something absolutely horrible. I imagined him to be in four pieces, or something, so that when I got there and found that perhaps it was only his chin blown away, as it was . . . on one occasion, then I was able to do something, whatever I could do with the bandages, until help could come for him.

Private Harry Patch
Duke of Cornwall's Light Infantry
The shelling was bad. You could hear the big shells coming, although if you could hear them that was all right, they'd gone over. You never heard the whizz-bangs coming, they were just there. And you never heard the shell or the bullet that hit you. Of course whizz-bangs were

Q2850

This dressing station shows some of the hundreds of wounded German prisoners from the battle of Menin Road Ridge.

Q2855

A padre gives comfort to a wounded man from the battle of Menin Road Ridge.

shrapnel and that was worse than a bullet. A bullet wound was clean, shrapnel would tear you to pieces. It was a whizz-bang that killed my three friends and wounded me, it was just bad luck. They had those four magazines over their shoulders, fully loaded. That's why they all got blown to pieces.

Lieutenant Hartwig Pohlmann
36th Prussian Division
On September the 20th the great attack of the Highland Division met our own regiment. The firing went on for several hours, even after the Highlanders had stormed our front line and were trying to get onwards through all these shell-holes. We sprang from shell-hole to shell-hole. The fire was so heavy I didn't notice the single shells. We advanced and drove the Highlanders back a bit, but we couldn't reach the front line where our third battalion had been vanquished. They were all gone, some dead, some taken prisoner, we didn't see any of them again. We happened to catch some of the Highlanders, and it was a funny sight for us to see soldiers with kilts and naked knees.

Corporal Jack Dillon
2nd Battalion, Tank Corps
At Passchendaele the smells were very marked and very sweet. Very sweet indeed. The first smell one got going up the track was a very sweet smell which you only later found out was the smell of decaying bodies – men and mules. After that you got the smell of chlorine gas, which was like the sort of pear drops you'd known as a child. In fact the stronger and more attractive the pear-drop smell became, the more gas there was and the more dangerous it was. When you were walking up the track a shell dropping into the mud and stirring it all up would release a great burst of these smells.

Captain W. Bunning
24th Australian Battalion
The attack on Broodseinde happened on the morning of October the 4th. We were in the leading wave for the attack on the ridge and

beyond. We moved into position at midnight, and zero hour – going over the top – was 6 a.m.

Just before 5:30 it rained a little but it was not uncomfortable. We were in position and everything was quiet, with many waves, no doubt, forming up behind us and to our right. Then at 5:30 up went – not the usual white flares from the Germans, but yellow ones. We didn't know what it meant at first, but in a few seconds we found out when down came a very heavy barrage right on our line. Most of us had to ease forward a bit because we found they were dropping just on our position.

We waited till 6 o'clock, and at that moment the Germans' barrage lifted and ours came down. As we always tried to keep very close to our own creeping barrage away we went, and to our surprise, as we went down the slope into the valley we could see Germans running about in our barrage. We also met some in no man's land, and it transpired that they were attacking at the precise moment that we were too. They were soon devastated by our barrage. We went on and took what was called the red line, forty yards below the actual top of Broodseinde Ridge.

There we were dug in and consolidated. Then some smoke shells came over, which indicated that the barrage was about to creep forward. The 24th went through onto their objective, which was the blue line. The casualties in my company were not really heavy, not as heavy as one might have expected from the early shelling. After consolidating, one would move forward carefully, checking to see the field of fire was suitable for the men and siting their positions.

What was really surprising was to look across and see before you the green fields of Belgium. To see actual trees and grass – of course the fields had been churned up a good deal by barrage shells, but as far as we were concerned it was open country. But then to look back to where we'd come from, Ypres – there was total devastation. And then at dawn we could see why our own gunners had had such a gruesome time. You could see the flashes of all the guns firing right from Broodseinde to the Menin Gate.

Lieutenant Charles Carrington
1/5th Battalion, Warwickshire Regiment
The noise would grow into a great crescendo and at a certain point your nerve would break. In a flash of time, in a fifth of a second, you'd decide that this was the one. You'd throw yourself down into the mud and cringe at the bottom of the shell-hole. All the other people around would be doing the same.

Sometimes you miscalculated and this wasn't a shell for you, and it would go sailing busily on and plonk down on somebody else four hundred yards away. When a shell arrived it would drop into the mud and burst with a shattering shock. The killing splinters flew off and might fly fifty yards away from the point of impact. You could find a fragment of red-hot jagged iron weighing half a pound arriving in your shell-hole.

They'd take another second or two before they would all settle down in the mud. Then you'd get up and roar with laughter, and the others would laugh at you for having been the first one to throw yourself down. This of course was hysterics! It becomes a kind of game in which you cling on and try not to let the tension break. The first person in a group who shows a sign of fear by giving way and taking cover – he'd lose a point and it counted against him. The one who held out longest had gained a point – but in what game? What was this for?

After eighteen months in France I was still trying to pretend to be brave and not succeeding very well, and so were we all. All the time one was saying to oneself, 'If they can take it – I can take it!,' the awful thing being that this was not an isolated experience but one which went on continuously, minute after minute and even hour after hour.

Bombardier J. W. Palmer
26th Brigade, Royal Field Artillery
It was mud, mud, everywhere: mud in the trenches, mud in front of the trenches, mud behind the trenches. Every shell-hole was a sea of filthy oozing mud. I suppose there's a limit to everything, but the mud of Passchendaele – to see men sinking into the slime, dying in the slime – I think it absolutely finished me off.

I knew, for the three months before I was wounded, that I was going to get it. The only thing was, I thought I was going to get killed. Every time I went out to mend the wire I think I was the biggest coward on God's earth. Nobody knew when a wire would go, but we knew that it had to be mended, the infantrymen's lives depended on those wires working. It didn't matter whether or not we'd had any sleep, we just had to keep those wires going.

There were many days when I simply don't know what happened because I was so damned tired. The fatigue in that mud was something terrible. You reached a point where there was no beyond, you just couldn't go any further. The night I reached my lowest ebb I'd been out on the wire all day and all night, I hadn't had any rest, it seemed, for weeks. It was very, very difficult to mend a telephone wire in this mud. You'd find one end and then you'd try and trudge through the mud to find the other end, but as you got one foot out the other one would sink down again.

It was somewhere near midnight. The Germans were sending over quite a barrage and I crouched down in one of these dirty shell-holes. I began to think of those poor devils who'd been punished for self-inflicted wounds – some had even been shot. I began to wonder if I could get out of it. I sat there and kept thinking, it's very lonely when you're on your own. Then in the distance I heard the rattle of a harness. I knew there were ammunition wagons coming up and I thought, 'Well, here's a way out – when they get level with me I'll ease out and put my leg under the wheel and I can plead it was an accident.'

I waited as the sound of the harness got nearer and nearer. Eventually I saw the leading horses' heads in front of me and I thought, 'This is it!' and began to ease my way out as the first wagon reached me. But you know, I never even had the guts to do it, I just couldn't do it. I think I was broken in spirit and mind.

Private S. C. Lang
My battalion went into the line in the middle of the night. It was raining and misty everywhere and we had to travel on duckboard tracks. Going in, the shells were landing amongst us and one man was killed in front of me. I was then blown off the tracks and had to be helped back

on, or I'd have sunk into the mud. The mud dominated everything in that attack. We were led into positions just in front of our front line, beside what once was a creek. We lay down in shell-holes waiting for the attack, which was due to start at 6 o'clock, when at 5:30 a sudden and tremendous barrage came from the Germans, right in our front line.

I think every one of us thought the Germans must have known of the attack and that they were going to wipe us out by this barrage. We all got very worried. But suddenly, as I lay in my shell-hole, I had a premonition – I became convinced, utterly convinced, that nothing could be done that day that would hurt me. I became perfectly calm and almost went to sleep. Then at 6 o'clock a magnificent sound started up, it was the 'swee swee swee swee' of our own barrage coming from behind, and it seemed to stop the German barrage immediately. We got up, sticky with mud, and somehow or other the whole battalion had not been wiped out.

We went up the hill to Broodseinde Ridge in perfectly good order, and by that time there didn't seem to be many Huns about at all. We went over the top and when we got there we saw the whole of the green plains of Belgium spread out before us. We could have gone on and on and on, there was nothing to stop us except a sea of mud through which no gun could possibly be dragged. If we'd gone on we'd have been annihilated by the German gunfire, so we had to stop.

Gunner Sydney White
Royal Artillery
The only way up from Ypres was by a plank road fifteen to twenty feet wide. All munitions had to travel a considerable distance up this plank road, and the mud was so deep that on one occasion, with drag-ropes on the wheels and something like a hundred men on the drag-ropes, it was still impossible to pull the guns out of the mud. The mud and the conditions were absolutely indescribable. You saw fellows coming down from the trenches badly wounded, covered from head to foot in blood, and perhaps an arm missing. You saw some of the fellows drop off the duckboards and literally die from exhaustion and loss of blood. Horrible, it was.

Private S. T. Sherwood

As I slipped to the bottom of the shell-hole I took my torch out, flashed it around and to my horror found I had a German companion – that was where the terrific stink came from. I thought, 'Heavens, am I going to spend the night with you!' I knew that without help it was impossible to get out, so I shouted, screamed and did everything possible to make someone hear me. I shone my torch up in the air in the hope that someone would see the light, but nothing happened.

I wasn't one to panic, I was always one to keep cool if possible, but for the next half-hour I struggled as hard as I could to climb up the sides, and in the process my trench boots were left at the bottom. But every time I would get within a yard of the top and then slide back into this terrible filth again. I reviewed my position and realised I'd have to keep myself going until the morning. First I decided to sing, and sang all the songs I could possibly think of. I sang, I cursed, I raved and eventually I prayed. I prayed that help would come before morning.

I was sweating from head to foot with all the exertion. Then as I lay back in the trench I remembered my old pipe and tobacco and smoked pipe after pipe. Gradually I found I was sinking further and further into this mire – the water had gone above my waist, and no matter how I struggled it was impossible to get out. I knew that struggling further wasn't going to help me so I continued smoking and singing and shouting as best as I could until my voice had almost gone.

I took my rifle and jammed it into the side of the shell-hole as far as I could to give me some support, putting my right arm through the sling. Then I either dozed off or became unconscious, I don't know which, because when I woke the bottom of my body was completely paralysed by the coldness of the water, which I could feel creeping further and further up. During this period the Germans commenced shelling the area. The vibrations made the shell-hole shake from one side to the other. I was rather pleased because it gave me something to interest myself in – it kept me awake and alive. I was still sinking further into the mire. I filled my pipe again then put my hand into my tunic pocket for my matches and found they were wet through.

It was then I began to despair. I thought, 'I'd sooner be killed with a

A panoramic view of Passchendaele shows the mud and desolation.

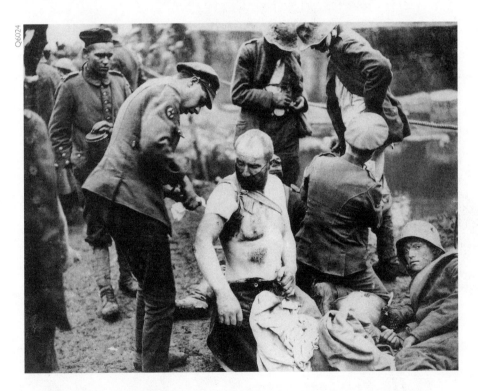

After the battle of Broodseinde, men of the Royal Army Medical Corps dress the wounds of German Prisoners.

A wiring party carries reels of telephone cable along narrow duck boards towards the town of Pilckem.

shell or a bullet than die in a bloody filthy shell-hole.' From then on I can remember no more until I thought, 'Can I be dreaming – there are footsteps somewhere.' Feebly, I tried to shout until I heard a voice say, 'Where are you?' I shouted, 'I'm here, in a shell-hole.' The footsteps went round again for a few minutes then looking up I saw a head appear over the top. 'Oh, my God,' he said, 'hang on, hang on, chum.' I remembered no more from that 'hang on' until I found myself in hospital between clean white sheets.

Lieutenant Ulrich Burke
2nd Battalion, Devonshire Regiment

It had rained and rained and rained. We even had to cease the battle for a few days before continuing on, while the ground we went over became more and more broken up. All this gave the enemy time to reorganise and reinforce, so it became even more difficult. And there were no trenches at all at Passchendaele. There were just a series of shell-holes that had been reinforced with sandbags so that you could hide inside them. If, for instance, you wanted to urinate and otherwise, there was an empty bully beef tin kept on the side of the hole, so you had to do it in front of all your men then chuck the contents, but not the tin, over the back.

I had to go round my sector once a night with the sergeant-major. And when we left one shell-hole we'd have to ask which way to go next, because each night the ground would have absolutely shifted. One night the people on our left were planning an attack and we were going to give them heavy covering fire. It was a night attack due to start at 10 o'clock, but at half-past nine an order came through that the attack was off. So my sergeant-major and I had to go round twenty-four of these front-line shell-hole posts, quickly and in the dark, to stop the men firing when there was nothing to fire at. It was awful. We didn't really know when we were going towards the enemy and at one point, when my sergeant-major was within about ten yards of them, a Very light went up behind him. Because of the kind of Very light it was, he knew damn well he was out in front. So he quickly doubled back and managed to find the post.

But the conditions were miserable. You lived cave-like. You can imagine a man after being in one those holes for a week, where he couldn't even wash. Each day he got a two-gallon petrol tin of tea given him, delivered in a small box of hay which was supposed to insulate the tin and keep the tea warm. Well those tins were baked, boiled – everything was done to them – but whenever you put a hot substance in them you still got petrol oozing out, and that gave the men violent diarrhoea. But they had to drink it because it was the only hot drink they had.

Troops had to go overland to all these shell-hole posts every day, the first time to deliver rations and ammunition and the second time, at night, to bring the tins and hayboxes back, because there wasn't room to keep them in the little shell-holes. You couldn't chuck them over the top because they were needed again.

It was a terrible experience for the ration parties to make two journeys. The troops were from other battalions, because it was realised that the battalion on the line couldn't possibly do it. And they couldn't care less how they did it. The butter came in a round flat tin but bread was just bread and sometimes, when the fellow had fallen about a dozen times, there was a thick paste of dirt and mud all the way round it. Well, chaps started cutting this crust off and throwing it away, but then they found they had no bread left, so they had to eat it.

Oh, the conditions were terrible. You can imagine the agony of a fellow standing for twenty-four hours, sometimes up to his waist in mud, with just a couple of bully beef tins or his mess tin trying to get the water out of this shell-hole. And he had to stay there all day and all night for about six days, that was his existence. And when he got a hot drink it was tainted with petrol, so he knew that for the next four or five hours he'd be filling a bully beef tin.

The men were hardened, but the life was terrible. Another extra chore was that lime had to be spread on the back of the posts because open excreta was being chucked out and if you didn't put down lime then when you came crawling out you'd be covered in it. A further great problem was trench fever and trench foot. When a fellow got a very high temperature, you could tell he'd probably got trench fever. It wasn't dysentery exactly, but it was constant diarrhoea and left him weak and listless. Trench foot was owing to the mud soaking through your boots and everything. In many cases your toes nearly rotted off. We lost more that way than we did from any wounds or anything.

Gunner Leonard Ounsworth
124 Heavy Battery, Royal Garrison Artillery

The rats used to pinch your rations at night, they'd gnaw through anything you put them in unless it was in a metal container. But the gas attack finished them. In the morning there were dozens and dozens of these rats crawling about on their bellies. We just stubbed our toe beneath them and sent them into the moat. Yet there were two swans which lived on the moat and they were up on the ramparts apparently unharmed.

Private Raynor Taylor
Welch Regiment

The battalion halted along the roadside for the usual ten minutes. Suddenly we were called upon to stand up because the King was coming along this road and we were expected to cheer him. This cavalcade came along, the King in his car, and the officers did cheer but I've no recollection of any of the men cheering. After a period in the front line, you weren't in any mood to cheer anybody.

Sergeant-Major Richard Tobin
Hood Battalion, Royal Naval Division

There was no chance of being wounded and getting a Blighty one at Passchendaele. You could either get through or die, because if you were wounded and slipped off the duckboards you just sank into the mud. I don't know how far the duckboards extended because it was such slow going up to the Front, but there were hundreds and hundreds of yards zigzagging about. At each side was a sea of mud, and if you stumbled you would go in up to the waist, and literally every pool was full of the decomposed bodies of humans and mules.

Then, when you got up to the Front, there was no front line to speak of, just a series of posts scraped in the mud. A machine-gun crew here, a few riflemen there, further on a Lewis-gun crew. In some cases the battle depth of your battalion was 1,000 yards of these posts bogged down. You couldn't get food or ammunition to any of them in daylight because the Germans were shelling the whole time. When shells started dropping you ran to the right or you ran to the left to get some cover, but if you were on the duckboards you couldn't run anywhere. You just had to face it and go on.

The men found the relief was hopeless. The battalion came from ordinary trenches but the men struggled back in twos and threes, some a day late. I have seen men going out covered in mud, they just scraped it away from their eyes. They carried in their hands what looked like a muddy bough of a tree – but it was their Lewis gun. Their only thought was that the Germans were in as bad a position as we were. In fact, there was one place where a little party of men was trying to make their hole more comfortable by scooping it out, and some hundred yards away the Germans were doing exactly the same, but both, in their miseries, didn't take any damn notice of each other.

Corporal J. W. Palmer
26th Brigade, Royal Field Artillery
I realised I wasn't dead, that I was alive. I realised that if these wounds didn't prove fatal, I should get back to my parents, to my sister, to the girl that I was going to marry – the girl that had sent me a letter practically every day from the beginning of the war. I was taken to a dressing station and given morphia, and then I must have had that sleep I so badly needed, for I didn't recollect any more until I found myself in a clean bed with white sheets, and I could hear the lovely, wonderful voices of our nurses, with their English, Scotch and Irish accents. And I think then I completely broke down, for next thing the padre was sitting beside my bedside. He was trying to comfort me. He said I'd had an operation, and he told me that he had some relatives out there who had been out there right from the beginning, and by God's grace they hadn't had a scratch. He said, 'They've been lucky, haven't they?' I thought to myself, 'Lucky? Poor devils.'

Sergeant Cyril Lee

I remember trying to help a lad in this copse about a hundred yards from our jumping-off trench. There was no hope of getting to him, he was struggling in the middle of this huge sea of mud. Then I saw a small sapling and we tried to bend it over to him. We were seasoned soldiers by then, but the look on the lad's face was really pathetic – he was only a mere boy. It pricked my conscience, I felt I should try and do something more for him, but I couldn't do a thing – had I bent it a little more I should have gone in with him, and had anyone else gone near this sea of mud they should have gone in with him too, as so many had.

Lieutenant E. W. Stoneham
Royal Artillery

One day when we were less active in the battery, another officer and myself went out across the battlefield to reconnoitre – to see if we could find an alternative position should we have to take one up. We'd walked about for some hours and were getting rather tired, so we decided to rest. There were no dugouts to shelter in but we did find, as usual, a huge shell crater. So we got into this crater and sat down. Presently my fellow officer, who happened to be something of a scholar, started reciting Shelley's 'Skylark' and I found myself frantically yelling out 'Stop!' I realised that if he'd gone on, I don't know what would have happened to my nerve.

Fusilier Joseph Pickard
1/5th Battalion, Northumberland Fusiliers

I remember being in this sort of advanced clearing station. And when I come round it was dark and I was lying on a stretcher, and I didn't know what was the matter with me. It turned out there was a blanket over the top of me and I'd been left for dead. My old lady later got the number of my grave and the King and Queen's sympathy, but fortunately I didn't know that at the time. I got rid of this blanket and then I saw a light near where I was, so I shouted down an orderly, and two of them eventually came down and had a look at me. They wouldn't give me a drink

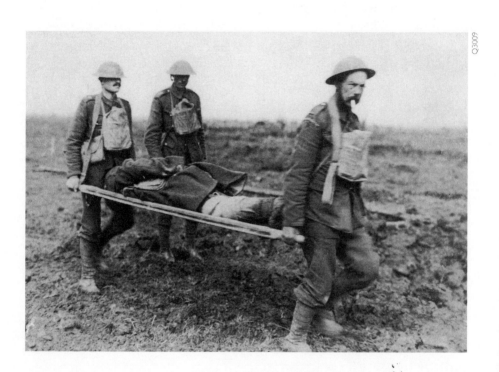

Guardsmen bring in a wounded soldier at Passchendaele.

of course, but they picked the stretcher up and put it straight on a hospital train.

BATTLE OF CAMBRAI

Corporal Jack Dillon
2nd Battalion, Tank Corps

The location of the battle of Cambrai was kept so secret that even my colonel didn't know about it. In fact I was told before he was, because I was company reconnaissance officer. It was my job to reconnoitre the route up to the Front. I thought that Cambrai was a splendid choice because it hadn't been fought over much and the going was very good, one couldn't ask for better conditions.

I planned the route in the usual way. We'd been allotted our frontage, so I knew where to go and it was just a question of how to get there. It was a fair distance, about three miles, and I walked some of it during the day and the rest at dusk. I did my trick of laying a tape from the front line back over the route I'd reconnoitred, dodging round things we wanted to avoid, and eventually ended up where the tanks would start. I was pretty tired by the end of the day and got an hour or two of sleep.

On the night of the 20th of November we started moving tanks up to the starting position. The tanks were driven up by relief drivers and relief crews to enable the crews to be fresh for the battle. I was guiding them, and during the guiding I had a very nasty experience. We had shrouded torches and I got caught up in some barbed wire. The leading tank was bearing down on me and I couldn't stop it or get free of the wire. I flashed my torch and held it up as high as I could, and the driver eventually stopped with a volley of oaths because it was an unheard-of thing to do. You should never flash a light at a driver because it blinds him. But that had been my purpose. I stopped the tank and got free.

The tanks were terribly noisy when you were inside one, but outside on soft ground they weren't too bad, and we'd arranged for the Flying Corps to provide cover for the noise. So we got to our starting position, about 150 yards behind our front line, and the tanks were lined up so when the whistle blew that morning they only had to drive forward. At zero hour the tanks moved forward and there was a creeping barrage that wouldn't damage the ground at all – our artillery had pinpointed the German artillery to stop them firing at the tanks. My job was to be on hand in case of further developments. Then, out of the blue, came a bullet that split my thumb and knocked my walking stick miles out of my hand.

But the Front opened up like a pat of butter. The trenches of the Hindenburg Line were our main objective. To cross that line with tanks was quite impossible, as it was enormously wide and deep, but the ingenuity of our headquarters staff produced the answer. Enormous bundles of fascines (in other words brushwood) were provided. They were about five feet in diameter, like enormous toilet rolls, they weighed about a ton and a half and were carried on the nose of the tank. As the tank came to the trench, this bundle was released and fell into the bottom of the trench. This enabled the tank to nose down, rest on it and crawl up over the other side, and in this way the uncrossable Hindenburg Line was crossed.

The Germans were very annoyed with us for this ungentlemanly trick. Many of them thought these tanks with peculiar things on their noses were some new infernal machines. However, it worked, and for the first time we had some form of tactical manoeuvre because there were plenty of tanks on the ground. It wasn't a very wide front and there were about 350 tanks, so the idea was to select a trench and at point X, the leading tank would cross and then move on up to the next trench. The next two tanks would cross over the same fascine and turn right and left, clearing the trenches on each side. The last tank would follow along and overtake the first one, so that the process could be repeated at the next line of trenches. The process of clearing the trench on each side was fairly simple, because each tank only had one side to deal with. The tank would stop halfway across the trench and fire a few rounds of 6-pounder down it, and that cleared it all right. The infantry would then come up and take over.

As regards crossing the barbed wire, this was a miracle to see. I'd never seen such a depth of barbed wire. It was ten yards deep, four feet high, and so dense you could barely poke a broom handle through it. It could never be destroyed by artillery fire in a month of Sundays. But the tanks went through it and I've personally followed the tracks and walked straight through as if it had been on a carpet. The tanks cleared the wire for the crossing of large numbers of people by driving into it two abreast, dropping in steel anchors then turning away from each other and going down the length of the wire pulling the anchors after them. The result was to drag the enormous barbed-wire fences into balls of wire about 20 feet high, and when they cleared the ground, it was as clean as a whistle. There wasn't a scrap of anything left, not even weeds.

We got through all four German lines without any serious opposition. The tanks reached their objective quickly, and when I caught up with them I found the crews sitting down drinking mugs of tea. The infantry were sculling about wondering at having got through so easily. It was a complete breakthrough. If the cavalry corps had been on the spot to carry on the attack, as was intended, it could have been a major British victory. We could have pushed through to the other side of Cambrai and there would have been a complete readjustment of the German line. But the cavalry weren't produced until hours too late and then there weren't enough troops on the ground.

It was obvious by about 10 a.m. that there had been three or four hours for the Germans to reorganise. By that time the tanks had been withdrawn, covered by the infantry, and I had no further reason to be there, so I found a spare ammunition mule, got on its back and got a lift back to a casualty clearing station where I got my thumb dressed. It was a nasty mess but it healed marvellously and I got full use of it back.

Captain Horace Birks
Royal Tank Corps
We had rough compasses in the tanks and set course for the enemy line. It was dead silent until we got to the enemy wire, which was zero hour for guns, and that again was a first-class show – Crystal Palace had nothing on it. There was no answer from the Germans at all. It was the

first time in our lives we saw the Hun being blown up all over the place, and the troops were frightfully pleased. There was no machine-gun fire so we opened up our tanks, but then we got into this belt of wire. It was quite terrifying because it was about seven feet high and very thick, and over 120 yards deep in places. Of course if we had stopped in that and got our tracks whipped off then we should have been for it. Instead the tanks made great swathes in the wire and the Jocks, who were playing with us, came through the gaps we made and we all emerged on the other side, into the deep valley known as the Grand Ravine.

Captain Douglas Wimberley
232nd Machine Gun Company, Machine Gun Corps
The wire at Cambrai was about four foot high and fifteen yards wide, but the tanks that had gone in front of us had ploughed through it like a ship in the sea, and we had no difficulty at all in following their tracks. We also got over the Hindenburg front line. That was an enormous trench, about eight feet deep and fifteen feet wide, but again we were able to get over quite easily. Getting our mules over wasn't so easy, but luckily there were quite a lot of Germans there who were more or less looking for someone to surrender to, so they helped us get them across.

When it became really light it was a wonderful sight. We could see the lines of tanks ahead of us going down the slope towards the Grand Ravine and the lines of Jocks slowly moving along behind them. As we passed, there were numbers of Germans in every direction. The ones near us were really just trying to surrender, but further down the slopes we could see quite a lot more running around trying to escape from the tanks.

They'd left their trenches and dugouts – probably rightly – because had they stayed they'd have got Mills bombs from the Jocks. They were a very poor type of German – they were small, unshaven and dirty, and quite a lot were wearing spectacles, rather like the cartoons of the time of what the Germans were supposed to look like.

Later on we got into position and began shooting 'overhead fire,' over the lines of the advancing Jocks. The extraordinary thing was that for about three minutes I had to stop firing altogether, as a great number of Boche came straight towards our machine-guns with their hands up, and it would have been absolute sheer massacre to have killed them.

Lieutenant Miles Reinke
2nd Guards Dragoons, German Army

When the first tanks passed the first line, we thought we would be compelled to retreat towards Berlin. I remember one tank, by the name of Hyena, which advanced very far then suddenly stopped about 1,000 yards from my little dugout. Some of the boys soon discovered they could stop the tanks by throwing a hand grenade into the manhole on the top. Once this was known, the boys realised that there was a blind spot – that the machine-guns couldn't reach every point around the tank, and these points were very important in the defence.

I was shocked and felt very sorry for those fellows in the tanks, because there was no escape for them. Once a man was on top of the tank it was doomed to failure, and the poor fellows were not able to escape. The fuel would start to burn and after an hour and a half or two hours we saw only burning tanks in front and behind us. Then the approaching infantry behind the tanks still had to overcome the machine-guns of our infantry. These were still effective because the British artillery had to stop shooting as the tanks were advancing, and naturally some of our machine-gun nests were still in full action.

Anyhow, the attack came to a standstill and we waited for several regiments of cavalry to sweep up and drive us towards Berlin. But this didn't happen, much to our surprise. When new troops were pulled together near this break-in of the British tanks, the situation settled down, we were formed anew, and afterwards we could clearly see the spot where the British tanks had driven into the German lines. Then after a few days we made a counter-attack. It didn't succeed on the first or the second day, but on the third day we were finally successful.

Sub Lieutenant William Benham
Hawke Battalion, Royal Naval Division

When I got to France there was snow all over the Western Front. There had been a very severe frost and there were lots of frozen corpses that couldn't be moved or buried. Before I got there the Germans had made an early dawn attack across the snow, wearing white sheets and using whitened rifles. They'd managed to drive back the last battalion with great casualties because they hadn't been seen, and we still had several bodies lying there frozen, unable to be moved because of the frost.

When at last the frost broke, we were able to get the bodies down, and one of them was Sub Lieutenant Alan Campbell, the son of Mrs. Patrick Campbell, the actress. We managed to get these bodies to a burial ground five or six miles behind the front line, and I had the unenviable job of being in charge of the burial party. We carried the men over the trenches until we got to where the transport could come, then the bodies were put in GS wagons and taken down for burial. Afterwards, I turned to walk the five miles back to the line. It was a pouring wet afternoon, with squally sleet going down our necks and the roads full of puddles and shell-holes.

My orderly, a dour Scot, was with me and presently we heard the sound of a car coming along. My orderly commented, 'Some ruddy staff wallah, Sir.' I said, 'Yes, I expect so,' but instead of swishing past us in a shower of mud and water, the car stopped and a cheerful young voice said, 'Would you chaps like a lift?' I was being offered a lift by the Prince of Wales, who was on one of his tours of the front line. My orderly sat beside his driver while he and I sat in the back with his equerry. We had a long talk and I found him more than interesting. After three or four miles his way was different from mine, so he put us down and we trudged on back to the trenches.

Gunner William Towers
Royal Field Artillery

I was one of fifteen drivers taking thirty horses to try and get ammunition through to our battery's guns. Each driver had two horses, and you had a pack for each horse with eight shells in it. The Germans were watching for anybody who tried to come through and the first few times we were shelled and had to come back. Sergeant Emsley said, 'Towers, I want you to come up front about six yards behind me and when I give the signal, we gallop.'

So I was following the sergeant, but just after we set off the Germans dropped a shell right by us and that was it. I remember going up in the air and landing on the floor. I wasn't in any pain but I could see that shrapnel had gone into my kneecap. It was a joy, actually, because I thought it wasn't too bad and therefore I'd soon be home and out of it all. Two men from RAMC came over and one of them got a bottle of iodine and tipped it into the hole in my knee. Oh! The pain was terrific. They ran some bandages round it and put me on a stretcher.

I couldn't see where we were going because all around was barren land, but all of a sudden they stopped and put the stretcher down. I said, 'What's up?' and they said, 'You're all right, don't worry,' and went to a trap-door. They lifted it up and they put the stretcher on a slide and lowered it down. There was a proper hospital underneath. It had been a German hospital. There was a full staff of hospital people there. They took me down to a theatre and a sister pressed a white mask over my face, the anaesthetic hit me and the next thing I knew, I was waking up on a train.

I was in a carriage on a stretcher fixed on the wall, and when I looked round Sergeant Emsley was next to me. He'd been wounded in the leg as well. They took us to a hospital at Étaples and then put me in a bed and fitted me with a Thomas splint, a round wooden ring with iron bars and a footrest. The pain from my knee was getting terrible, so when I saw an officer coming up with his arm around two sisters and laughing, I said, 'Excuse me, Sir, could you have a look at my knee? The pain is driving me crazy.'

He came over and he stank of whisky. When the nurses took the bandages off he said, 'Oh, there's fluid above the knee. We'll tap that tonight.' So they came for me to go to the theatre and I thought, 'Thank God for that.' But when I woke up in early hours of the morning I thought, 'Oh my God. My leg's gone.' They'd guillotined it off without saying a word. There had been no hint at all that I was going to lose my leg. They hadn't even looked at it until I asked the doctor.

That day, I prayed to die. All I could think of were the men who stood begging on street corners with a crutch with a tin can. And I was a footballer and that was finished. It was terrible. Late in the afternoon, a nurse came up, took the blanket off and started tearing the gauze off that had dried on. As she was pulling it I think I called her every name I knew. I said, 'You're inhuman, woman!' but she didn't take any notice, she must have been deaf. She could have wet it, which would have made it come off easily, but she wouldn't. I was in agony.

After that, they put me on a boat and I was taken to Stockport General Hospital. A civilian doctor, Mr. Fenwick, came to look at me and when he took the bandages off the smell was terrible. The flesh had receded, two inches of bone stuck out and it had gone black. He said, 'Send a telegram for his mother and father to come right away.' He thought I was going to die. He told a sister to get a bowl of sterilised water with peroxide in it and that my leg had to be syringed with this solution every four hours. And then it started to get better. The wound became beautiful clean red flesh. Mr. Fenwick said, 'We're going to win, Willie.' My parents came, and my future wife, whom I'd met when I was home on leave. I think it was her that pulled me through. And Mr. Fenwick was an angel. He arranged for a friend of his, a surgeon who specialised in amputations, to re-amputate the leg and make a proper stump. He did it and it was perfect. Everybody seeing it said, 'What a beautiful job.'

1918

In that trench came up Field Marshal Haig's famous message 'Backs to the wall. Every man will stand and fight and fall. No more retreating.'

By transferring many of their divisions in Russia to the Western Front, Germany enjoyed a temporary numerical advantage over the western allies, with 192 divisions against 169. The German army was recognised to maximise its chances. The youngest and fittest soldiers were concentrated in special 'attack' divisions; the oldest and weakest were concentrated in second-line divisions only really capable of static defence.

On March 21 the British Fifth Army was subjected to the most intensive artillery fire of the war so far: 6,600 guns pummelled the British positions and an early morning fog meant that the stormtroopers leading the German attack were on top of the British before they knew what was happening. The attack broke down in several places where the fog lifted or local resistance was well coordinated, but the line was penetrated to considerable depth elsewhere. Some units were surrounded. Others were compelled to fall back as their flanks were left 'in the air.' By March 24 the Germans had advanced fourteen miles, the greatest advance on the Western Front since 1914.

The British were driven back to the old battlefields of the Somme. However, if the British were finding some disagreeably familiar sights, the Germans were staggered at what they discovered. British supply dumps were packed with foodstuffs not seen in Germany for years. Told that the Allies were on their last legs, the Germans were appalled to find their enemies living in what was, by comparison, the lap of luxury.

The perennial problem faced by attacking forces on the Western Front was how to advance over a battlefield, even if the enemy withdrew. The great artillery pieces that destroyed all before them were mostly horse-drawn, and to get them across the churned-up fields they created required new roads, if not railways. Ludendorff planned a succession of blows at different parts of the Front to avoid sustained assaults across the old Somme battleground. The main phase of his offensive was scheduled for March 28, an attack near Arras intended to drive all the way to the Channel coast at Boulogne, seventy-two miles up the road. Preceded by an equally ferocious barrage, nine German divisions attacked four British ones, but were stopped in their tracks. Although a thrust at Amiens made better progress, the Germans were compelled to admit the failure of their offensive on April 5.

Ninety thousand British and French soldiers had been taken prisoner during the great German offensive. The Germans persevered, launching another, smaller-scale assault near Ypres on April 9. Again the British were driven back, prompting Haig's famous Order of the Day on the tenth: 'With our backs to the wall and believing in the justice of our cause each one must fight to the end. The safety of our homes and the freedom of mankind alike depend upon the conduct of each one of us at this critical moment.' Further German assaults took place on the Somme on April 24, where Villers-Bretonneux fell and was retaken by a prompt counter-attack that involved the war's first (and only) tank versus tank engagement – thirteen tanks a side. The British won.

The Germans attacked the French on May 27. The chosen battlefield was the Chemin des Dames. In three days the Germans advanced forty miles, and by the beginning of June, German soldiers were back on the banks of the Marne, the high water mark of their 1914 campaign.

The mood of crisis in the Allied camp was grave, but General

Foch blocked a direct attack towards Paris and the senior commanders on both sides began to recognise that Germany had shot its bolt. German casualties from March 21 to June 1918 were not far short of a million. German advances had driven deep salients in the old front line, almost doubling the length of front that the much-reduced German army had to occupy. On July 18 the French counterattacked, with 750 light tanks supporting their assault, and the Germans – as in 1914 – found themselves driven back to the river Aisne.

The British Army lost a thousand artillery pieces in the retreats of 1918, but so massive was British industrial superiority that they were replaced by the summer. On August 8 the British attacked and smashed through the German front line at Amiens to a depth of eight miles. Not that success was obtained by weight of numbers but by superior operational ability: better artillery tactics, air superiority, and the coordinated action of infantry and tanks. Germany never recovered: the British Army stormed every successive defensive line it encountered. By the end of October with the French now revived and the Americans more than earning their spurs the game was up. Germany requested an armistice on November 3, thus averting the spectacle of an Allied offensive across the German frontier. The armistice came into effect at eleven o'clock in the morning of November 11 – 'the eleventh hour of the eleventh day of the eleventh month.'

Gunner Leonard Ounsworth
124 Heavy Battery, Royal Garrison Artillery
The thaw started on January the 15th, with rain as well – it was so complete that the ground just collapsed. The end of the dugout just fell in and buried one of the cooks – he'd have suffocated if we hadn't got him out in time.

Four of the guns were moved to Sorel that day. They couldn't have picked a worse one for it, because by the time we got there the ground was an absolute quagmire. We used the gun planks, which we carried in the wagons. These planks were about ten or twelve foot long. We ran the gun on these: you would pick them up and put them in front again. It was a bloody nightmare of a job.

Corporal Ivor Watkins
6th Battalion, Welch Regiment

An officer along with a company sergeant-major would come round with your ration of rum every night. A lot of people were under the impression that you were given rum to make you mad, to build up your confidence, but that was not the case. The rum was given to keep your tummy warm during the night. We never got enough to get drunk. But while we were in the Béthune sector in March two chaps stole a jar of rum. They were dead by the following morning. They drank so much that they regurgitated and killed themselves. I remember looking at them: their faces were white as marble, white as marble.

There was always the fellow who wanted to flog something or scrounge something. I remember one chappie who had a broken pocket watch which he tried to flog to the Chinese Labour Corps. He was telling us about it. 'What did they say, Taff?' 'Oh,' he said, 'no bloody bonny-la, no bloody goody-la.' He got so fed up he threw the watch up into the air. He said there was one damn big rugby scrum to try to get it. They wouldn't buy it off him, but once he threw it up in the air they all wanted it.

Captain Cyril Dennys
212 Siege Battery, Royal Garrison Artillery

Well of course I was very young. I think that the sexual aspect worried some of the older men quite a lot. I mean, it made them jumpy. I remember there was one case where a captain who was getting on in age applied for special leave. You could get a week's special leave to go to Paris or somewhere. On his leave chit he was asked for his reason. He put quite boldly, sexual starvation. And to everyone's surprise and delight he got his leave. He went off and we hoped he satisfied his needs in Paris.

Major Andrew Bain
1/7th Battalion, Argyll and Sutherland Highlanders

There was a shortage of metal at home so they wanted anything easily transportable brought back from the Front. I made a list, a sort of salvage-price list, and distributed this to the four battalions in my brigade. It said 'For every rifle you'll be credited with two pounds; for a shell case six pence; for ammunition about two pence a dozen for spent cartridge cases.' And that mounted up enormously. One month the 6th Gordons, by just combing over the ground and picking up everything that was there, collected about six thousand pounds.

Private Hubert Trotman
Royal Marine Light Infantry

It was time for leave. We travelled in a boxcar to Calais. We were as lousy as cuckoos. When we got to Calais we had to head for the fumigator. But there we saw a queue a mile long. We were told the boat sailed in half an hour and if we didn't make it we would lose a day of our leave. So those of us at the tail end of the queue broke off, went down to the docks and, damn me, we just walked onto the boat. We hid down below until it had sailed. So we disembarked unfumigated. That night I got as far as Paddington and the next day I caught the first train to Didcot. When I got home, just to take it in and breathe the familiar smell of the bakery again, I stood outside the shop for a while. Then I opened the door and shouted, 'Mother, I'm outside. I'm home.' What a sight I must have been. I hadn't changed my clothes for months. I had a beard and I was in a hell of a state. She took one look at me and tears rolled down her face. She said, 'I'll clean you up.' 'No,' I said, 'You can't do that yet.' I put my hand in my armpit and took out a handful of lice. 'Look,' I said. 'Lice, hordes of them, I can't come in like this.' I put them back where they came from and went up to the hospital to see the matron. She knew me well, because I had visited her on my rounds when delivering bread to the hospital. She said, 'Hubert, we will soon fix you up.' She put a large sheet on the ground outside. 'You stand on that. Empty your pockets and then take all your clothes off.' Then she put me in a big bath. When I got out I asked about my clothes. She told me she had put them in the copper, lice and all. I had to spend my leave in civvies.

Lieutenant Colonel Alfred Irwin
8th Battalion, East Surrey Regiment

We got huge drafts after the actions, and they all became 8th East Surreys in no time at all. I always made a point of greeting a new draft by telling them a bit of the history of the regiment and what it had done and so on. We were a successful battalion. We always felt that if a particularly horrid job had to be done we were chosen for it. We and the Suffolks. We only once failed to take our objective. There was a very strong battalion feeling. The chaps we got were gradually getting nearer and nearer to the dregs of the nation, of course, but they all seemed to become 8th East Surreys in an extraordinary short length of time.

Captain Charles Carrington
1/5th Battalion, Warwickshire Regiment

In the last year of the war I was sent home to train recruits at a camp in Northumberland, where we used to take in what were called A4 boys. These were boys who were fit but underage and untrained. They'd been called up under the Conscription Act and had to be made into soldiers in six months. As soon as they were nineteen years and trained, they were pushed off to France in batches. By these days the regimental system had quite broken down. They came from any part of England and they might be sent to any regiment. I didn't altogether enjoy this experience, I didn't much like being a young, fit man and pushing off these other young, fit men to fight instead of me, but I suppose somebody had to do it. When they came to us, they were weedy but they weren't when they left us.

Corporal Ivor Watkins
6th Battalion, Welch Regiment

At Houplines near Armentières, in March 1918, we were going up by night as a covering party for an Australian tunnelling company, which meant if Jerry come over we'd have got it in the neck before the tunnellers. We got into a house where there was a cellar, got some mattresses and a brazier and made ourselves comfortable. There were some 18-pounder batteries behind us and the Germans were going at them. On the night of the 16th of March he started shelling those batteries with mustard-gas shells. Our gas guard must have got killed because we had no warning. Gas is heavier than air and it must have got down into the cellars because when we woke up in the morning, we felt our eyes burning terribly and thought it was the smoke from the brazier. We started rubbing our eyes but what we were doing was rubbing the mustard gas into them. We soon realised with the smell, which is akin to horseradish, what we had done. We all came up and were rushed down to the casualty clearing station. Our eyes were watering profusely. Nothing but water running from our eyes. They were burning like hell. I could just see a mist in front of me, but I hadn't rubbed as hard as some of the others.

From the clearing station I was rushed to the 2nd Canadian Hospital. Within four days, I was at St. Luke's Hospital in Bradford, where they were clearing out the casualties as quickly as they could. They attached to me a sign 'Gas Shell. Very Severe.'

When I got to Bradford, I couldn't see. It was the most terrifying experience I have ever had. Was I going to be blind for life? What was I going to do? My trade, my employment gone. It hit me very, very hard. For the first month or so, I couldn't recognise anything, then there was a gradual haze. I had a Scottish army sister and I'll always remember the intonation, 'Taffy, I'll get your sight back, don't worry.' I was given goggles to wear to keep the glare out. I also had burns to the tender parts of my body which they treated with ointment. I had a steam kettle as well, to inhale. And then I started heavy smoking as I thought to clear my chest, but it was obviously just soothing the nerves. It was fashionable to smoke. We were given cigarettes in hospital. We were treated right royally. I recovered my sight. But so many didn't. I had my 20th birthday in that hospital.

THE GERMAN BREAKTHROUGH, MARCH 21

Sergeant-Major Richard Tobin
Hood Battalion, Royal Naval Division
We took the line in the spring of 1918 – tough, grim and determined.
We were hardened veterans of many battles. Our constitutions had sur-
vived the winter. The battalion wit said we were quality not quantity.
The collapse of Russia had released a huge German army. Some said
half a million, others said a million.

On March the 20th my battalion was lying in Havrincourt Wood on
the Cambrai front. We were brigade reserve, the front line was being
bombarded. The enemy showed every sign of being ready, his guns had
registered on all important positions, and mid-March soaked us with
gas shells – thousands a day fell. Mustard gas had lain in the hollows for
days and the gas that affected the throat reduced the voice to a whisper.
This affected our communications 'phone and word of mouth. We were
a whispering army. But we would go back foot by foot, inch by inch,
fighting and killing – we were determined.

That night in the trenches, when the wind was in the right direction
we could hear the German trains and transport rumbling up with their
great army that was going to sweep us into the sea. We were grim, we
were determined, for behind us lay the Somme battlefields, every yard
soaked with British blood shed for almost two years of hard fighting.

I made a bed in the bend – I couldn't sleep. A quietness I knew so
well falls over fronts just before an attack – the quietness was on. I fell
into an uneasy sleep and about 5 o'clock I was awakened with a roll of
drums – gunfire. I knew this was it. I knew in a few moments the
enemy's long-range guns would bomb the rear areas to prevent reinforcements. I woke the band sergeant and we cleared out and got into a
dugout – we sat and listened to the thud of shells – the ground trem-
bled. When it quietened down I came out. No orders had come from
the brigade and nothing from the battalion.

I decided to get back to the wood. When I arrived there I found my
battalion had been sent to support another. There was a plank road
through the wood and slowly troops began to trickle down the road. I

gathered what information I could but there was none of my battalion. I had heard that our division had held its front except in one small sector. But on our left flank the Fifth Army had had a rough time: They were weak and had a hell of a position. They had suffered many casualties – rather than holding on, they were just clinging on. I sat and awaited orders – soon the trickle of troops had stopped coming through the wood. I sat looking up the road, waiting and hoping. Suddenly, I heard a muffled shout from my rear, 'Sergeant-Major.' I turned – it was one of our officers. 'Come in as quickly and quietly as you can.' We moved back out of the wood to our battalion – they had withdrawn round the side of the wood and not through it. Then for days it was solid fighting.

Major Hartwig Pohlmann
36th Prussian Division

On the 19th of March we got our orders to go into the preparation positions. During the night behind the front line, there was a lot of traffic carrying ammunition and bringing into position the guns. There was very much life and a lot of people moving in the trenches. On the 20th we got the order, tomorrow morning the attack will start – we got a high feeling. We were in high spirits because we hoped for our victory in this battle. That night about 3 a.m. I got out of my dugout to look round. The night was silent, nothing was to be heard, and there was a clear sky, stars shining and glittering. I thought these are the same stars that my family at home will look at.

At 9 a.m. I stood up and had a little breakfast and then left my dugout. I could see nothing. It was thick fog. I thought how can we attack in this? Nevertheless we had to attack. I told my soldiers to hang on with one hand to the belt of the man in front, but they couldn't do that for long because the ground was very rough and we had to creep through barbed wire. So soon there was a pell-mell, but everyone knew that they had to go straight on. The soldiers that lost their own companies made contact with other companies and followed them. Soon I had soldiers of several companies of my regiment together and they followed me. As we advanced through the fog we suddenly heard guns firing behind us. We realised that we had come out behind a British battery which was firing barrage fire. They didn't know that we had broken through. One of my men laid a hand on the shoulder of the British officer and said: 'Cease fire.' They were stunned.

Lieutenant Cyril Dennys
212 Siege Battery, Royal Garrison Artillery

Apart from a bit of gratified conceit, I did realise that it was going to be not like, but much worse than, the battles of Ypres, because the odds were much greater against us. I felt sure that the Germans would make a strong effort when the time came.

Well, on the evening of the 20th of March I went to the billets to spend the night there and wait for the orders to go forward. We knew the attack was coming the next day. I felt awful. There were no other officers of the battery in the billet. I was entirely by myself, and was trying to face up to what I knew was going to be a very unpleasant morning and probably my last.

At first I played the gramophone. In those days I had a young man's taste for rather lush music, and played Puccini. Then I went to bed. At 4:45 the telephone went, and a voice said, 'Orders to man battle stations.' Then I heard a curious noise in the sky overhead. It seemed to me that it was just as if some giants were carrying huge strips of canvas. It was caused by German long-range gun shells passing over on their way to the railway junctions and places behind our line. But apart from that noise, there was a very serious rumble from the Front. I quickly ate some food, got some equipment and went outside. I could see first of all that it was thick fog, but it was not thick enough to prevent my being able to see that there were a regrettable number of explosions up front. I could see points of fire thrown up and that small birch trees were continually being thrown in the air. They were the birch trees in D'Holnon Wood.

I went straight to the battery and reported to the major in command. He said it was important that someone got to the forward man observation post; I was to take one signaller with me and send two signallers to go up to the post by a different route. Then perhaps one or other party would make it. As I left, I felt a slight trembling of the ground as this barrage went off, and that didn't improve my morale.

Well, the two signallers going by a separate route never got to the observation post. They were caught by a shell, wounded and evacuated. I never saw them again. I took a perfectly splendid young corporal called Burn, an Irishman who didn't have to be in the war at all, because they had no conscription. He and I started towards the battle zone, and the high ground in front. As we walked the fog became slightly thinner, which enabled us to see slightly more easily. And we didn't enjoy what we saw. I thought to myself well, the only thing that's absolutely certain is that someone's got to be in the observation post and ought to be there as soon as possible.

What we had seen was a very great number of shell bursts. As we got further they got thicker, because we had walked right into the German barrage. I had a strong temptation when I met a particularly intimidating shell-hole, still smoking, to get down into another hole and wait for it to get better. But I knew that it wasn't going to get better. I thought to myself that if I'm hit it was better to be hit trying to get to the post than hiding somewhere.

So my corporal and I got into the outskirts of D'Holnon Wood, where we met a colonel and two other officers. I said, 'It's pretty nasty this morning, isn't it?' He said, 'Yes it is, but I don't think it can go on very long at this rate. I mean there must be some limit to the ammunition they've got.'

Just at that point, there was a very loud crash in the air caused by the burst of a high-explosive shell and I couldn't see anything for mud, dust and smoke.

After it cleared, I couldn't see the colonel at all but the subaltern was lying on his back. I put my hand under his head, in fact I put my hand into his brains, which were out. He had been hit by a fragment that had come through the front and taken his brains away at the back. I thought, 'What shall I do now?' Just going away and leaving him isn't very good. On the other hand, it was quite clear that even if he could have been got to an advanced dressing station, he had only minutes to live. I thought he'd be dead already but he wasn't, he was still breathing. However, I thought to myself, 'That's all very well, but there is really no excuse at all for not trying to get to the observation post. You must do that. You don't have to hang about here.'

Then Burn came up and he and I went on through the wood and finally we found the post where we were supposed to be. And it had not been hit, that was the astonishing thing about it. Moreover, when we took the line, we got through to the brigade. I was now the forward observation officer for the brigade.

I spoke to the brigade and told them that the barrage had lifted over me and was now in the British battery area. Still strong, but gradually dying away. I also couldn't see any breaks in the battle-zone wire that would make it possible for anyone to get through. On the other hand there were practically no troops. I thought – I didn't say this on the line – there is no reason why the Germans shouldn't just get up with wire-cutters and methodically cut their way through the wire. We couldn't have stopped them. Why the Germans didn't massacre the lot of us at that point I don't know. The Germans of course like to stick to their plans.

By now it was a fine afternoon and I could see the Germans had brought up their field kitchens and were determined that their chaps were going to have a hot meal that day. Then I saw something rather closer, grey figures, obviously German, going to and fro in a couple of copses. This struck me as a target worth having. I phoned through to brigade and said that I could see German infantry massing in these copses. I think they were preparing to make an attack on one of the surviving redoubts. Brigade turned all their surviving guns – that's two batteries out of six Howitzers, and two heavier guns in another battery – onto the two copses. This was a most gratifying sight from my point of view, the place was filled with Germans.

Sergeant Ernest Bryan
17th Battalion, King's Liverpool Regiment
We knew what the orders were; they must not break through. If retirement, and it will be necessary, retire but don't let them break through. That was all our orders, and that's what we did, that's what we did from

21st March, nine days and ten nights of scrapping and retiring, scrapping and retiring round the villages. We got to Ham eventually. That was the biggest town there was outside St. Quentin. When we got into there nobody knew anybody. We were a nondescript pool of all sorts of regiments, bits and pieces, anybody at all; sanitary people, cooks, everybody, they were all in it.

Lieutenant Ulrich Burke
2nd Battalion, Devonshire Regiment
Then we halted, stayed where we were. We did as much defence work as possible and waited for them to come. Then they'd come on and we'd get the order – after we'd shot and killed quite a few – to retire. Well, we were retiring and retiring and we were never still. You never knew where you were going to pick up any food, where you were going to pick up ammunition, and some of the men got windy and really would have run. Now if an officer or a sergeant had behaved like that, the whole lot would have panicked. The only thing that kept them there was respect for your bravery and your attitude; you knew what you were doing and you were saving them all you could. And that kept them steady.

Sergeant-Major Richard Tobin
Hood Battalion, Royal Naval Division
On March the 26th we dropped into a trench. It was a trench we knew of old. We had started to retreat on the 21st of March, 1918, and here we were back in the trench we had started to attack from on November the 13th, 1916.

Corporal Sidney Amatt
7th Battalion, Essex Regiment
We were given instructions to retire. As we looked over we saw that the Germans had advanced on our left flank and on our right and they were behind us only a hundred yards away. Somehow we arrived at what had been a reserve trench. There a sergeant of the Machine Gun Corps told us to go down the dugout out of the way of the shellfire. We all bundled

These are two British soldiers who were killed in the German advance of March 21. Someone has taken their boots.

This is a view of the devastation after an 18-pounder battery was caught by shell-fire on Corduroy Road.

down this dugout and when we got down there we saw an officer who said: 'Next time you're relieved, you'll be relieved by the Germans,' and he made some coffee for us. We had left one man as a sentry at the top of the dugout. Suddenly he yelled down to us that the Germans were in the trench. As we made ready to go up the steps, he came down and joined us. I expect he was terrified.

Next thing, we heard a German voice up above. One of the chaps with us who knew a little German said he's calling down that we've got to surrender. Anyway, the next thing we heard was a grenade bouncing down the steps – it was a rather terrifying experience – as we knew it was going to explode at the bottom. There was nowhere for us to go. We cowered there. It exploded and a corporal close to it was splattered with a lot of small pieces of this grenade but everyone else was all right. We were ordered to come up with our hands up. When we got to the top he said we were ordered to say 'Kamerad,' which we did because there was a big unter-officer – like our sergeant-major – with a Luger pistol which he pressed into your ribs and looked at you with a mean look. If you said 'Kamerad,' he'd nod you on and you went up the trench and were all collected together. When we got to the top of the trench I was astonished to find that the whole area we'd occupied a few hours before was swarming with Germans. The whole army was moving forward.

APRIL

Gunner George Cole
3rd Northumbrian Brigade, Royal Field Artillery

We were cut off from everybody else, repairing telephone lines. We took shelter in a dugout for a time and the next thing I knew when we came out was there was Germans there. They'd broken through and come round both sides of us. They were standing there and one of them had a trench mortar bomb. A potato beater, that's what we used to call it. We had no arms. We never carried rifles or anything. He's standing there with a bomb. We were flabbergasted. We then met other people who'd been taken prisoner. The Germans told us to carry their wounded to a casualty clearing station.

In hastily dug rifle pits, men of the French and British Army await the advancing German Army.

Marky and me were carrying a big fella with a wounded leg. We didn't have stretchers so we were just carrying him in blankets. All he kept saying was 'Wasser, wasser, wasser.' He wanted water. As we trudged along we saw one of our lads lying wounded, one of the 6th Durhams, and he was conscious. I said, 'Marky, put him down.' We just tipped the German into a shell-hole and picked the 6th Durham lad up. He was easy to carry and we were hurrying back with him. I said, 'For God's sake, don't ever mention this. We'll be shot out of hand.'

Sergeant-Major Richard Tobin
Hood Battalion, Royal Naval Division
My battalion had withdrawn around the wood and now, for days, it was an infantryman's battle. Even our divisional artillery joined us as infantry, often firing alongside of us over open sights. Our major-general and his brigadiers were with us, controlling the troops, Wellington like. It was leapfrog in reverse. Battalion went through battalion. Company through company. But always a company, always a battalion standing facing the enemy, ready to fight. And so we came back to the Somme battlefields, these old battlefields. In that trench came up Field Marshal Haig's famous message 'Backs to the wall. Every man will stand and fight and fall. No more retreating.' But still, we had a little joy in our hearts, the infantrymen, because although we had not won, we had not been beaten. The only lead in our hearts was the thought that we were back to the old trench ding-dong. No signs of an end. So the weeks and months went by. April, May. We even did one or two small attacks.

Captain Maberly Esler
Royal Army Medical Corps
When the battle of Villers-Bretonneux, near Amiens, started, first of all we were gassed heavily. We were down the valley when it got so full of gas that we had to clear out. We went to some support trenches which were very primitive and took up our position there. The only place I could find as a first-aid post was a large quarry, and we took up our position there. We found a cave at one end of the quarry. In a much

Q6595

The Queen's Royal West Kent Regiment awaits the advancing German forces.

bigger cave at the other end I put all the stretcher-bearers, the stretchers and all the drugs. Unfortunately, a shell fell short and hit the top of the quarry and buried all these fellows and killed them. So we finished at night without any stretcher-bearers at all.

Captain Toye, who was awarded a VC later on, came round to my shelter in the quarry and said, 'Where are all your stretcher-bearers?' I said, 'Under that lot,' pointing to the pile of rubble. He said, 'You've got to get out of this as quick as you can. You're going to have a hell of a walk because they're putting down a tremendous barrage between here and Villers-Bretonneux.'

And we did do that. We started a hundred and eighty strong and we arrived twenty-one. People ask me if I was frightened. Of course I was frightened, but it was so like a nightmare that I thought it must be a nightmare. That such a thing couldn't be happening. I thought that I'd wake up suddenly and find it was a dream.

I had a sergeant beside me. Suddenly a shell went up, and as the smoke cleared I saw him sitting with his two stumps waving in the air, his legs completely shot off. I said, 'Well, we'll take you to the side of the road.' He said, 'You're not going to leave me here?' I said, 'I'm afraid we can't do anything about it, we've got no stretcher-bearers, we've got nothing to carry you with, we've got nothing to give you, but we'll put you out of the way of the tanks and I hope you'll be picked up.'

It was an awfully painful decision to make. People who could walk helped them along. I had about five people clinging to me, one with a jaw blown away, bleeding all over me, and that's how we ended our march. It was a nightmare. Getting through that was a miracle really, a miracle.

Captain Henry Oxley
23rd Battalion, Middlesex Regiment

My first experience of giving instructions to my particular men in my post on how to wear gas-masks was in early April 1918, when we were occupying a post immediate to a German pillbox in front of Passchendaele itself. The conditions there were a quagmire of mud and shell-holes. This particular night we were being shelled by German shells of very big calibre. One particular shell landed under a pillbox and disturbed some of the decomposing casualties, left from the battle of Passchendaele. The disturbance of these bodies by the shell gave off an obnoxious odour. In my inexperience at the time I gave the order to don gas-masks.

When day broke, after wearing our gas-masks for quite a time, I thought I'd take another test. I thought, 'Well, it doesn't seem to be dangerous.' So I took my gas-mask off and I felt quite all right. So I instructed the other lads to take their masks off. And then I thought, 'Well, I don't know. This is peculiar.' Then it suddenly dawned on me. This heavy shell had disturbed the casualties and dead bodies around and given off a kind of a gas of some odour from their bodies. I thought to myself, 'Well, it's a good job that it's not quite daylight.' Otherwise my face would have been shown up red.

Captain Stefan Westmann
German Medical Officer

One day we got the order to attack these brickworks in the Lys sector and take them. The only possible means to take them was by a surprise attack in full daylight. We had orders to do this. We cut zigzag lines through our barbed-wire entanglements and at noon we went 'over the top.' We had run approximately a hundred yards all the way under machine-gun fire, which was so terrific that the losses were staggering. We got orders to lie down and to seek shelter. Nobody dared lift his head because they would machine-gun us for any movement. The British artillery opened up and the corpses, the heads and the arms and legs flew about and we were cut to pieces.

Private William Hall
2nd Battalion, East Lancashire Regiment

We were manning an isolated position in the Aisne area of trenches with a mixed body of men on a hilltop and expecting Germans to come in from any direction, as they had broken through.

One of our staff officers rode up on a horse and said, 'Now men, I want you to stand firm on this hillside – you've got a good position you

Q6659

Men of the Worcestershire Regiment hold the southern bank of the Aisne in May.

should be all right.' The men didn't take any notice of him whatsoever, they began to stampede and they said, 'We've no chance, Sir, we've got no chance whatsoever, the Germans are coming up, they've got tanks.' So he started appealing to us. 'Men of the East Lancashire Regiment,' he said, 'now you have got a good reputation.' I said, 'It's not much good here, is it, Sir?' Just at that moment the German tanks came up the hillside from the village and started firing. Well, that started it. The staff officer and his horse got off his marks as quick as he could and all the men started running down to this wood at the hillside, down into the wood.

Captain Maberly Esler
Royal Army Medical Corps

When we were having our fortnight's rest out of the line, which was a habit – when one was occupying the trenches you had a fortnight in and a fortnight in a village two or three miles behind resting period – it was during one of these periods that the colonel sent for me and said, 'I have a very unpleasant duty for you to perform which I won't like any more than you do,' and then he told me what it was all about.

Apparently one of our men, our own men, had absented himself from the front line on two occasions when a battle had started, and after the battle was over he came back and made some excuse that he'd mislaid the way. Well, of course, I realised that this was a very serious offence and the first time I sentenced him to some severe punishment myself, but when it happened again I realised he must be sent up to Army headquarters for a court martial.

They court-martialled him and sentenced him to death by firing squad, and the unpleasant task the colonel set me was to attend the shooting and to pin on his heart a piece of coloured flannel so that they'd give the marksmen something to fire at.

The following morning he was to be shot at dawn and I lay awake thinking of it all night and I thought, 'Well, I'll try to help this fellow a bit,' so I took down a cupful of brandy and presented it to him and I said, 'Drink this and you won't know very much about it.' He said,

'What is it?' I said, 'It's brandy.' He said, 'Well, I've never drunk spirits in my life, there's no point in my starting now.'

That to me was a sort of spurious sort of courage in a way. Two men came and led him out of the hut where he'd been guarded all night. As he left the hut his legs gave way, then one could see the fear entering his heart. Rather than marched to the firing spot he was dragged along. When we got there he had his hands tied behind his back, he was put up against a wall, his eyes were bandaged and the firing squad were given the order to fire.

The firing squad consisted of eight men, only two of whom had their rifles loaded. The other six carried blank ammunition – that was so that they wouldn't actually know who had fired the fatal shot. I wondered at the time, 'What on earth will happen if they miss him and they don't kill him completely?' and I was very anxious about that, but when they fired he fell to the ground writhing as all people do – even if they've been killed they have this reflex action of writhing about which goes on for some minutes.

I didn't know whether he was dead or not but at that moment the sergeant in charge stepped forward, put a revolver to his head and blew his brains out, and that was the coup de grâce which I understood afterwards – I learnt afterwards – was always carried out in these cases of shooting.

Sergeant-Major Richard Tobin
Hood Battalion, Royal Naval Division
When we were out of the line we used to stand by the road and watch the fresh, strong, plump and new American battalions swing by. They waved and laughed and shouted. Our boys stood by the side of the road and grinned back – but we wondered, 'Did they know? Could they do it? Would they do it?'

Sergeant Melvin Krulewitch
United States Marine Corps
We left New York and sailed in a convoy of seven or eight ships, including some very important warships. We were, of course, under twenty-

four-hour alert; we had submarine warnings about halfway across, and several submarine attacks during the trip. As we neared the French coast and the coast of Ireland – in that general line from Ireland to France – we were met by a group of camouflaged destroyers. It was a most welcome sight, because we were in a danger zone, and they would flit in and out between the ships, giving us an assurance of safety.

We came through all right, with no losses, and landed at Brest. On the trip across we'd had to impose many restrictions: sleeping quarters were tight and we all slept in hammocks; and we had an allowance of just a small amount of water each. That water was used for brushing the teeth, then washing the face, then for washing your hands and finally for washing your clothes – all in the same bucket.

We had submarine attack exercises every day, when some men went to the gun crews and others to the boats in order to prepare us for an emergency, should it come about. Some of the men hadn't had any experience of sailing abroad and they were a little – shall we say – queasy at times. But by and large the crossing was a tremendous success, and all the men in my platoon were well trained and active, and ready and eager to get into the battle itself.

When we got to France there was intensive training from French and British instructors, who had already had three-years' experience of the war and could give us the benefit of that right at the start. We learned trench practice and how to handle ourselves in night raids and night marches. We learned how to handle a knife, which we hadn't learned before, although all of us carried a dirk. We also learned the raider attack, which was common in trench warfare, because both sides would occasionally make a night raid to a part of the enemy line to get a prisoner, or some information or documents.

So we were trained right down to the bone. These men were like eagles newly washed, which I think is what Churchill called the British soldiers landing at the Dardanelles. And our boys were ready for war; we awaited the call; we were no jingoes, we were no screamers around for this or that, but we were regular marines and we were trained for war – that was our profession. We didn't like the waiting behind the lines. We heard in March or April that one of our brother outfits – the 1st

Division – had had a raiding operation up north, and we waited for our opportunity. And then the day finally came, and we loaded into the famous forty-and-eight box cars. And there we were, shouting and gay, the finest type of young American.

Private John Figarovsky
1st US Division
When we landed, one of the first things we did was to parade through the town of St. Nazaire. The French people were just delirious with joy, because in the Americans they saw hope for the future. As we marched through town, the sidewalks and even the gutters on both sides were full of people – and we felt so proud and important that such a fuss was being made over us. The mayor even proclaimed a holiday.

Most of us were young fellows, and we must have made a good impression because the French girls would jump in the ranks and throw flowers at us and scream and even kiss some of the soldiers. But we kept on, you know, with army discipline, we tried not to notice too much of that. It was such a wonderful reception – we never imagined anything like that would happen, that we'd be welcomed so warmly. They must have admired us a lot. And of course we were looking forward to a great adventure ahead of us. We were looking forward to the fight – we didn't know how serious it was because we'd never been to war before. But we didn't stay in St. Nazaire for long, we were marched about three miles out of town where they had some cantonments.

When we trained with the French troops they were very cooperative. Most of them were short, and it seemed they'd had their clothes on for a year – they hardly ever changed their clothes. But they were very nonchalant about everything, I guess they were tired after four years of warfare. And they were surprised to see that we were so eager to get into the fight.

Corporal Clifford Lane
1st Battalion, Hertfordshire Regiment
I think if the Americans hadn't come in it would have been stalemate, in which case – because the Germans had had enough, too – there

would have been a negotiated peace. But the fact was that suddenly there were all these Americans, hundreds of thousands of strong, healthy, well-equipped lads whose strength hadn't been impaired in any way. They were ready to go – just as we had been in 1914. So you can just imagine what the Germans thought, they knew what was going to happen. That was why they were so desperate to capture Paris before the Americans got established over there. I'm sure the Americans had a profound influence on the outcome of the war.

After the Bolshevik revolution we knew that eventually they would release hundreds of thousands of German troops. But we weren't bothered. Life was so precarious anyway, you only could live from day to day. You never thought, 'Well, in a few months' time they'll be after us,' because we didn't expect to live that long. The general strategy, if there was such a thing, seemed effective to us, but we knew nothing about it. We trusted our generals to a certain extent, but we really didn't know what was going on.

Private Murray
2nd US Division
The Frenchmen would take off their shirts – their undershirts – in the evening, and by candlelight – which we had in the dugouts – they would run the seams of their shirts over the candle-flame, and there'd be a flick, flick, flick. They were cooking the coodies (lice) and knocking them off. Well, we got great pleasure watching them doing it; we were free from vermin at that time and didn't know what a coody was. But by the next morning we were overloaded with them. We had hundreds and thousands of coodies ourselves and we went through the same pastime with the French in the coody situation.

BATTLE OF CANTIGNY – MAY 28

Private John Figarovsky
1st US Division

We got there just about five–ten minutes before it was time to go over the top. The company commander was there with his watch in his hand – all the watches were synchronised; he was ready to give the order to go over the top. Everything was just as quiet as anything; you could hear a pin drop.

And then, finally, five thousand guns started to fire over our heads. And we jumped from our trenches after getting a signal from the company commander. We jumped from our trenches, and he warned us not to go too fast because we had to follow our barrage. The barrage moved at the rate of about a hundred yards in two minutes. Four minutes, and we followed that barrage. Well, it was just like the 4th of July, there was so much noise going on, what with the soldiers all in line marching forward, following the barrage.

We got to the first trenches there. A lot of Germans were dead already from the barrage, from the artillery, and we jumped over the trenches, went on to the second line of trenches, they were captured. We travelled through the wheat fields; wheat was up to our hips. We travelled through the wheat fields, and we were under fire, terrific machine-gun fire after the first half an hour or so. The Germans began to send a counter-barrage towards us. They fired their machine-guns through the wheat, and we started out, we started out five paces apart. Before long we were fifty yards apart, and then even as much as a hundred yards apart because of the losses. We got to the third-line trenches of the Germans, and there were stopped for a few minutes. We stopped while they moved our guns forward and then that was the first objective. And then we went on to the second objective; and all that day was terrific fire.

The next day we went forward, we relieved the first and second battalions – we went forward, and that's where we met the strongest opposition, the second day. We went forward as usual close together, about five–ten paces apart. Before long we had so many losses that you

Q61343

An American bombing party starts out on a raid.

Q21214

A Land Army girl says farewell to American soldiers as they leave Winchester for the Western Front.

could hardly see the men on your right or left. I was behind the captain, and he told me to go and tell the fellers to come to the right, to close in to the right. So I started across the wheat fields parallel with the front, to do my mission. And as I started out, one German machine-gun there, in high ground there, he had me spotted. He started to fire, and I could tell by the bark of the gun when its bullets were just firing on me, he had the muzzle of the gun just on me. So I pretended that I got hit; and he turned his gun in another direction. I got up after about ten seconds or so and I continued another twenty–thirty yards. Then again he noticed that I wasn't really hit, that I was just fooling him: he turned his gun on me again, and again he fired. So I fooled him twice. The third time I got close to where the man was, and I waved my left arm to, to tell him to, to come to the right, to close in to the right, because you couldn't possibly hear a voice even if one shouted in your ear with all the firing going on, and the artillery, the machine-guns, all that – you couldn't hear anything. The only way, it was only by signalling, only by movement of the arms that you could. So I moved my arm, and just as he got my signal to close in to the right, that same German machine-gun that tried, that tried twice before to get me, finally got me.

Lieutenant Robert Poustis
French Cavalry
After one month with Americans we were quite close with them. Unfortunately there was a German machine-gun always firing. We heard always the noise of 'Whizzling, whizzling' of the bullets. There were three or four 'Sammies' as we called them in front of us, and I shouted to them, 'Lie down, lie down,' and they replied, 'Oh, monsieur, ça ne fait rien – It's all right.' Then I heard the rattle of a machine-gun again. All of them were, I would say, I hope not killed, but I would say put down.

Sergeant Perry Webb
7th Battalion, Dorsetshire Regiment
The NCO would look up and say, 'Here's so many biscuits for you.' We used to put it all together, and if you had six men you knew that was a

Q8847

'Well, it's not exactly cricket' seems to be the expression of the British troops as the American soldiers try to explain baseball.

Sergeant Perry Webb, 7th Battalion, Dorsetshire Regiment.

sixth each of everything that was there. If there was, say, a pot of jam, you had your part issued to you when you had a meal in your billycan. That's what the Americans couldn't understand when they came with us. They said, 'How on earth can you have rations dished out like that? Our fellows would eat the lot.' I said, 'Well, our fellows don't.' They all had their proper rations and it was up to the NCO to see to it that they had, because they were in trouble if you didn't.

Bread was very, very scarce. You might not see bread for two months, so mostly it was just big square biscuits, like dog biscuits. They were nutritious no doubt, but we'd have to break them up with a trenching tool handle to make them small enough to eat.

There were potatoes though, and Maconochie vegetable rations. I don't know if it was a form of greens, it was concentrated. You'd get a round tin each of sliced potatoes and a little lump of fat pork in the middle, and you'd just jack-knife it open and eat them as they were. Then there was bully beef, which was more or less plentiful. I think everybody had a fair share of bully beef. I did see bacon once or twice, but it was very rare. You might get a bit of cheese occasionally, but not often, and you got margarine but never butter. I only ever had hot food once or twice in the trenches, and that was when we were on a very quiet front and our kitchens were able to get right up to the reserve line.

Sergeant Melvin Krulewitch
United States Marine Corps

We got into the trucks and we moved up to the Front. In the rear as we went up, we passed little villages and the people would come out and cheer us and give us their blessing. You could see a look of fatalism in their eyes, because they'd been through this year after year. They'd seen their own men go up, and they knew by now that the Germans had broken through between the British and the French on the big Paris–Metz road and were on their way to Paris. It looked as though a second battle of the Marne was building up. We got there, the fresh, new Americans, getting their first baptism of fire, which they would get within a few hours at Belleau Wood. But we got it even before, because

The United States Army arrives in Le Havre in July to reinforce the unit, which has already been in action.

all the way up the road we were shelled by the German artillery on both sides of the road. Occasionally there would be a hit, but we got through, and we got to the Belleau Wood area. We unloaded just off the road, the highway to Paris, and got into the woods under cover – 'Take cover, take cover,' was the order of the day.

As we began to dig in other armies retreated through our lines. Some of the French came through, some of the Senegalese calling, 'Beaucoup Boches, beaucoup Boches,' which meant many Germans. Our people dug in on the edges of the wood to give them a good field of fire so that they could defend. And after all the other troops ran through us, passed through our lines – we were the only defence at that point between Paris and the Germans.

We moved into the edge of Belleau Wood, and there facing us from the hill opposite, not more than a few hundreds yards away, were the German positions. We could see Germans from where we were: we could see the ambulances driving along the ridge to pick up their wounded. We dug foxholes first and then later a trench system. It was a quiet day and we worked to strengthen our position, to get our ammunition ready, our hand grenades in a position where we could use them for defence and do everything that we could without making the actual attack.

We were ready for either advance again on orders from top command, or for a defence against a counter-attack. Now this was the kind of fighting that many Americans knew of: no longer trench system but open warfare. The way our ancestors had fought on the frontiers and in all the wars of our country. And we knew it. But the difficulty with Belleau Wood was you never knew where the front was. Little groups of men – Americans, little groups of Germans – got together to fight each other. While we were fighting in one direction all of a sudden without any warning you'd find there were some Germans to the rear of you who had to be mopped up. We had to clean up, mop up, and move ahead. Move ahead with the unyielding determination to enforce your will on the enemy: that was how we moved in Belleau Wood. We saw every indication of the defeat that the Germans had suffered in that battle. The second-hand equipment, the used equipment, the shell cases, everything all neatly put in piles to be sent back to the factories for renovation and re-use. We even found some German rolling kitchens there, with food all ready to eat. A hungry marine wouldn't think too much of a booby trap, and would help himself to some of their beans and stew. In the rocky crevices and in the little foxholes that the Germans had made – we found the German dead. We found not only the German dead from the day before, but dead from four or five days before, that the enemy hadn't had time to bury. That was Belleau Wood. Fighting from hand to hand; from position to position; not knowing where the next attack would come; but the steady moving forward until we cleared the entire woods.

Gunner William Maher
US Artillery

When we arrived in the Château-Thierry section, our battalion guns immediately went into action in support of the marines and the infantry who were in the Belleau Woods. We were firing continuously day and night – high explosive, gas and shrapnel. And we realised the importance of saving Paris, and the Allied army itself was at stake. There was a lot of heavy work going on there hauling ammunition day and night. We had to keep off the roads in the daytime because we were under the constant observation of the enemy. So during the day we had to hide in the woods and clean our horses and equipment and get ready for the next night's work. This went on for about forty-four days and nights. Our division suffered very heavy casualties – about nine thousand eight hundred officers and men; but we felt we helped, turned the tide, and we did a good job.

Captain Herbert Sulzbach
9th Division, German Army

On July the 15th our offensive started towards Rheims. Preparations were enormous. The bomb barrage and the gun barrage started at 1 o'clock at night and went on for four hours. The infantry moved on after the barrage ended, but we soon realised that the infantry could not move on very far. The first French prisoners came in and told us that they knew of our offensive. Our mood was not too good after we heard this, and especially at night when we were told that our division was to be withdrawn back into camps. During this night we found that many regiments were already in camps moved from the front towards the so-called back line. We were full of doubt. Suddenly came the order that our division had to move towards Fismes, about forty kilometres away. This order was rather more depressing, because it seemed that our offensive had failed entirely.

I never forgot this night. After terrific heat, thunderstorms, downpours, it was regiment after regiment moving towards another place. We were drenched wet and fell asleep on our horses. We arrived at Fismes a few days later and then came the Order of the Day, of July the 18th, telling us that enormous attacks out of the Bois de Villers-Cotterêts had started. It seemed too that the Americans had arrived, because the orders said that the forces were so great that they couldn't have been French and British alone. After the 18th of July we moved into the front line and were attacked by a barrage which was absolutely unbelievable. It was the worse barrage and the worst gunfire I ever heard, and I had been through the Somme and everywhere else since then. The night came and the infantry moved a little backwards, we moved forwards, but we moved more backwards than forwards. It went for days like this, until the retreat came at the end of July. It was hardly possible to get through the gunfire of the Allies. Their aeroplanes were flying very low and seeing everything that we were doing and bombing us in daylight. So it went on until we moved to a new line far further back. We realised that something had gone wrong, our losses were enormous and the gas attacks fearsome. The gas stuck into the high grass so that even our horses had gas masks. We realised it was the beginning of the end.

Major Hartwig Pohlmann
36th Prussian Division

In July 1918 we tried to cross the River Marne, but after three days we had to fall back. The resistance of the enemy was too heavy. We also met the first American troops and we saw from month to month more and more American troops would come to the front line. The enemy became overwhelming for us. But we knew that we had to do our duty as soldiers. It was a matter for the politicians to find a way to a fair peace. So we did our duty as long as we could and most of the German soldiers did so. We had very heavy losses in that year, and the units became smaller and smaller. We were forced to form one company out of two, and so on. The number of our guns diminished and so we had to fall back from one line to another.

JULY 18

Captain Reginald Thomas
Royal Artillery
It was a magnificent sight as the French cavalry came out of the forest at Soissons. Their uniforms were all new, bright blue, every bit and spur-chain was burnished and polished; their lances were gleaming in the sun; and as the bugler blew the charge the horses went into the gallop in a fan attack – two regiments of French cavalry. They went along beautifully, magnificently, through the wheat field in the afternoon sun, until they hit the German machine-guns which had just come up and unlimbered. The machine-guns, they opened on them at close range and aimed high enough to knock the riders off the horses. Riderless horses went all over the field for two or three hours. At the end of that time there was practically nothing left of those two cavalry regiments.

BATTLE OF AMIENS

Private James Southey
Australian Corps
The morning of August the 8th started very foggy indeed, and as our barrage opened, a tremendous barrage, we were wondering how we were going to get on. But, forward we pushed, and met comparatively

slight opposition. Some Germans surrendered quickly, others fought to the end. As we pushed on wondering where we were, the sun broke through and we began to see countryside that we hadn't seen for quite a time. It was unscarred, all sorts of cultivated land, and we began to feel, 'By Jove, the war's coming to an end. We're getting through.' And we had a feeling of great uplift about the whole job.

Fusilier Tom Bracey
9th Battalion, Royal Fusiliers
We took a lot of prisoners there. We were there for about three days and then they shifted us up towards the quarry. I was wet and cold and they were shelling us on this blinking road – out of Arras. We came up with the Scotch Division. I was carrying this bloody 48-lb. tripod, I mean it's heavy. I was there wishing a bloody shell would drop on me. The only time in the war I hoped a shell would drop on me. But it didn't drop on me, so on I had to go.

Major S. Evers
Australian Corps
Before the 8th of August took place, for every offensive up to then, the guns always had to be brought up into position so that the advance would be halted. General Monash thought that if we could break through and have the guns in position so that the Germans would not be able to fortify their positions, it would be a breakthrough. Of course the problem was to get the guns into position without the Germans knowing. It had to be carried out with utmost secrecy, otherwise the Germans would be able to fortify their positions and stop this attack. General Brudenell White thought that if we could get a noise to drown the noise of the guns coming up, they could get the guns into position. It was arranged for a fleet of bombing planes to go up and down the line a fortnight before the actual transferring of the guns and tanks into position. On the night before this particular operation the guns were brought within a hundred yards of the front line and the Germans never knew. To complete the success of this breakthrough there had to be the surprise and disorganisation behind the German lines. This was

accomplished by a fleet of armoured motor cars which traversed no man's land and got behind the German lines. This was a highly successful move, because once they got behind their lines our armoured motor cars simply shot up every transport they could see, and wherever troops were concentrating the armoured motor cars mowed them down and completed the disorganisation and rout behind the line. In the meantime the tanks were going forward and taking position after position. The infantry followed up behind. Even though the Germans brought their artillery out of their pits, it was of no avail. The Australians got all round them. While this was taking place, the Horse Artillery with the howitzers and the 18-pounders galloped into action. The horses would be turned round, the guns turned and then they would fire. The Germans were surrendering everywhere. I saw one Australian private actually prodding the rear of a German brigadier, much to the amusement of everybody else. But it was a morning of victory. You could feel the hair pricking up your spine with excitement because we knew that it was going to be the end of the war. That was the only time I saw Australian troops enthusiastic and pleased that they were in the war.

Captain Montague Cleeve
Royal Garrison Artillery
I had a phone call one morning from General Alexander on August the 8th. He said, 'You're going to be inspected by a VIP this afternoon. Go into action on the Spur Maroeuil and be prepared to shoot at 2:30.' We thought it might have been the army commander or someone from GHQ.

Anyway, I got the men all tidy, we put on our best clothes and all like that and got the gun into action, everything all perfectly ready, a model of how it should be done. Come 2:30 and a whole cloud of dust arrived as a motorcade drew up. Out of the first car stepped His Majesty King George V and all his staff, including General Alexander VC.

His Majesty came round and he was terribly interested in the gun, which was then depressed. He walked all over the mounting with me, asking all sorts of questions, and then he asked if he could see the gun loaded. So, of course, we said yes. All the VIPs by that time had

Q6646

This 12-inch howitzer is ready for action.

climbed up onto the mounting and were standing on the load platforms. I said, 'I'm awfully sorry, Sir,' to the King, 'but I'm afraid nobody's allowed to stand on the platform while the gun is fired.' So very reluctantly the King agreed.

The gun was loaded by twelve men, six either side of the rammer, and they had to squash up together at the far end of the platform. A little railway carriage carried the shell, weighing about 2,500 lb., into the breech. It was terribly important to ram it home otherwise it would have slipped back at high elevation. So on the word 'go' from the number one, the twelve men pushed with all their might and rammed the shell into the bore. The King was very thrilled with that. When the gun was loaded it had to be laid.

When all was ready, I saluted the King. 'Gun ready, Sir.' His Majesty turned round to me and said, 'Fire the gun, please.' The Navy always says please, so I immediately ordered fire. Many of his surrounding staff cupped their ears and turned away from the gun because they were frightened of the shock. His Majesty stood as still as a statue and seeing all these cowed heads turned round and said in quite a loud voice, 'I consider it makes no noise at all, no noise at all.' His staff all looked awfully sheepish after that. But it did make an enormous bang. It was a gentle bang, but a very gigantic one.

The King then said, 'May I look at the map?' So we took him into the command post wagon and he pored over the railway map of the front line. He turned round to his staff and he said, 'You know, gentlemen, I've just come from the launch of the Fourth Army attack at Amiens, down south. I see from the railway system that the Germans will have to rush there – in any case, the Germans will have to rush there with their reinforcements, now at Ypres, to resist the attack of the Fourth Army. And I see from the railway line system that they'll have to go through Douai station to get there. Why not keep Douai station under harassing fire from now on?'

Later I went into Douai and spoke to a local woman. She said, 'Well really, Douai was a very peaceful place until early in August. Then all of a sudden one afternoon there was a terrific explosion in the station and nobody knew what it was. We thought we were being bombed. Well, it so happened that there was a German troop train in the station at the time and a shell fell right on top of it. The people of Douai were delighted.' That first round, the first of anything that happened at Douai, was the King's shot. So his idea worked extremely well, but unfortunately he never knew about it.

Sergeant-Major Richard Tobin
Hood Battalion, Royal Naval Division
In the summer of 1918 came the breakthrough. We had left the trenches behind, those mud-sodden trenches that we had hated for so many years. We were out in the open country. We almost felt victory in the air. Admittedly the Germans were standing and fighting here and there, but they were going back and we were following them. The breakthrough had come. It was open warfare. We were in green fields once again. However, open warfare brought its difficulties. This was the test of the trained soldier and junior officer leadership. The battalion commander had to watch his flanks, wondering when to stop, when to dig in, when to go on. We also had our ration problems. But it looked like the end and the peace we had longed for.

Major S. Evers
Australian Corps
We crossed the Somme marshes on the afternoon of the 31st of August and made our way to the place where we were supposed to be for the night. About midnight we had our meal and the shells were falling about there. In the complete darkness we were eating, eating dirt as well as food. About 2 o'clock we went to battalion headquarters, where a conference was held with candlelight. We were then given our dispositions where we were to attack at 6 o'clock. This meant time was getting very, very short indeed to get into position.

We wended our way as quickly as we could to the place where we were to meet our guides, who were to take us to the position where we were to attack. When we got there, there were no guides. But eventually we found our way to the front line into our trenches. Another company found Germans in their trench before, so had a sharp fight

Q3214

Four wounded Canadian troops pose cheerfully at a Casualty Clearing Station after the Battle of Arras.

German prisoners carry their wounded after the Battle of Arras.

and ejected them. I sent a message to the OC to say that I was in position. In the meantime the Germans must have sensed that we were coming over, because they put down a barrage of machine-guns which were hitting the back of our trench with terrific thuds. It was a dreadful sound, and made more frightening because we knew that we'd have to get up and charge into it in a few minutes.

We'd advanced too far, so that the artillery did not know where our front line was, we wouldn't have any artillery to protect us when we launched our attack. I felt very much like refusing to allow the men to go over that morning, because it was sheer murder, but, of course, when the time came we had to do our duty and over the top we went. There were terrific casualties, men were going down right and left all over the place. I was with a sergeant-major just preparing to run from one position up forward when a machine-gun bullet got me through the thigh. I fell on the broad of my back and couldn't get up, the bullets were zipping all around me, and I could see over my toes the poor men of my company trying to get through the wire. Then the miracle happened, suddenly the Germans came out with their hands up! They were calling 'Kamerad.' All firing ceased. Had they fired for another few seconds, there wouldn't have been a man alive. That morning I went in with four officers and a hundred and eight men. By nightfall there were only eight men alive. But my remnant had joined up with B Company, passed through the wood, and had succeeded in capturing Péronne.

The incredible surrender of the Germans at that moment was probably due to Private Currey who, under heavy machine-gun fire, killed the crew and captured single-handed a field gun which was holding up our advance. He then took out another post with a Lewis gun. He got a well-deserved VC. Another man, Crank, turned round a captured field gun and, at a range of two hundred yards, instead of the usual five or six hundred yards, fired directly into the German lines. That must have been the only reason why the Prussian Guard – who were the flower of the German Army – surrendered. They had volunteered to stay and protect that place at all costs because it was the last bastion before the Hindenburg Line. Those huge men, brave soldiers that they were, actually surrendered to the Australians. That was the astonishing part, how the flower of the German Army surrendered to the Australians. And that I think goes down as one of the greatest annals in the history of Australia, that the Prussian Guards surrendered that morning.

BATTLE OF ST. MIHIEL

Private Di Lucca
42nd US Division
When we finally reached our trenches it was raining a deluge. So we had to form a line by holding each other by our raincoats, to get through the trenches, and we marched through, during a terrible barrage which had started fifteen minutes earlier by the Americans. Everything was coming down – trees, stones, rocks, everything came over our heads in the trenches: it was a dangerous spot to be in. We came forward until we reached our dugouts, where we rested for two or three hours.

At dawn we got the order to go over the top. We had to get out of our trenches and meet the enemy, who was only twenty feet from us. We didn't know this. They come out of their trenches; we come out of our trenches. We met one another, faced one another like a bunch of animals. We lost our senses; we charged them with our bayonets. I saw a German, a six-footer, coming towards me – why he picked me I don't know. Anyway, I saw him coming. I don't know what gave me idea, what gave me the strength, but as soon as he came near me, I turned my rifle by the butt, broke his thrust and I hit him on the chin. All of a sudden he was bleeding. He let go his arm, put his hand towards his chin to find out where the blood came from. That gave me a clear spot: I turned the rifle and I hit him in mid-chest with the bayonet. I left the bayonet there till he fell down. Looked at him, pulled out my bayonet – I know what happened to him, I know the conditions – and I just left him, and I kept following my other friends – they were going ahead of me. We chased the enemy, which was in full retreat, from trench to trenches, from place to places, all the way down the embankment from the hill of St. Mihiel.

When we reached the city of Château-Thierry I joined my division. The place was littered with dead. Only a few days before, the marines had met the onslaught. The ground was full of holes: dead all over the place; dead mules, dead horses – everything was putrefied. The place smelled terribly. The rain, it rained constantly, which never helped any, didn't help decompositions of the body. I had never had any training for this. In my first action, I never expected to find anything so gruesome.

SEPTEMBER

Lieutenant Stuart Hastie
Royal Tank Corps

The first wave of battle tanks passed over the wire of the Hindenburg Line. Behind that was a collection of tanks which were fitted specially for dealing with the wire. They were equipped to clear this wire off the ground to enable the cavalry to pass through. Each tank was fitted with a grapnel and a steel cable. The tank passed into the belt of wire, dropping the grapnel as it passed through. It then turned to the right and proceeded up parallel to the belt of wire. The effect of this was to roll the grapnel and roll up the wire, also pulling up the stakes and everything until it had a mound of wire as high as a cottage, at which point the tank would go no further on account of the tremendous weight of the wire. The cable was then cut and the tank left to join the other fighting tanks in the battle, leaving behind it a gap of sixty yards from which every strand of wire and every post had been torn up.

OCTOBER

Private McGuire
US Artillery

Upon arriving at Villsey Soutray I was disappointed to find that the battlefield was nothing like I had expected. There was nothing but mud, fallen trees, and bodies which hadn't been picked up yet. It sent a cold chill up my back because I wasn't expecting anything like this. When we arrived at the Front we had to get our guns into emplacements through heavy mud, which was almost impossible. We had to get trucks to help us push them into position and then get them camouflaged. We were expected to start firing that night. 200-lb. shells were rolled into position; we loaded the guns and prepared to fire. We were all scared, because it was something different; we never expected to find the very, very heavy conditions of mud, rain and cold. By 1 o'clock we had something like thirty shells shot off from our position. Then the sky reddened terribly because of the return fire which was coming over. Shells were bursting into the ground throwing mud up into the air a hundred feet almost which was coming down and hitting us on the head. We were full of mud and filth.

On arriving at our new positions in the Argonne Forest, we found out that the devastation at this position was worse than Villsey Soutray. The fighting at this point must have been terrific. Thousands of trees were splintered, crushed down into the mud, and it made it hard for us to travel. We got our guns into position quickly because the amount of shelling that was done by the Germans had every man of us scared. We had never heard such cannonading prior to this position.

At the end of October we were trying desperately to get to Metz. The situation at the Front was getting worse all the time. Because of the mud, we couldn't sleep. Our kitchens were getting left behind, so we were hungry. It was a case of do or die now. Then we heard that the Germans were sending over, by railroad to Metz, enough ammunition to make the war last another couple of months. We were ordered to fire on all trains coming into Metz. We fired off a fusillade and blew up their trains. The sky lit up very, very bright red. We even thought the Germans had some kind of flame-thrower because the flames seemed to be creeping closer towards us all the time because we didn't know that we had hit the target. We thought they were using some terrible new weapon against us.

Then we found out that we had destroyed all the ammunition the Germans were bringing into Metz to make the war last longer. Then we

The American Balloon Company confidently moves forward on October 1.

heard there was to be an Armistice, so we were to fire off all our shells, otherwise we were going to have to take them back home. When we met some Germans later they said, 'What did you do? Those shells came so fast. Did you send them out by machine-gun?'

Corporal Clifford Lane
1st Battalion, Hertfordshire Regiment
We made this attack just in front of Le Cateau. It was a night attack, and preparations were made to avoid chaos as far as possible. Well, chaos occurs in broad daylight attacks, so we knew what the risks were at night. We all wore a silvery bit of metal on our backs so that anybody coming from behind would know who we were. We also carried red sort of candle things that would light to indicate our positions.

We went over the top, and we met no resistance. They came out with their hands up. One came running out of his trench waving a white shirt, he nearly knocked me over – he was screaming his head off – it was pathetic. You would never have seen that in the old days.

Major Philip Neame
15th Field Company, Royal Engineers
Just before the end of the war we attacked with an American division on our left, and we reached our objective and took thousands of German prisoners. The British divisions on our right – we were on the left of the British line – the British divisions again succeeded and got all their objectives. The two American divisions on our left were very slow in advancing and didn't get their objectives until long after we did. Then we were told to be ready for the next attack within forty-eight hours; we were ready and the people on our right were ready – the Americans weren't ready. The whole thing was delayed for four days because the Americans had got their rear area leading up to the captured trenches in such a congestion and muddle that they couldn't get their reserve troops up, they couldn't get their fresh ammunition up.

We heard afterwards that they'd got their food supplies mixed up – in fact ahead and blocking all the roads. This meant they couldn't move their artillery forward. It was a complete muddle.

NOVEMBER

Sergeant Melvin Krulewitch
United States Marine Corps

Every piece of artillery in the American Army and the adjoining French units opened up. This action produced a symphony in colour: you had the red artillery flares; orange flames coming out of the cannon; green signals indicating possibility of gas attack, and you had the shells bursting in the air creating a white colour. On top of this you could hear the thunder of the guns. It was a great support to our morale to know that this extraordinary barrage was going on behind us. On we moved in the usual way, in a long skirmish line; men five yards apart, moving along at a leisurely pace, just making sure that you wouldn't get into our own barrage fire. The artillery fire had almost wiped out the first row of trenches, so we were soon in them and taking prisoners. One or two of our boys were wounded. A great shout of triumph went up and down the line when we made the German prisoners carry our wounded back on stretchers. Then we pushed ahead. Occasionally some of the boys would kneel and take a shot at a German, but they were retreating. Then another great shout of triumph went up because we'd captured their artillery: that was about two and a half miles behind the line.

We were attacked then by long-distance machine-gun fire and we had some casualties. The fire came from the heights of Bayonville, which was part of the Kriemhild Stellung defence line. That night we moved up and took the heights of Bayonville, so there was nothing ahead of us except the retreating Germans. And we pursued them relentlessly, night after night, day after day. The Germans were losing food; losing their artillery horses and their baggage and ration wagons. They were so hungry that they would shoot a horse and cut steaks out of the rump. At first we thought the horses had been hurt by shellfire: then we saw the skilful butchering of the steaks, and we knew what they had done. Finally we reached our objective, which was to cut the Metz–Malmédy railroad on the heights looking down to the Meuse river below Sedan. We cut that on the last night of the war – November 10th – and we put a footbridge across the Meuse river under withering gunfire. We crossed the river that night and made an attack on the other side. To us the fight was just like any other fight – the fight of the 9th, the 10th. That morning we found our wounded and gassed boys lying around on the ground and we took care of them. We expected an infantry attack, but the Germans never came that night, because there was too much gas in the woods and they took a chance of being killed themselves by their own gas if they attacked. So they let go with a box-barrage of the high-explosive shelling and mustard and phosgene gas. The following morning when we collected our unit, all I had was eleven men out of a company of over two hundred.

Captain Herbert Sulzbach
9th Division, German Army
In October I had leave to go home to Frankfurt, my home town, to my parents. I was very much looking forward to this leave after the terrific battles we had been through. I went through the streets of Frankfurt. I was not saluted. I was a commissioned offficer, yet no one saluted. Everything was rationed and there was hardly anything to buy. Dance halls were closed, the streets were dull and the mood of the people was really bad. We hadn't realised at the Front how bad it was at home. People were fed up with war. They wanted the war to be ended as soon as possible, victory or no victory. After a fortnight I went back to the front line, to my comrades, to my guns, and I felt at home amongst the mud, the dirt and the lice.

In spite of our retreats for weeks and months, we still received mail, bags of it, even some with parcels. Parcels didn't come from Germany but from Belgium, where there was still some food and chocolate. The letters I received were not depressing, but some of my comrades received letters which were most upsetting. Their families wrote, 'We have nothing to eat, we are fed up with war, come back as soon as possible.' You can imagine how it affected the morale of these poor chaps.

On November the 1st we were at Étreux not far from St. Quentin, where we had started our big offensive on March the 21st. Then we were so full of hope and broke through the British 5th Army. Now it seems a million guns of the American, French and British were bombing us. The war was entirely lost. As adjutant I had to give the order of the day. On the 11th of November it was: 'From noon onwards our guns will be silent.' Four years before, full of optimism, now a beaten army.

ARMISTICE

Private Hubert Trotman
Royal Marine Light Infantry
We were still fighting hard and losing men. We knew nothing of the proposed Armistice, we didn't know until a quarter to ten on that day. As we advanced on the village of Guiry a runner came up and told us that the Armistice would be signed at 11 o'clock that day, the 11th of November. That was the first we knew of it.

We were lined up on a railway bank nearby, the same railway bank that the Manchesters had lined up on in 1914. They had fought at the battle of Mons in August that year. Some of us went down to a wood in a little valley and found the skeletons of some of the Manchesters still lying there. Lying there with their boots on, very still, no helmets, no rusty rifles or equipment, just their boots.

Major Keith Officer
Australian Corps
At 11 o'clock on the 11th of November I was sitting in a room, in the Brewer's House at Le Cateau which had been Sir John French's headquarters at the time of the battle of Mons. I was sitting at a table with a major in the Scots Greys who had a large, old-fashioned hunting watch which he put on the table and watched the minutes going round. When 11 o'clock came, he shut his watch up and said, 'I wonder what we are all going to do next!' That was very much the feeling of everyone. What was one going to do next? To some of us it was the end of four years, to others three years, to some less. For many of us it was practically the only life we had known. We had started so young.

Nearby there was a German machine-gun unit giving our troops a lot

The Commanding Officer of the Irish Guards reads the news of the Armistice to his men.

of trouble. They kept on firing until practically 11 o'clock. At precisely 11 o'clock an officer stepped out of their position, stood up, lifted his helmet and bowed to the British troops. He then fell in all his men in the front of the trench and marched them off. I always thought that this was a wonderful display of confidence in British chivalry, because the temptation to fire on them must have been very great.

Trooper Alexander Jamieson
11th Battalion, Royal Scots Fusiliers
As we advanced we saw the terrible state of the Ypres salient. There were wrecked tanks from 1917 all over the place. I was used to dead horses and mules but not in the numbers that we saw up there. Of course it was just shell-holes everywhere. By the end of the first day we were clear of Ypres and on a ridge where we could look ahead and see trees and a landscape that had not been affected by war. It was just unbelievable. We knew then that things were going well.

We came back out of the line at a place called Vichte and had gone to bed in a hay loft. Our sergeant came in shouting that the war was over. Everybody got up and went down into this wee village. The estaminet owner opened his pub and issued free drinks and then went back to bed. We were paraded at the usual time. We were made to do slope arms by numbers till 11 o'clock. Then we were disbanded. That was the Armistice.

Corporal Reginald Leonard Haine
1st Battalion, Honourable Artillery Company
It wasn't like London, where they all got drunk of course. No, it wasn't like that, it was all very quiet. You were so dazed you just didn't realise that you could stand up straight and not be shot.

Corporal Clifford Lane
1st Battalion, Hertfordshire Regiment
As far as the Armistice itself was concerned, it was a kind of anticlimax. We were too far gone, too exhausted really, to enjoy it. All we wanted to do was go back to our billets, there was no cheering, no singing.

On the eleventh hour of the eleventh day of the eleventh month, officers and men of the United States Army give tribute at Winchester Cathedral, England, to their fallen comrades.

That day we had no alcohol at all. We simply celebrated the Armistice in silence and thankfulness that it was all over. And I believe that happened quite a lot in France. It was such a sense of anticlimax. We were drained of all emotion. That's what it amounted to.

Sergeant-Major Richard Tobin
Hood Battalion, Royal Naval Division
The Armistice came, the day we had dreamed of. The guns stopped, the fighting stopped. Four years of noise and bangs ended in silence. The killings had stopped.

We were stunned. I had been out since 1914. I should have been happy. I was sad. I thought of the slaughter, the hardships, the waste and the friends I had lost.

Index of Contributors

General Index